THE CURIOUS ADVENTURES OF A POLYMOTH

First published in 2025
by The Black Spring Press
An imprint of The Black Spring Press Group (BSPG)
Maida Vale, London W9,
United Kingdom

Cover and interior design by Edwin Smet

ISBN 978-1-915406-94-1

BLACKSPRINGPRESSGROUP.COM

FSC www.fsc.org MIX Paper | Supporting responsible forestry FSC® C014540

To Emma & Rupert

THE CURIOUS ADVENTURES OF A POLYMOTH

The life of an ordinand, banker, serial volunteer and *laterpreneur*

Julian Sturdy-Morton, BEM

with love and best wishes

Julian

B G S P
THE BLACK SPRING PRESS GROUP

To Maria, in every sense my 'other half'.
To the memory of Bejay.

To Sam, Sophie and Charles, Tilly, Bella, Lyra and Wilf, and to my wonderful family of friends.

'I am a part of all that I have met'
Ulysses—Alfred, Lord Tennyson

'Hope is being able to see that there is light despite all of the darkness'
—Archbishop Desmond Tutu

CONTENTS

INTRODUCTION

Everybody wants to belong; it is one of the most natural of human needs, researched and discussed at length by anthropologists and psychologists. 'To belong' we follow flags, teams and all manner of affiliations. For some, it seems easy: they are born with clear ties, loving parents, a close-knit society or family, strong historical links, bonds of kinship or conflict.

For others, affiliations are ephemeral. For centuries, people have travelled for adventure, business, diplomacy or war, leaving their family or tribe to do so, or bringing up their children in many cultures away from their notional home. Migration and war tear people away from their roots and such people absorb many traditions and belong to none.

The travel may span many regions, until such people emerge as polycultural beings: not 'immigrants' or 'migrants' but, in the word coined by Prof. Nina Glick-Schiller, *transmigrants* – people who bring 'together their societies of origin and residence'. That resonates with me.

If we were trees, I think transmigrants would be mangroves, which exist on every habitable continent, in most countries, with roots that feed from salt and fresh water or air. Cut one root and a mangrove draws on others. Dr Arne Fjørtoft, of Worldview International Foundation, calls mangrove trees 'a dawn of hope for our fragile planet'. Their survival has been hailed as 'symbols of hope'. No two mangroves are alike.

In that sense, I am a mangrove and have learnt to draw on many roots. These pages hold the memories, brief encounters carried visually in my mind, of my roots, of how I was formed and people I have met, often by chance more than by my own efforts. Some people are famous, one or two are infamous, most are not well known. Several are a part of history or contribute to shaping it. While I may not have impacted them, collectively all have enriched or affected my life and allowed me to experience a connection with the past, the present and the hopes of the future.

With few exceptions, I like people. The best adjectives often belong to the least likely people, more than to those upon whom praise is publicly bestowed in obituaries. I prefer people who bring hope to others; my memories may appear naïve and uncritical. I am a hopeful optimist.

In his touching autobiography, *The Shaping of a Soul: A life taken by surprise*, Richard Harries quotes Samuel Johnson: 'The only end of writing is to enable readers better to enjoy life or better to endure it.' It is typical of Richard's kindness that he should think of others. I prefer Cecil Day-Lewis's view: 'We do not write in order to be understood; we write in order to understand.'

A QUICK OVERVIEW

A few facts. I'm a Londoner, born to the west of the capital in 1952, a handful of years after the end of World War II. London was a colourless, struggling city with smog and a small airport. We lived in a farmhouse in Cranford, overlooking fields, surrounded by trees, and a five-minute walk from what is now Heathrow's main runway. We had a Border Collie.

Papa (Nicol Morton) was born in Darvel, a thinly stretched town in Ayrshire that was then packed with Farming Mortons and Weaving Mortons. I did not get to know any until I was much, much older, mostly after Papa had died. Over centuries of diligence, the family spawned a 1600s Covenanter blacksmith, John Morton, who fought the English and was summarily executed; Sir James Morton, inventor of fast dyes, who chose not to patent his invention because of its national importance; and Nobel laureate, Sir Alexander Fleming, a distant cousin who gave the world penicillin. During my childhood we went once to Scotland, fleetingly, and met a few members of Papa's family.

My mother (née Muriel Constance Sturdy) said she was born in Neuchâtel… but more of that later.

My sister, Alison, was almost four when I was born.

I remember little of my English infancy, other than the palette of dull greys that made up my hometown. I had a ration book, chilblains in winter and hand-me-down clothes from my sister; for two years nothing happened that I could describe from memory. From the only photograph I saw while growing up, I now know that Alison and I helped in the campaign to promote National Dried Milk; I was chubby, a few months old and a poster baby for the fattening powers of the powder. Our images were later cut out from the advertisement and stuck inexpertly onto a smart domestic setting, so it was many decades before I learnt of my brief modelling career. No other photographs were ever on show at home.

We left Britain before I had learnt about family, class, Empire and those tricky nuances that led George Bernard Shaw to write, 'It is impossible for an Englishman to open his mouth without making some other Englishman hate or despise him'.

We went to Lebanon. There I discovered a world in glorious Technicolor; Beirut was light years away. Flying, which now takes less than five hours, involved changing planes at Milan and again at Athens. If you left on Monday morning you would arrive on Tuesday afternoon. It was paradise and, for five turbulent and occasionally war-torn years, it was home.

As the years accumulated, we moved to France, Cameroon in West Africa, Germany and Sri Lanka; finally, my father retired from the Foreign Service in Turin, which had once, for a few years, been the capital of the newly united Italy.

Throughout childhood, work and leisure I have experienced more than 4,000 take-offs, more than one flight for every week of my life – a statistic that, even if I am grounded, will remain true until I am in my eighties. I used to deflect the question 'What do you do?' by saying, 'I test seats for airlines.'

Sent to board at a day school in Britain at seven, I have always been a foreigner in my own head, even if I am not in the eyes of many.

I trained for a vocation in the Anglican priesthood but, once qualified, I chose to pursue a career in finance. Making that rather strange decision, I wrote myself a letter – one of those toe-curling moments of growing up that you hope will never resurface. It did. I re-read my adolescent thoughts forty years later and I am incredibly lucky; after several bumps along the way, I now largely do what I would have wanted to do from the beginning.

Only once, aged nine, was I shown my school report. My teachers conspired to deliver a message by each using the word *dilettante* – I was untouched as I had no idea what the word meant, although my parents' anger indicated it was no compliment. Mr Lazenby broke ranks – he taught art (pots and daubs) and declared that my ingenuity could lead to 'success or jail'; the trigger, as we cleared up after class, was my decision to carry more glass jars than I could reasonably hope to manage just to avoid a second trip. Nothing was broken.

Recently a friend mistakenly described me as a polymath; I am not, although I may be a 'polymoth' because I have nibbled away at many occupations and hobbies. It is said that 'a specialist is one who knows more and more about less and less until he knows everything about nothing; whereas a generalist is one who knows less and less about more and more until he knows nothing about everything.' I am a generalist.

A polymoth devours a portfolio of passions and occupations, nibbling away at anything that appeals, not in a superficial way but not in the long term either. We are not academics pursuing perfection in many fields, nor are we butterflies, flitting aimlessly from blossom to bloom. We are polymoths.

I have had a go at every experience offered with the enthusiasm of a habitual observer, often returning for a second try but seldom for a further bite. Instead, I store hopes and memories, relishing them, learning from them, replaying them like video clips in my mind, using experiences to inform future hopes. What is lacking in consistency or belonging is richly compensated in diversity. There is always another distraction, another opportunity to create and draw on new roots. In childhood that is fragility; yet, as I age, it becomes strength.

CIVILISATION AND CIVIL WAR

1955 to 1960

We went to Lebanon because of Papa's work – until recently a serving RAF officer and in charge of a London airport, he was appointed Military Attaché to the British Embassy, which led to a career as a diplomat. I think we always called him Papa.

My mother's name changed with the winds and whims of her self-projection. She celebrated her grandchildren but did not like being a parent or being called anything maternal. She was christened Muriel but called Lulu, Michael and Mike. After her death, I encountered a tired pseudonymous paperback, *The Greatest People in the World* by Flying Officer X, inscribed in the author's hand: 'Michael, who turned out to be even more lovely than had been supposed by H. E. Bates, Oct. 1/42.' They worked together in the Air Ministry through much of WWII.

She settled for 'M', pronounced in an almost Italian way as Emma, the name I shall use.

Beirut in the mid-1950s was a city filled with beauty and adventure, freer from the scars of war than now. The country had been independent for scarcely 10 years and yet its history stretches back almost to the birth of history itself. It is a nation that schemes and trades, cheating its own demise as its politicians cheat its people. It is also a nation that loves and feeds like no other culture I had encountered… until I met my Armenian wife.

Our first flat was on the sixth floor of an attractive, modern block in the predominantly Christian area of Achrafieh. On the ground floor lived a family with one of Beirut's first televisions, the size of a large postcard and displayed in an open window for all to watch broadcasts of Gamal Abdel Nasser addressing crowds with anti-British slogans.

Above us lived Queen Dina of Jordan's dress designer, who died in a helicopter crash. The flat became the focus of ritual mourning, which was not good for the family (us) living below. Furniture was removed in vans and replaced with items that shifts of hired mourners could smash while wailing day and night for a week. We watched his coffin being carried on shoulders, ostensibly up to his home village in the mountains.

Everyone in Beirut seemed to have a home village in the mountains. Beirut was a city that people 'came to' and not a place that many 'came from'.

The city is on the Mediterranean's eastern shore, its back against one of the two ranges of mountains that run the length of Lebanon. Within 30 minutes of leaving the fashionable Corniche, one is in the mountains at more than 3,000 feet with views stretching forever.

While Papa worked, Emma attended an art course at AUB (the American University of Beirut), entertained and broadcast children's stories on English radio. I do not remember her ever reading stories to us at home. Alison went to the Collège Protestant, and I was looked after by a Syrian nanny until I went to kindergarten in September 1956.

There were endless drinks parties and, by the time I was six, I could stay up for the early stages. Guests included glamorous Lebanese, Arabists, journalists, diplomats from other countries, Queen's Messengers with their silver greyhound badge, and employees of the great oil empires, such as the boisterous Douglas Bader.

My 'job' at parties was to offer cigarettes or cigars and to hold a silver candlestick, flame blazing, for guests to light their choice. I shudder at the thought, but it must have seemed normal then. Cigars intrigued me so much that I once took one to bed, pulling it to bits to find the chocolate that I believed there must have been in the middle or why else did people chew on them so happily; disappointingly there was none, and it made a horrible mess.

In summer, when the atmosphere was sultry and airless in town, the mountains were warm and the air pure and clear. The mountains were also busy, vibrant and welcoming. As a child, I almost experienced the glamour of water-skiing after breakfast and skiing on the snow-clad slopes after lunch – almost but not quite. Lebanon is truly a self-destructive paradise.

We spent our summers in Shemlan, which hangs in the mountains at a greater altitude than any village in England. Shemlan's unpaved streets were lined with cedars. From our garden we could see the mountains, the sea and the capital, about 20 miles away. The view embraced hundreds of shades of green, mixed with yellows, blues and greys, broken by the regular shapes of red-tiled roofing. Pollution blurs the view now, but it remains spectacular.

Shemlan was the home of MECAS, the Middle East Centre for Arab Studies. MECAS is the reason for our 'Camel Corps' diplomats and their unparalleled mastery of Arabic. George Blake was at MECAS at the end of our time in Lebanon; Kim Philby visited him there occasionally. Villagers still call it the 'Spy School'.

At AUB Emma found an artistic talent. Among others, Kim Philby commissioned a portrait, which he apparently took with him when he fled some years later to Moscow. Emma seemed to forgive his treason but not his failure to pay her fee, which she would bitterly remember.

The British Community School (BCS) taught me the basics of English, maths and French. Its playground included a beautiful, Italian garden with low box hedges and gravel paths. In a rough-surfaced yard by the large metal gates were playground toys, and there I learnt to ride on a sprung rocking horse, cantering alone across wide-open spaces on an immobile steed while watching and listening to the squeals and laughter of others.

From early school reports found among Emma's papers after she died, I was numerate and literate, artistic and musical, cheerful and keen – a proper little teachers' pet. It didn't last; my concentration slipped, and I became increasingly detached from the class, pre-occupied in my own world. Each report, from almost four to seven, talks warmly of my 'imagination' although from six onwards my mind wandered, and I seemed absent.

Playground battles involved 'our gang' and 'their gang' – I was in neither, an outsider. It was a lonely place where I learned to observe and store memories. I went to school each day with a snack box – bread and cheese and a greaseproof paper twist of currants that I can taste now, with the crunch of desiccated, bitter grape seeds and sharp sugar hits.

Lebanon is known for conflict and food, fight and make up. The burning smell of grilled meat and fresh parsley, lemons and watermelons, apricots and rain on the fertile earth, cordite and rubble – these smells linger and defy description. The same words are used for Lebanese food in London as are used in Beirut, but the smells and tastes are extravagantly different, experienced against a background of unfiltered cigarettes, diesel and freshly ground Lebanese coffee. This was my nursery diet, my comfort food, *kibbeh* with a squeeze of lemon or a mouthful of *tabbouleh*, rather than cottage pie or fish fingers.

Some food was delivered, even during a short civil war. Not quite Ocado, goods were lifted from the street in a basket that was lowered from the balcony. Down went the basket with empty bottles (for the delivery boy to reclaim the deposit) and a shopping list; back came the basket full of groceries and a bill; down again with payment. I was mesmerised by the drama of deliveries and the street's shouts and noises. Much later, throughout my career, I preferred city centre hotels amid the bustle.

Treasures and antiquity were visible everywhere: sometimes fenced off and venerated like the temples of Jupiter and Bacchus at Baalbek; otherwise incorporated into other buildings as part of everyday life. In the 1950s there were churches, mosques and synagogues throughout Beirut.

Few other countries are more burdened with legacy, both architectural and religious.

In the 1950s, Lebanon was a Christian country with two large Muslim communities and a Druze minority. The Jewish population was growing, as Jews left other Arab countries but were not yet ready for the hardships of the newly formed state of Israel. It is remarkably a land of crosses and crescents, happily together in childhood, uncomfortably co-habiting from their late teens, antagonistically on opposing sides of real or imagined divides in adulthood.

After church, our Sundays were spent on the Corniche or at Hotel St Georges with its salt-water pool beside the sea – eventually I bought one of Emma's watercolours showing that Sunday setting and it hangs on my study wall.

On beaches south of Beirut, near the airport, I would run barefoot on the sand; tar stuck to my feet, to be washed off with petrol, yes petrol, before going home. My toes often met Roman coins beneath the surface. The collection grew. I became blasé about 2,000-year-old currency and would discard duplicates. I had not learnt, as any child knows, to keep duplicates to swap.

The mountains of Lebanon, especially near Byblos, are rich with some of the best-preserved fossils in the world. They were recorded with amazement by pre-Christian travellers, by which time they were already tens of millions of years old. Split open a chunk of limestone and, almost inevitably, there is a fish or crustacean like a rusty red, beaten, metal skeleton against the creamy stone, sealed in a moment of life as though caught by an X-ray camera.

When we lived there, parts of the coast between Beirut and Byblos were more glamorous than Saint Tropez and a magnet for the greatest screen stars. The ancient port of Byblos, one of the oldest continuously inhabited cities on earth, was first populated 3,000 to 5,000 years before Stonehenge or the great pyramids were conceived. The greatest of the pyramids are closer in time to us than they were to the foundation of Byblos.

Time and distance mean different things in differing contexts. Americans think 100 years is a long time; we think 100 miles is a long distance. Huh! In the Middle East they reckon history in thousands of years, and in Australia distance is measured in thousands of miles.

Although the family car was an amiable VW Beetle, we were driven everywhere by Papa's driver, Joseph, in a black Humber Super Snipe. The Humber was a supercilious car with a radiator that resembled disapprovingly pursed lips, not a thing for leisure. When we were not in the car, Emma persuaded Joseph to read: 'Don't just stand about waiting; read a book and we shall find you.' He began to devour books, in English, French and Arabic.

Emma returned to Lebanon only once, weeks before the start of the civil war that lasted from 1975 to 1990. Joseph met Emma at the airport; 'as usual, Madame' he had written to her, but this time he had a driver of his own. He had become a senior civil servant, respected for his grasp of literature in three languages. 'This position I owe to you, Madame, for insisting that I read.'

Artemis Cooper grew up in Beirut at the same time as I did; her father, John Julius Norwich, worked alongside mine. My path and his crossed from time to time for decades until the month he died, still working on another biography of a nation.

Alison had a doll's house with each room made from a wooden Gordon's Gin crate and walls decorated with wrapping paper. On my sixth birthday, Artemis arrived with a present for Alison – a beautiful, antique miniature tea service on a porcelain tray. I thought it the most precious thing I had seen and hers the most beautiful name I had heard.

Our flat overlooked an open park, with a raised copse to the right and, on the other side, a large walled area protecting preposterously large villas. I spent hours on the balcony looking neither left nor right but straight across the green at the poverty beyond. In this small park, people gathered and played. In the spring of 1958, as civil war erupted, our modest park hosted clashes between the military and impoverished shantytown residents.

Should you need to know, you best avoid the unpleasant effects of tear gas by lying on the bathroom floor with taps running and a damp towel wrapped around your head, covering your face. That was our Syrian nanny's solution. I unwisely stood on the balcony, watching the running battle, and feeling immune to the fire-cracking danger of shooting. However, a cloud of tear gas rose to our level and, just as anywhere, nanny knew best. She ushered us in, but not before I had been bitten by the neighbour's pet monkey that leapt from flat to flat while my screams of pain were drowned out by gunfire. Life skills acquired in Beirut were unlike anything required by most British schoolboys.

There was a wonderful greengrocer that we called French's, although that was possibly the nationality, not the name. I would sit on the ground, shelling and eating fresh peas, while business was concluded. During the troubles, there were impromptu gun emplacements on every street corner and outside all such shops. One low wall of sandbags sheltered us when a car was blown up further down the street.

After such an explosion, there are several seconds of personal silence as ears adjust and then, gradually, the rattling sounds of falling debris and screaming return – by which time I had been dragged back inside the shop, where I hid by the fresh peas. Being ignored in the chaos made me feel both isolated and secure.

The car bomb victim was, I soon heard, the father of one of the boys at school. Like most people growing up outside the comfort of the western world, I witnessed death in public long before I understood the concept of dying.

BRIEFLY BACK IN BRITAIN

1958

In the early summer of 1958, French and American naval vessels moored off the coast in Operation Blue Bat. Then we saw hundreds of American troops and tanks on the beach and taking positions around the city, beside the Lebanese army's sand-bag fortifications – exciting for a five-year-old.

The civil war grew in intensity. When bullets hit our building, we were evacuated and filmed on newsreel as we reached London after two days crossing grey Europe. Alison and I had joined the BOAC Junior Jet Club shortly after it was formed in March 1957. We went everywhere (as unaccompanied minors) with the enamel wings on our clothes and the logbook with our passports – it was a great way to travel in the 1950s and 1960s, even when fleeing a civil war.

In our London exile we stayed briefly with cousins in Finchley. It was a strange land for me.

Apart from this short stay, kindly taken in by cousins, I scarcely knew my wider family until after Emma and Papa had died. I only met my maternal grandparents a handful of times, and they were not with us when we were in London.

Emma kept us apart, with the strange explanation, 'They're my, family; it has nothing to do with you'. I do not write that with self-pity – Emma was ill-equipped to be a parent, so I grew up ignorant of the simple syntax of relationships and with no expectations, which is the reality for hundreds of millions. Parental love provides stabiliser wheels on life's bicycle – a child can learn to live with confidence rather than a fear of falling. Life without that love, without stabilisers, means learning to fall before learning to ride, distressing but not life-threatening. However, a child without a secure sense of parental love may always be vulnerable.

In November 1958, back in Beirut on Universal Children's Day, I stood in the wings of a large auditorium dressed in shorts and a white shirt with a striped tie on an elastic band. We watched as pairs of children from the whole alphabet of other nations marched onstage holding high fluttering flags far larger than they were, and then I held the hand of an English stranger as we stepped on stage, each with a small paper Union Flag taped to a ruler.

'The children of Great Britain send their greetings to the children of the Rest of the World,' I shouted audibly to the crowd of children, parents and officials. The applause sowed the seeds for a love affair with the stage that did not bear fruit for forty years.

Other young delegates called for peace, weeks after a short civil war. More than six decades have passed; all the children who paraded that day will have retired or, sadly, died and still there are few, if any, signs of peace in a region where healing is a fading illusion although there are so many people who work tirelessly to create hope.

CROSSING BORDERS FROM LEBANON

1957 to 1960

Lebanon is so compact that borders are unavoidable: to Syria in the north, Jordan beyond Syria to the east and Israel to the south.

Driving south we would see, from the road, the vast Palestinian refugee camps and their air of hopelessness. In my childish ignorance, I misheard the names and called them Chivers (like the marmalade that I ate at weekends); years later, the two main camps visible from the road are towns with tens of thousands of stateless residents and I know more of their sadness and volatility – they are Sabra and Shatila.

We entered Israel with a blank sheet of paper between the pages of our dark blue passports to avoid stamps appearing on our return. The scars of the 1948 Arab-Israeli War were raw, in some ways more so than now, and they are still unhealed after 70 years.

I think we visited every church and religious site in and around Jerusalem. The rule of my childhood was Emma's relentless determination to visit every available museum. We had no choice, but it offered some closeness to a woman without maternal instincts.

In the tiny Chapel of the Ascension on the Mount of Olives, there was only one other person visible in the dull candlelight. As we leaned over to touch the footprint on the stone from which Jesus rose to the heavens, we met the other presence, also British – a charming, earnest, learned vicar, Ronald Smythe. Ronald was, intermittently, important in my life.

Ronald was at once interesting and terrifying, both characteristics growing with age. He was a man of almost ascetic self-discipline and learning, with little time for frivolity. He became a guardian for much of the time that my parents were abroad, and I am grateful for it.

When we met him in Jerusalem, I was five or six; it was shortly after he had been ordained. Before that, he had spent two years teaching history to young Palestinians in Israel. Ronald was one of three children. His older brother died, gradually over several years and very young. His younger sister, Pat, was one of the most famous showjumpers of her age. They were close in so many ways, right down to both needing hip replacements in the same year.

We drove 1,400 feet below sea level to the Dead Sea, the lowest surface point on earth. We had the place to ourselves and swam in the thick salt water, Papa reading a newspaper while floating on the surface. There was no holiday industry then, no shower for visitors, no café. We returned home, stinging from a coating of salt. Hundreds of Dead Sea Scrolls had already been taken from the Qumran caves that we passed on our way to the lake.

On other occasions, we crossed the River Jordan, a modest stream with vast significance. In 2010, I met the three regional joint-heads of Friends of the Earth (an Israeli, a Palestinian and a Jordanian) and saw their anxiety about abuse of the river. They recognised differences that could have divided them, but chose instead to value what brought them together, in outlook and philosophy. They were angry about exported water, such as dozens of litres of water used to grow an avocado eaten in a London café. What a waste, where water is short, to squander 'the source of all life' on one smashed avocado on toast.

We passed King Solomon's Pools – reservoirs the Romans used to feed water to Jerusalem and where people swam before the birth of Christ. There we found a tortoise crossing the road and, calling it Solomon, we adopted it – things were done differently then. We provided lettuce leaves from our picnic and bottled water from the River Jordan for Solomon; it must have worked because Solomon lived a long life and, I like to think, a happy one.

Emma and Papa attended a ball in Damascus so, as nanny was Syrian and Joseph was driving, Alison and I joined them. Damascus was about as populous as Beirut, older than Byblos and people lived and traded within ancient ruins patched up for modern use. The roads were not well made; people walked in mud. While in Beirut most dressed stylishly, in silks and European clothes, in Damascus women wore headscarves and men wore cotton *dishdasha* and *keffiyeh* or military uniforms. Perhaps glamour was confined to those in cars.

We were sent to bed early in a vast, tired room in a grand hotel. Creeping out that night, we saw our nanny kissing a soldier – the first time I had seen anybody kiss with passion.

Nobody hindered our first visit to Krak des Chevaliers in 1958. Sitting on a 2,000-foot hill just north of the Syrian border, it was an astonishing fortified city built in the 12th century. Home then to thousands, it was deserted when we visited. No sign of life in a castle as large as the Cité de Carcassonne. T.E. Lawrence, Lawrence of Arabia, described it as 'perhaps the most admirable castle in the world' and we had it to ourselves.

Alison and I ran through cavernous, vaulted cellars that had stabled 3,000 horses. We scampered up long flights of stone steps and ate our picnic on ramparts overlooking a valley that had changed little in a thousand years. We peered through the arrow loops and shouted in the vast, arched, gothic chapels and halls, chasing the echoes of our voices and imagining them to be the sounds of crusader ghosts.

We drove back to Beirut after dark. Along the rough track, the hill rose sharply to our left and dropped steeply away to our right and our path was blocked by a large, well-positioned tree trunk. A fire burnt on the hill, and we saw the red dots of cigarettes; suddenly soldiers fired into the air and laughed. Papa nudged the tree with the bumper and eventually it rolled down the hill and we passed, to shouts of laughter and the sharp snap of celebratory gunfire.

Borders were always awkward, and we were often held for hours. Recently, reading *The Story of Syria*, kindly given me by its author, Syrian diplomat Ghayth Armanazi, I appreciated that life in Syria and Jordan was always much harsher than life in Lebanon.

Boys were better treated than girls in 1950s Lebanon, so Alison complained. Certainly, at borders and roadblocks, my cheeks were often pinched and my hair ruffled, apparently both good things. However, it may have been my one phrase of Arabic that caused the laughter.

Arabic is a gender-specific language; different words are used when addressing a woman or a man. The first song I could partly sing was by the Egyptian star, Asmahan, singing '*Ya habibi, ta'ala li haqni*' ('Come quickly, my love, and follow me'), words that I sang repeatedly to the amusement of all who heard. These are words whispered by a woman into the ear of her lover and decidedly not sung by a small boy to a burly border guard!

Regrettably, when we left Lebanon, I knew almost no Arabic. I could say little more than *shukran, yellah, ya habibi* and the most important word… *amahl* meaning hope.

LONDON AND BOARDING SCHOOL

1960

Papa was posted back to London. Alison was at Châtelard, a school above Montreux on Lake Geneva, and I had mumps in Beirut. Our return was delayed until the swelling cleared and we could cruise across the Mediterranean, the VW sitting on a vast string 'shopping bag' in which it had been hoisted from dock to deck.

I was by far the youngest person on board. Dressed like a marionette in *lederhosen,* I walked the decks watching adults smoking, drinking, gambling and getting much, much better acquainted.

Unsupervised, I reached out my childish hands, trying to touch the walls of the Corinth Canal as we passed through. I watched tables being set for dinner, meals being prepared in stainless steel kitchens, scarlet ribbons spewing from the top of Stromboli. Effectively alone, I stored sights, sounds and stories in my mind's library, to dip into and enjoy over the years.

The ship moored at Civitavecchia. We walked and walked in Rome. We were the only people in the Sistine Chapel; I lay on the cold floor with binoculars scouring the candle smoke-scarred ceiling. Even then, I probably felt that it was the most perfect assembly of painting I would ever see – the characters looked familiar as portraits of people we'd met in the mountains of Lebanon and on trips to Syria and Israel.

After a week on board, we reached Marseilles, and the Beetle was lifted off the deck for our drive across France and into Switzerland to collect Alison. In Montreux, Neuchâtel was sign-posted, and we pleaded to see where Emma had been born. She said 'No'.

Back across the channel, I spent a term at a local school in South London, preparing for prep school. Emma dressed me in those *lederhosen,* and I soon found that British antipathy towards Germans was strong 15 years after the war had ended; I returned home, daily, covered in scrapes and bruises, having been kicked on the ground by other boys. One, little older than me, wore metal callipers on both legs; his kicks were the most painful. Emma sent me back each day in the same outfit. Only my *lederhosen* remained untorn that week.

We are tribal; clothes are uniforms denoting membership of different groups. Clothes, like accents and language, divide us. I am not alone, I'm sure, in growing up in a home where jeans were prohibited. Emma dressed me to cultivate an image of herself as a sophisticated voyager, not to enable me to fit in. I wished never again to be that child in the playground wearing *lederhosen.* I filled a wardrobe with uniforms, matching the kit to the occasion.

I was still seven when I arrived at Colet Court, (now called St Paul's Juniors) essentially a day school in Hammersmith. It was a strange choice as I was not destined to go to St Paul's, and I had no family or friends in London. Alison's godmother (Alison Munro) was High Mistress of St Paul's Girls' School and that maybe informed the choice more than the school's suitability. In 1960 there were, I think, only three other boarders in my year: Bill Bear and Danny Danziger, both Americans who returned there; and Geoffrey Thorpe-Young, who went on to St Paul's.

At weekends, we had the run of the school. We watched *All-in Wrestling* and *The Black and White Minstrel Show* on a tiny TV in the housemaster's study. Once a term, after dark at weekends, we had fire practice. Small boys in pyjamas abseiled from a fourth-floor window on a rope attached to a 'picture hook'; even 007 would have thought twice.

In class I had periods of excellence and of indolence, topping the class or gazing out of the window and scraping through. At school and at home, I was beaten with a cane for misdemeanours I can no longer remember; at school, however, I also received praise and prizes – for writing, photography, history, French and other subjects where I occasionally excelled. I sang well and performed solos in church services and life happened to me while I watched hopefully.

I was ferried by Universal Aunts between school, the airport and places where I was parked for exeats or holidays. Emma and Papa never visited Colet Court while I was there. However, Emma attended a carol service in my last year, at Emmanuel Church in Finchley. I was to sing a solo and like to think that was the reason for her unexpected presence. After she died, I discovered it had been her neighbourhood church while growing up; it was where she and Papa had married.

PARIS, EUROPE AND MORE BOMBS

1960 to 1964

In 1960 Papa was posted to Paris.

I first visited Paris in 1956, staying in a house in the courtyard of the Ambassador's residence. I have returned almost every year since. I admire and am exasperated by Paris. It is grandiose with trappings of pomp, inequality, and coldness, with airs and graces and cosy corners yet even its romanticism can feel synthetic. While I love Rome, a muddled accumulation of past glories dressed in shades of apricots and peaches, salmon and poached haddock, my dial rarely gets beyond 'admire' with Paris – the heart of it was rebuilt, under Napoleon III, to impress and intimidate, not to comfort, beguile or function efficiently.

You can walk across Paris in less than a day (I have done so often) and see some of the most bewitching architecture and beautiful urban vistas of any city I know. Much like a painted and powdered *grande dame*, it deceives us. At its heart is a bickering, socially dysfunctional political village with some of the sharpest brains in Europe. Paris is in my blood, like oxygen or a virus.

We lived in the 16ème, a very correct arrondissement, in a modern block of flats near the Métro; we had a narrow corridor-like kitchen where I learned to cook. I grew up in many cities under siege, Paris among them. Paris was defaced with ubiquitous graffiti expressing OAS anger; *plastiques* (homemade bombs) exploded with unnerving regularity, killing people, damaging buildings, and destroying cars. The bombs occasionally stopped the electricity supply but, living near a hospital, our utilities were uninterrupted. As we cooked with gas bottles, had no television, Hi-Fi or Wi-Fi and went to bed early, it was merely a theoretical advantage.

Among Emma and Papa's friends, I remember Bill and Magda Hampshire; he was the Paris Correspondent of a London evening paper – indefatigable, kind and fun. 'Julian,' he once said, 'this is not for the girls.' I rather wish it had not been for me either; in his study, he showed me an unpublished photograph of a dead man with a hideously deformed face, crossed out with the angry blue pencil X of a censor or editor.

Bill had a press pass at the Nuremberg Trials and took a photo of Hermann Göring in his cell moments after he swallowed cyanide. In those seconds after death, muscular distortions are repulsive, vile, sick-making – it is not surprising that the photograph was suppressed.

Magda was Czech and the Hampshires drew back the Iron Curtain every summer to see her family. They drove with cases full of clothes and simple household goods to return, two or three weeks later, with empty luggage. Stories from their holidays taught me more than any schoolbook about the ravages of war and deprivations of communist occupation.

We went to Switzerland on holiday in 1962, encouraged by Bill and Isabelle Harpham (she really did come from Neuchâtel). That year I won my first photographic competition aged nine with a photo of the St Cergue railway station, near Geneva, using a 20-year-old box camera. Without wishing to sound ungrateful, the prize, a Kodak Brownie Cresta 3 camera, was rubbish! It was years before I took another reasonable photograph.

I love photography – 'writing with light' from Greek words φωτός ('*photos*' – light) and γράφω ('*grapho*' – I write). I love the shapes and colours, the intimacy of unexpected moments, the ability to see close-up from afar. I love the shadows and diamonds of light reflecting on water. It is one of my joys; a camera allows a photographer to hide and observe in plain sight; photographs keep memories alive although there were none visible at home as I grew up.

Naturally I love cameras, but not all cameras. I did not love that useless Brownie Cresta 3; nor Emma's ostentatious leather-clad Leica that rarely contained film; nor the vital but miserable diagnostic trio of the colonoscope, cystoscope and trans-oesophageal endoscope!

Tony Gamble, a friend who is a talented photographer, says that the best camera is the one you have with you; nowadays that's usually a mobile phone. I regret two missed shots, with no camera to hand. A shabbily dressed shoeshine boy, at Memphis airport, polished the shoes of an elegant businessman in a cream linen suit and silk tie. 1980 Tennessee was still racially divided yet the client was African American and the boy with the brushes was white. The second was on the steps of London's National Gallery – a rough sleeper, torn coat belted with string and surrounded by his possessions in tattered plastic bags, was giving the full 'spit-and-polish' to a pair of shoes with holes in their soles. For me both images speak of hope.

When we arrived to live in Paris, it had been blackened by generations of smoke and diesel fumes. In 1962 a decade of cleaning (made mandatory by the *Loi Malraux*) began to turn the black buildings white. Suddenly there was a reason to take photographs, although that was short-lived for me, with the arrival of that wretched Brownie Cresta 3.

In 1963 we went to Elba, and I finally learnt to swim. Something had happened in Beirut; I had apparently fallen into the Med and almost drowned. The fear of salt water in my throat has never really left but it has been mastered. Elba triggered a life-long fascination with Napoleon, following a visit to the very modest island exile home of the Emperor. Returning to mainland Italy, we saw old Roman amphitheatres, monuments, palaces, churches and museums that have become more familiar since. In Verona, we found that the huge pillars for the opera *Aida* were made of painted sponge. In Vicenza, we stepped onto the 1585 stage and set of Palladio's Teatro Olimpico. In Venice, we explored canals, glass works and museums and looked across St Mark's Square standing by the four horses plundered in 1204 from Constantinople. In Ventimiglia market, we bought trinkets I can no longer remember.

Back in Paris, I went to a fancy-dress party with a Beatles theme. I was in school uniform, badged jacket and tie, and took the Métro with a cardboard box painted like a TV covering my head and shoulders. I recently saw a photograph, and it makes me shudder. Who makes a child travel on public transport in school uniform with their head inside a box?

There was an ice rink nearby, Michel-Ange-Molitor, where I raced and played tag with other children. I skated faster than I braked... I once miscalculated the distance to the barrier – a large part of my front teeth was embedded in the wooden rail as I somersaulted over the top. Root canal treatment and dental work continued between Paris and London for two years of memorable pain and the lasting smell of tobacco on the dentists' fingers.

Christmas, as a family at home, was rare; it involved a foot high, folding plastic tree that was assembled on Christmas Eve. More often, I stayed with Papa's colleagues such as the Overtons, or with Ronald Smythe, godparents Oz and Ernest Shattock, or Dominique Cavey's family – a language exchange although he spoke only French everywhere.

The Caveys lived in Nonant-le-Pin, birthplace of Rose Alphonsine Plessis, the inspiration for Violetta in Verdi's *La Traviata*. Their home was a working farm at the heart of a village. They bred horses and trained them on their racetrack among fields of beet and apple orchards. Racing is in their blood; the Cavey Cup is raced at Vincennes. Dominique's father lived on the farm throughout the German occupation, defiantly burying shotguns and rifles in wax cloth in the orchards. He also distilled Calvados illegally, burying bottles with guns. They gave me a bottle in the 1980s; it was sublime.

I went shooting birds with those guns around the farm, failing to hit anything. We also went on 'formal' shoots, walking steadily across fields and through woodland, shooting as we went. Dominique, now retired, travels the world photographing camera-shy birds.

During my first stay with Dominique, I was introduced to their trotting horses. Most horses race flat out, galloping to the finish. In some parts of the world[1] the horses trot, surprisingly elegantly, either ridden or pulling a two-wheeled contraption, a *sulky*.

I have ridden since I was a child, so Dominique asked if I wanted to have a go.

'It isn't possible to flip these things over, is it?'

'*Non*. But try not to!'

I set off at a gentle pace and each time I lapped, Dominique yelled, '*plus vite, plus vite!*'. So, I upped my speed, lap after lap, and eventually answered my own question – it is possible to flip! It is no fun being tipped over and dragged, but there was no lasting harm to the horse (Dominique's priority) or me.

I spent one New Year's Eve in Caen with Dominique's grandparents. Oysters are the traditional NYE fare in much of France, and I firmly said, 'Thank you but no thank you'; '*pas de problème, il y a toujours des escargots*' and they were surprisingly good.

When we lived in Paris in the early 1960s, we visited Caen and Ouistreham, saw the Bayeux Tapestry and walked the length and breadth of the Normandy beaches, scrambling over the Mulberry Harbour at Omaha and Gold and playing among the rusting wreckage abandoned on the beach. I did not learn, until after Emma's death, that her two brothers, Ken and Norman, fought on those beaches on D-Day.

1 France, the UK, Scandinavia, Australia, New Zealand and the USA

CAMEROON, A DIVIDED NATION

1964 to 1967

Each continent has its own sounds and smells; however, ask anybody who has lived in Africa, and they'll say it stands head and shoulders above the rest. We moved there in 1964.

In Cameroon, on the western coast, the earth is a deep red laterite, laden with metals and minerals; in the damp heat, it smells dank and rusty – a richly truffled background to the scent of beautiful flowers, fruits, animals, food and the stench of waste. Africa is a continent of primary colours; clothes and vegetation come in loud tones. Squeaks, squawks and squeals came from animals I never saw; voices were always raised.

Initially we lived in the Francophone capital, Yaoundé, with its ultra-modern cathedral and active masses on the rough verges of unmade roads. Men carried very little; women walked straight-backed with water canisters worn like hats, babies strapped on backs or heavily laden boxes on their heads.

When we first drove through, I saw the street used as a lavatory by people, goats and cattle. Long flowing bright robes were busily printed with pictures and political messages. So much clashed with European sensibilities; gradually the sights form the exhilarating backdrop, without ever fading into the background. This is Africa.

Our first African house, in Yaoundé, had a large garden and expansive terrace, partially shaded by the first-floor balcony;

the terrace went all round the house, the grounds dropped away on three sides. At night, a watchman would sit on the terrace and gut fish to be dried the next day in the sun; after a couple of hours of smelly work he would drift off to sleep. Emma was advised, very early in our stay, to let sleeping night-watchmen lie. The French ambassador's man slept and was fired, with disastrous consequences for the French until he was re-instated; he was, they discovered, such a notorious criminal that nobody would dare to raid the grounds or house while he was there, albeit fast asleep.

The two house-staff that I remember were Valentin and Dieudonné. Dieudonné was an old-fashioned retainer, attentive and reserved. Valentin was like a Cockney market trader – quick, intelligent, witty and impossibly cheeky.

Emma heard a vacuum cleaner asthmatically struggle to inhale dust: 'Valentin, you need to empty the bag.'

'Oué, madame.'

'You unhook this panel and pull out the bag, which is too full.'

'Oué, madame.'

'Not in the kitchen, there will be dust everywhere; do it on the side terrace.'

'Oué, madame.'

'Not onto the tiles; put the dust on a sheet of newspaper.'

'Oué, madame.'

'And Valentin, you need to shut the kitchen door, or the dust will blow in.'

'Oué, madame.'

And with that Valentin walked into the kitchen,

shutting the door behind him, leaving Emma to empty the hoover. I rather admired him.

Castella, our second African home (in Buea, capital of the English-speaking west), had tall, wrought iron gates protecting the house, office and staff village. Here I was pampered – aged 12 with my own valet to lay out my clothes and bring me breakfast. We had gardeners, drivers, houseboys, cooks and valets, a butler, a night watchman – about 20 people in all. It was shamelessly and shamefully absurd – a legacy of the house's previous industrialist owner.

From the gate, a sloping drive rose to the house. Behind the house was the dark silhouette of Mount Cameroon, towering over an acre of kitchen garden with fruit, vegetables and trees bearing delicious, ripe avocados (which I disliked at the time; what a waste). Below the vast terrace of the house, a copse of Bougainvillea bushes hid a swimming pool and blushing hibiscus flowers turned from white to pink during the day (or over dinner, if they were kept in a fridge all day). I never tired of the exotic fly trap leaves that snapped shut on impact.

The Queen's official birthday was usually celebrated on the second Saturday of June throughout the world. Because of the soggy climate, Buea marked her actual birthday, 21 April. Every dignitary in West Cameroon, and a few more besides, would march up the hill to the martial sound of an out-of-tune police band playing almost familiar favourites.

The Garden Party required full mobilisation. The head gardener, a wise and experienced horticulturalist with minimal formal education, oversaw stocking the bars and clearing the empties. 'Make sure the champagne is kept in a bath full of ice, so that it is cold when we drink it, please,' instructed Emma. Some moments later she heard gunfire in the house and, surprisingly, rushed to find the source. She arrived to witness the fifth shot, as a champagne cork hit the bathroom wall, and bubbles were poured into a rapidly filling bath of fizz.

The day after the event, we read a local newspaper describing the Garden Party hosted, 'by His Excellency the British Consul, his honourable wife and their issue.' My press debut appeared next to an item headed, 'Girls These Days Tell Lies Like Rats!'

Cameroon was home for three years – three visits, 12 weeks in all, yet those experiences colour my thinking. Most of our travel was in the north-west, near the Nigerian border, where the Bamiléké peoples live, their kingdoms boasting long, distinguished histories. They are artistic, cultured, and intelligent tribes – Oprah Winfrey is of Bamiléké descent. However, they have been in opposition in Cameroon since independence in 1960 and conflict has been part of their history for centuries.

Dschang, a large town, is a place of fierce rivalry – the name means *clash* or *dispute* in the Bamiléké tongue. At a junction in the dark red earthen road entering town, we saw three poles made of split branches rising from the ground; crammed in the cleft of each was a human head, recently severed in public executions, dripping blood and not yet damaged by the sun or the birds. It was a revolting, medieval mark of death that I can still see.

We drove to the Centre Climatique, a remarkable collection of thatched houses within a safely walled estate. Being predominantly from the Bakweri tribe near Buea, our drivers and support staff were fearful and distraught; they slept in the Land Rovers outside our thatched hut, the crested Union Flag fluttering protectively on each vehicle.

That night Alison and I were trusted for the first time to fetch the family passports from reception. Returning, we peeped inside to read our parents' dates and places of birth. Emma's claim to have been born in Neuchâtel, unexplained but well-suited to the mystery of her personal narrative, was unmasked – she was born in Newcastle-upon-Tyne.

Another Bamiléké kingdom, Bafut, achieved fame in Gerald Durrell's book, *The Bafut Beagles*. Alison wrote to ask his advice when we knew we would travel there and meet the Fon of Bafut. He was the undisputed ruler of a mountain nation the size of the Isle of Wight with as much autonomy as possible for a man with more than 100 wives. Durrell's kind response sent greetings to the Fon, described how we would be welcomed and advised, 'make sure your parents take the right tribute; the Fon particularly likes whisky and gin.'

Having driven through lush mountain scenery, we reached the Fon's palace or *Ntoh*. It was rebuilt 120 years ago, with a vast thatched hall and bow-to-get-in door for commoners. King Achirimbi had his own full height door and greeted us with an exchange of diplomatic niceties; it was an awesome moment. Papa presented a wooden case containing bottles of Johnny Walker and Gordon's. The delighted Fon clapped his hands and horn beakers appeared. Durrell was right. The Fon liked whisky and gin – he mixed the cocktail 50/50.

Bamiléké slit drums are short logs of light wood, hollowed out to different thicknesses so that a drummer, with sticks of varying weights, creates a tuneful rhythm or sends messages over great distances. The phrase 'jungle drums' implies gossip – in 1960s Africa, the slit drums substituted for telephones or radios in emergencies.

There were no meaningful local maps, and navigation coupled with tribal discord was a nightmare. When policemen stopped us, drums had told them we were coming, and drums reported a collapsed bridge on our route. We were diverted through the bush, bouncing along beaten mud paths with branches slapping the windscreens. We crossed streams or went through clearings; it was in one of these that I shouted, 'Stop!'

There was a crowd, slightly away from our track, and the sounds of drums and singing. Tentatively, we got out of the Land Rovers and several people approached. An African priest greeted us in French while others patted our arms and faces gently with their open palms.

The priest had just finished a service in this village that long ago converted to Christianity. In his sermon he announced that the Diocese would fund a simple church and a school room. The villagers were celebrating this news. He said he was the only person in the crowd who had ever seen a white face and the elders had told their people what they themselves believed, that we were angels come to confirm the priest's promises.

The dancing drums did not falter as villagers manhandled Alison and me gently into the circle. The drums' crossing rhythms subtly changed with no signal – four beats to a bar then three, like a waltz, or five, like Dave Brubeck or, mostly, two like a human heart resting or racing, flighty or fearful. The crowd swayed; we danced as well. The Twist was popular in Britain then, imitating the motion of using a towel after a shower. In this remote village, with neither showers nor towels, we danced the Twist as though we had wings.

Albert Schweitzer lived and worked for much of his life in a leper colony in Lambaréné, 250 miles south of Yaoundé. His story caught my imagination; I read what I could – a biography, an old encyclopaedia. Recitals of his achievements sounded like hyperbole or fiction and turned out to be understatement. Schweitzer was remarkable; with four doctorates, he was a musician, philosopher, theologian, man of medicine and a Nobel Laureate who dedicated his life 'to God's work'. A Lutheran, he was rejected by the Catholic mission to which he first applied. He was 38 when he began his mission. The more I read, the more this complex man fascinated and influenced me. His story of hope underpinned my eventual vocation.

In 1965, Emma and Papa met him and promised we would go on our next visit, the Easter holidays in 1966; sadly, Schweitzer had died by then.

In 500 BC, Hanno the Carthaginian Navigator recorded seeing Mount Cameroon's volcanic activity from the sea. It is the fourth highest mountain in Africa and remains active. The peak is 14 miles from the Atlantic – its slopes sweeping down to the sea at Limbe where beaches of soft black volcanic sand carry hot channels from underground torrents into the sea, making it our favourite beach. The mountain's western slope records 10 metres of rain annually, 20 times more than London; it is one of the world's wettest spots.

Not now meeting Dr Schweitzer, we set out in 1966 to 'conquer' Mount Cameroon. The climb goes through dense tropical rainforest, into undulating grasslands and onto a harsh moonscape scattered with basalt plugs, reaching a bare, cold summit. Beside the chilly upper path, there were hot pockets exuding steam from which we scooped lava, malleable and uncomfortably hot. We walked and scrambled above 13,000 feet, within 200 feet of the top, when we were enveloped in cloud. Visibility fell to nothing, and we stopped overnight, almost choked by an open fire on which we cooked a meal of tinned soup. I was the youngest white person to have reached that high, the guide said. So what? It's not the top!

The next day, we descended in a tropical flood of rain. The porters undressed completely, bar a small *cache-sexe,* and put their clothes in plastic bags inside the boxes. We put on everything imaginable to keep dry, to no avail; we were soon soaked, giving the porters the last laugh. Paths vanished in the rain, so Alison and I each made a banana leaf canoe and, sitting, floated bumpily down streams that had usurped the paths.

Tribal clashes in Cameroon did not make European headlines, despite tens of thousands of deaths in a civil war; we saw those severed heads and saw the smoking remains of burnt-out villages where the residents had been encircled and cremated while alive. At birth, life expectancy was about 40. By contrast, the neighbouring Biafran War was well covered, probably because of the potential impact on oil supplies as well as the tenacity of Frederick Forsyth, who was embedded as a journalist. Papa apparently went into Biafra twice in 1967 to 'rescue' Forsyth, returning without him on both clandestine incursions.

CHORAL WORKS AND WORKSHOPS

1964 to 1970

Back in the UK, Emma, Papa and I did a three-stop tour to find a school – Marlborough was dismissed by Emma, who opted for Oundle because, she said, it had a river and sailing. In hindsight, knowing better how her mind worked, I suspect it was because the ambassador in Yaoundé, Sir Edward Warner, was himself an Old Oundelian.

The third leg of the journey was that single childhood visit to Darvel, where I met some of my Scottish family for the only time while Papa was alive. It was decades before I again spent time with cousins Nicol, Billy and Joe.

While there, we went to a wedding in Largs; knowing no-one as the reception groaned on, I wandered into formal gardens where I was joined by the local MP, Fitzroy Maclean. He was used to the limelight but, for a magic moment in that garden, I was his audience. He told me great tales such as boys love. Decades later I learned that he may have been a model for Fleming's James Bond and had written *Eastern Approaches*, the ultimate adventure.

Oundle is a pretty Cotswolds-style town in Northamptonshire, with nothing to protect it from the ice-cold Russian winds. The school was part of the town but did not swamp it. I arrived on the first day of a new school year alone, aged 11, knowing nobody, having visited the school briefly once, and with my parents in Africa. On that first day I met Benjamin Rhodes, who has been a wonderful friend ever since.

Otherwise, I just tried to follow the flow.

The first weeks were spent in a haze, learning the names of houses, their house colours, routes from A to B, the names and functions of different buildings – in brief, something akin to the London cabbies' Knowledge. Every new boy had to pass this 'tick's test', essential for basic survival. I gradually found my way around.

I became a chorister and discovered the importance of music both at Oundle and for me personally. That term, the whole school sang Bach's Mass in B Minor; I sat in the middle of the front row of trebles in the very small Chancel Choir, the group who sang most. It is a vital part of the school's annual traditions to sing a major choral work and over the years I sang the *Messiah,* Requiems by Brahms, Fauré and Verdi, Vivaldi's *Gloria*, the *Matthew* and *St John Passions*, the *Nelson Mass* and Rossini's *Petite Messe Solennelle.*

My 12th birthday coincided with my first half term at school. Emma and Papa were out of touch in Africa and forgot the niceties of the school calendar, so I was left with nothing planned for the *exeat* week. After the other boys departed, I was found by 'Chaps' Anderson, the housemaster, alone in the silent common room. I was a lost parcel with no forwarding address; he 'made arrangements'.

Chaps, so-called because it was his word for everybody, had been with Orde Wingate's Chindits in Burma where he served with Arthur Hearne who lived in the next village with his wife Ursula and four daughters. I had a date for tea on Sunday.

I arrived in my best suit and ate chocolate cake before

the Hearnes drove me back to the empty school boarding house. 'Come again, any time; just bicycle down and remember to wear your roughest clothes.' I went back the next weekend, the next and the next. The Little Manor House had a large garden surrounded by collapsing dry-stone walls and gradually, between impromptu games of football in the paddock with the girls, we repaired the walls and then found other projects over the years. It was a slow week alone at school, eating at a long refectory table for one, but it soon passed whereas the friendship lasted.

When Arthur died, two years later, Ursula insisted that the visits continue. I had taken other boys down with me and they in turn took siblings who took their friends and, over 20 years, Ursula hosted dozens of boys; most were at her funeral, more than 30 years later.

By Christmas, Emma had sorted out the diary. I stayed with Ronald Smythe at his vicarage at Belhus Park, in East London. I went to the youth centre each Saturday and church each Sunday and otherwise spent my time on my own.

The modern brick vicarage housed an incongruous grand piano bearing silver-framed photographs of family. Lost in my own world, I did not read Ronald's sorrow. He was barely 20 when his father died, and he lost his wife within months of marrying in 1961. Canon Sydney Evans officiated at their wedding and anointed Gill in hospital before she died. Ronald was always a generous, yet restless, soul. His autobiography, *Not One Sparrow,* was published when he was 76. It uncovers a lifetime of financial and emotional setbacks and insecurities. He was committed to his spiritual and psychological ministry until his death not long ago.

When young, we do not recognise who is important in our lives until it is too late to thank them. I wish we could talk now. Unlike Ronald, I was not unhappy or depressed as a child; I was simply bewildered and muddling through; there, but not really part of things.

The next term I knew my way around at school. I sang, occupying the same central front row seat in the Chancel when Oundle hosted *Songs of Praise*. I loved it; I had a voice but soon discovered I lacked the basics of sight-reading and musicality.

The end of term train took me to London, and I flew unaccompanied to Cameroon.

On my return to Oundle, a month later, I was in such pain that eventually the school doctor was called. 'It could be worse;' he joked, knowing nothing about me, 'you could be in a jungle without a hospital!'

'Yesterday, sir, I was in the jungle'. He stopped laughing. An ambulance blue lighted me 30 miles to Northampton where I was rushed into surgery for an emergency appendectomy.

The hospital stay lasted for more than a week, including the Sunday when *Songs of Praise* was broadcast from Oundle. A TV appeared in my room; I was surrounded by doctors and nurses. A cameraman may have slept; a lens rested excessively on me, hogging more than my quota of the limelight. None of the family ever saw the broadcast.

There were complications with a post-operative infection and persistent abscess, so I spent the summer term isolated in the school sanatorium with books and prep brought to me, essays and exam papers taken back. Initially a coal fire was set and lit in the room before 7 a.m. and the Light Programme (now called Radio 2) listening time was strictly rationed – I healed to two tracks… 'Paint It, Black' and 'River Deep – Mountain High'. I had occasional visits from boys, masters and Ursula Hearne; otherwise, I was alone.

That summer, while healing, I began sailing at the Tamesis Club in Teddington. I crewed a 14-foot Merlin Rocket (sail number 1266) owned by the father of a school friend; we raced regularly on the Thames and sometimes entered regattas off the south coast, launching off the beach. I had fun off the water and tried in vain to win on it – the competition included future Olympic sailor Chris Law and his brother Tim.

I sailed a bit at Oundle when not running cross country or rowing. Oundle's Third VIII was wisely coached by Mr Philips and we did well, rowing a heavy, clinker-built boat when our competitors were in slick shells. We were accustomed to sneers at the start. Luckily our old boat was very stable while the shells wobbled uncontrollably with an inexperienced crew; we won races that we should have lost and with the victories came silverware and tankards; you can have the best equipment in the world, but it is worthless in the wrong hands.

I have spoken French almost since I could speak. It was the main language in Beirut, Paris and Cameroon and children absorb languages, almost by osmosis. The British think it may confuse a child to face more than one language; my in-laws were vocal on the subject. That misses the point. The pace of a child's learning is determined by their grasp of concepts; having learnt the idea of 'a door' or 'pain', a 'pair of shoes,' or 'hunger', it makes little difference to their development if they add two or three words for each. Children can differentiate between languages, speaking French with one person and English with another. That is in part because each language has different physical characteristics in pronunciation that set them apart. It is easier to learn as a child than later. I was hardly a teenager when a teacher said, 'You now have a greater French vocabulary than the average *ouvrier dans La France profonde*'.

Oundle's Combined Cadet Forces exercised on Wednesdays. Some were Navy or Air Force cadets; most were Army, with camps, rifles, marching and raw fingers from polishing.

In 1968 a group who enjoyed riding formed a cavalry, cycling three miles to Barnwell each week. We hacked across some of Britain's most beautiful countryside, crossed mercifully low hedgerows, learnt to jump over rickety red and white poles, cleaned tack and had tea, surrounded by our riding teacher's acres and pets. We only attended two formal parades a year and riding is more fun than spit-and-polishing a pair of boots.

Barnwell's most famous residents were the Duke and Duchess of Gloucester. Their oldest son, Prince William, was a British diplomat in Nigeria and a passionate pilot. At some point he called Papa to say he'd like to stay for a few days. 'I'll be flying myself so would you meet me at the local airport, please, Nicol? Just to smooth the way.'

On the day, Papa received a call from Customs. 'Come quickly. We are about to arrest a British smuggler.' Papa arrived and asked for details. 'A man is flying in and says he carries whisky. He is a smuggler; we will arrest him.' In the nick of time, Papa established that they'd heard 'Grant William, like the whisky' instead of 'Prince William'.

'Quite a long journey but all OK. Why the large reception committee, Nicol?'

'Oh, don't worry about that – the story will keep.'

The prince settled in for a long weekend at Castella, causing happy chaos by popping into the kitchen for a chat whenever he wanted a cup of tea.

When Prince William transferred to Japan, his parents invited us to tea at Barnwell Manor – a 'Thank you' for hospitality offered to their son in Africa. The Duke drove a Mini Moke for the short walk to the sheltered garden of rose bushes within the walls of a ruined castle.

'Come on, legs, why won't you take a Royal command? Two of my brothers were kings, young man; I'm jolly glad I'm not.'

He was Colonel Blimp in the flesh: a ruddy, round face and a moustache, victim of multiple strokes. In his 60s, he was cheerful and grumpy in one breath without an ounce of unkindness. He was easy to like.

The Duchess looked delicate and beautiful, with an enigmatic smile, seeming to prefer the company of her dogs. After a house and garden tour, we sat at a table heaped with foil-wrapped biscuits, a hopeful sign. Then a dozen or more dogs arrived: 'Julian, would you unwrap the biscuits, please, and make sure each dog gets one.' I never tasted the biscuits.

Prince Richard joined us, looking impossibly cool in jeans and a white T-shirt. Both garments were banned at home; Emma called them 'common'! The young prince was studying architecture and showed us the galley proof for his first book, *On Public View,* a coffee table extravaganza of his London photographs. He took us through each photo's history; I remember one story clearly.

The statue of Achilles behind Wellington's house on Hyde Park Corner was given to the victorious Duke by the Ladies of England. Prince Richard tried every angle to get the right photograph: 'I even tried a shot behind the fig leaf, but there's nothing there.' When the warrior was unveiled, several ladies fainted at the statue's outrageous nakedness. A hat was passed and funds collected for a strategic leaf. So incensed was the sculptor (Sir Richard Westmacott) that he may have chopped off a bit or wrapped the offending item in a fig leaf like a Greek *dolma* so that, when it was unveiled again, nothing could cause offence; Achilles' heel was clearly not his most vulnerable spot.

Prince William, heir to the title and the reason for our visit, died a short while later in a tragic air race accident. Fred Marsh (about whom, more later) was also a competitor that day.

After one African visit, I returned unaccompanied to school, stopping in Chad, with the final leg of the trip on the school train. In our first lesson of term, we learnt about water distillation. The technique seems simple, involving a ditch, plastic sheeting, and a bowl to catch water.

'Imagine,' our teacher said, 'you're on the edge of

Lake Chad. There's water as far as the eye can see;' (my hand was in the air) 'you can't be certain that the water is safe, so you distil it.' I may have been waving by now, forgetting that some things are best left unsaid. 'You dig a hole, and do as I describe… – yes, what is it, Morton?'

'Excuse me, sir, but yesterday morning there was no water in Lake Chad – I was there, and it was completely dry.'

Workshops were mandatory at Oundle. For one week each term, rotating around the school, we would don brown overalls and casual clothes and work with our hands while everybody else was in class. The training was so thorough that the Rolls-Royce apprenticeship was a year shorter for Oundelians and, in WWII, the school manufactured ammunition boxes.

There were four main workshops while I was there: pattern making, foundry, engineering and carpentry, with a growing area for electrical and electronics work and fibreglass or composites. First, we made our own vice, pattern, cast, machining and finishing. I then branched out into rather chunky and ill-finished bits of furniture that lasted for decades. Other boys made hovercraft and dinghies, musical instruments and Hi-Fi sets.

An unloved or lonely child, as I was, often lacks confidence or boundaries and is vulnerable to predators. Abuse presents as relief from isolation, a reward for being noticed, or it nurtures a child's sense that they are unloved for a reason, it's their own fault. Often, only luck protects or saves the child from lasting harm. While I was at Oundle, a teacher that I risked getting to know too well disappeared under a cloud, pursued by rumours; a predator was removed. I was, perhaps, lucky. Much more important than that, I believe that I am defined by what I do myself and not by somebody else's actions towards me.

Emma and Papa bought a house in Claygate, near London. When it was not rented out, we spent holidays there while Papa remained in Africa. At times, I did not see Papa for a year at a stretch.

A local family advertised in a shop window. 'Help needed to prep, serve and clear a family Sunday lunch for twelve'. The family had fun from the first drinks that I served to the moment I left. After clearing up, I took a tray piled high with coffee, cups and saucers into the sitting room; I had taken on too much.

I entered the room and the father, Brian Rix, was in full flow as an increasingly inebriated Majordomo announcing guests at a ball. Straight-faced, he called preposterous names while tears of laughter rolled down every cheek, including mine; the tray rattled dangerously. Still in character, slurring his speech, he took the tray; 'Let me help; we don't want to shpill champagne on the Duchesshh of Tiddlypush, do we? Ladiesh and Gentlemen…' I sat and watched. He was very funny, in private as in public, and unusually considerate and kind.

I joined the orchestra at school and lasted a term as a violinist before moving to percussion. Whenever I hear the overture for *Die Meistersinger* or Sibelius' *Finlandia*, the physicality of drums and cymbals rushes back. Our cavalry eventually stopped, and we reverted to marching. My indifferent percussive skills qualified me to be a Colour Sergeant and to lead the band. There were two highlights in a Drum Major's calendar.

The CCF parade was Emma's second appearance at a school event; holding her beautiful Leica, she clicked as I marched in my red sash, bellowing commands and marshalling the troops with a large silver-headed mace. She had no film; no photographs were taken.

That year I led the Remembrance Sunday Parade slowly to allow WW1 survivors to keep up. We still went too fast so, to counter march the band, I threw the mace confidently in the air. It crashed to the ground. The band still turned, and I recovered the shattered pieces. Nobody noticed. The teacher in charge heaped praise on the quick-thinking process… praise that evaporated when I gave him the broken bits of ancient wood and silver.

In 1969, seven of us took against an anthem we were due to sing in chapel. Given Oundle's strong musical tradition, each pupil had a folder for sheet music. One was classified in our folders as Setting 14, a wretched dirge *Jubilate,* which, without irony, droned incessantly on a single note the words 'O, be joyful'. One Friday, we secretly collected all but three of the 800 copies. The next morning, after a futile appeal by Head of Music Robin Miller, Setting 14 was heard no more.

Within an hour, we'd been shopped and beaten by the squash-playing headmaster. Ouch! Well thrashed, we returned to our quarters and found the housemaster waiting. 'My study, now please.' Nervously we followed but, once there, he handed us a glass of beer each. 'I'm sure you'd rather not sit. I wanted to thank you for getting rid of that dreadful piece of music.'

I am grateful for the broad musical taste that formed at Oundle. Initially it was Bach, Beethoven and the Beatles; gradually I heard and learned more: Mozart, Brahms, Richard Strauss and Verdi. It was decades before I began to value Wagner's relentless intensity, the Great American Songbook's clever delight or, after I saw them in concert, the wanton letting go of Deep Purple and hard rock. Music is a universal language of pain and joy.

The school's skill was to offer boys a balance between academic, cultural, sporting and manual options, and each had a chance to shine. It taught hope and a sense of community.

MUNICH AND THE PRAGUE SPRING

1967 to 1970

There was no pause between Cameroon and the next posting, Munich. Emma and Papa moved into a large house in Harlaching, a leafy suburb. It was my twelfth home and full of potential adventure. A network of tunnels, blocked with metal doors, connected our cellar to other diplomatic houses. There were sinister basement rooms with drainage and hooks on the walls. In the 1930s, notorious Nazis lived in Harlaching and the houses in our 'secret' network had been seized in the 1940s.

Mid-1960s Munich was a capital of pretention and joyous frivolity. In Germany's strictly classless democracy, Munich was where real and spurious titles were flaunted: a magnet for jaded nobility from central Europe and for the vast, bejewelled new wealth of post-war reconstruction and the *Mittelstand*-driven industrial revolution. Munich rebuilt its opera house, won the right to hold the 1972 Olympics and hosted HM The Queen. The city was permanently in party mode, and I was in a ring-side seat.

Hjalmar Schacht was an economist and banker, admired on both sides of the Atlantic. He had also been a president of the Reichsbank and Hitler's Nazi Minister of Economics until 1937. He was tried at Nuremburg and was one of the few who were acquitted. He lived in Munich, until his death in 1970, and visited us at home one evening when I was 14.

Back at school that autumn, our history teacher described the term's syllabus, looking at the inter-war years, and rhetorically asked, 'Who was the architect of the economic miracle that consolidated Hitler's hold on power?'

My hand rose unwisely; I replied insufferably, 'Hjalmar Schacht, sir.'

'How the blazes do you know that?' demanded the usually imperturbable historian.

'Because I met him last week, sir, and he told me so himself.'

Munich enjoys a near perfect climate: snowfall in winter and hot summers – hot enough for part of the 900-acre Englische Garten to be dedicated to nudists since the 1960s, although I never had the courage or the physique. I loved the dry tranquillity of a blanket of snow, softening all sound except the crunch of boots, but I did not ski after my first attempt.

We went with a group of Munich's consular corps to Garmisch-Partenkirchen in 1969. The nursery slopes were shut, marking Eisenhower's death, so my first experience was from the top of the mountain, quickly slumping to sit on the back of my skis the whole way. One of our group, Fabrizia Giovinazzi, did not stop laughing until we had returned to her aunt's house in Munich. As the adults hit the drinks, Fabrizia and I discovered that we each made a good ragù; together we cooked for the whole party.

When we met, Fabrizia was a Communist, a budding scientist and a good tennis player (ranked 15 in Italy at the age of 16). We seldom played tennis. She thrashed me right-handed and trounced me left-handed until she said, 'I can't tie both hands behind my back,' so we found other things to do. I stayed with her in Naples or in the large, fortified family house in Puglia, an insight into a feudal world. She stayed with me in London.

We spoke and wrote for years in French because her English and my Italian could not reliably say what we wanted. Her independent-mindedness and sense of justice never faltered. Through her eyes, I first witnessed the radical changes in Italy into the 1970s, the rise of the Red Brigades and violent extremism, worsening divisions between north and south, and the growth in Mafia activity as Sicilian and Neapolitan families collaborated against the law. One evening in Naples, dozens of her family friends came to drinks. Outside, several armed men waited; each youngster arrived with a guard. When Emma and Papa moved to Italy years later, I already knew about the country's civil war.

Emma's great friend in Germany was Esther Bloch. The two of them talked almost every week for more than 30 years. Papa got on well with Friedl, a distinguished businessman who had served as a submarine commander in the war, and I met Martin, the younger Bloch son, with whom I share a birthday. Martin was my first friend away from school and the first person anywhere with whom I had an ordinary relationship that children take for granted. More than fifty years on and we are closer than ever.

Dominique, my French language exchange, came to Munich. We visited the concentration camp at Dachau. Five of us lunched that day: the others were Dominique, Fabrizia, and a young German (not Martin) and his father, an academic living nearby. After sausages and shandy, we approached the camp, where the academic stopped his son, 'Not here, not for you; *das hat nichts zu tun bei uns* – this has nothing to do with us.'

Dachau was the first concentration camp – a prototype for what was to come. Here, the chilling words *Arbeit Macht Frei* first appeared in wrought iron. The site was neither a memorial nor wholly abandoned; original huts remained *in situ*, not in good condition but in little danger of collapse. Nothing was off-limits. We walked through unattended gas chambers and climbed onto the roof to where the cylinders of poison were fed into the shower heads.

In a hall, while leaving, we saw hauntingly repulsive pictures of murder, described as medical experiments: people tethered under water and photographed with a stop clock until they drowned; others timed being frozen to death by hypothermia. The three of us toured the site all afternoon, unaccompanied, in uncharacteristic silence with no other visitors. It had by then turned windy and wet and the place was Godless and desolate.

For years I have re-run those images of Dachau, and my revulsion is unchanged. Tragically, it is no better now, with thousands of killers in modern war zones of staggering barbarity.

I spent two Easter holidays grilling *hendl,* as Bavarians call chicken, at a *Deutsche Supermarkt*. Aged 15 and with no experience, I had an assistant, a man some 25 years my senior. He was anxious to please, emotionally fragile; his German was faltering. Born in Germany, forced into the Wehrmacht as a teenager, he was captured and not repatriated from Russia until 1956 (or later, according to him). His pain remained fresh after the trauma of more than a decade in frozen labour camps. Forbidden to speak German, he had no contact with family or countrymen. Eventually, he talked of the hell of slavery. After my second stint, he had the confidence to run the grills himself, a shattered shell rediscovering purpose by patting paprika and herbs on a chicken and grilling it to perfection.

Martin and I sailed regularly on Starnberger See in his father's beautiful 20-foot day-boat with highly varnished wood and a small cabin. We had Swallows & Amazons adventures, including one night to the Lake's only island, Rosen Insel. We took the tender to an isolated beach; I stood, just as Martin gave the painter rope a quick tug, and I toppled into the water.

Germany is regulated. Sailors must have a licence of proficiency in one of three categories: A is for rivers and lakes. Martin and I studied in Lindau for our *A Schein für Segler* at the Bodensee Yachtschule, an intensive course with serious exams and very serious playing. One evening (actually, at 3 one morning) we overstepped the mark. Into a darkened room of contented teenagers burst the old-school commandant, Kapitän Kühn. Lights on, situation assessed, and concise command loudly given, *'Morgen früh, koffer packen*[2]*.'*

Lake Constance, or Bodensee, sits at the juncture of Germany, Switzerland and Austria. 40 miles long and 10 miles wide, it is Europe's third largest lake. The surrounding

2 As KK spoke there was no ambiguity: those four words meant 'Pack your bags first thing tomorrow morning and leave by the earliest available train.' By breakfast time he had a chance to rethink. We stayed.

mountains create their own weather system with unpredictable storms and warm summers. We were taught to handle boats in all winds, in German. We were also taught First Aid with tips for Oktoberfest injuries, such as a hit on the head with a tankard. I got my *A Schein* certificate.

Sailing was the perfect sport, requiring concentration, strength, agility, and teamwork… all qualities that I decidedly lacked or needed to improve. Sailing has something for everyone.

That summer I did a CCF camp – pony trekking in Devon. The cavalry thing still had a bit going for it. Then I joined Emma and Alison for the journey across Europe from London on the couchettes of a sleeper train.

We met Prof Dr Auer on that train. He was a director of Munich's Deutsches Museum, the world's largest museum of science and technology. Hermann Auer was professionally admired around the word; privately he was an enthusiast, an eccentric and a complete petrolhead, even before the war. Shortly after our train journey, he came to drinks, met a countess with a wonky knee and offered her a lift home. 'Yulian, come and see my new car,' said the Professor, leaving with the countess on his arm. The only car in the street was a brightly coloured Lamborghini and into this we lowered the octogenarian aristocrat with difficulty. I must have looked concerned because his parting words were 'Don't worry, Yulian – *keine Sorge*. We'll work out how to get her out by the time we reach our destination!' and with that he roared off, leaving rubber on the road.

Boarding school, long absences abroad and frequently being away from home for holidays meant that I had not observed or expected the deterioration in my parents' relationship. I was woken by fearsome screams and shouting at 2 a.m. one morning. Emma had packed a case, donned a fur coat and was leaving to take a waiting cab to a hotel in central Munich. I followed in pyjamas and bare feet into the snow and carried her back to the house. Neither parent spoke of it; nor did they really live together again.

In fact, I saw nothing clearly. I could never read what was on a blackboard or see road signs but assumed that was normal. At 15 I had my first eye test and have worn specs to correct middling myopia ever since. Sometimes I take them off to enjoy the watercolour wash of imperfect vision; it took time to get used to seeing properly.

The *Nijmegen Vierdaagse* consists of four marched marathons on consecutive days, with a pack. It is only really enjoyed when you have finished. In the 1960s, almost 25,000 people were involved each year, mostly soldiers from almost every country in Europe and North America – countries that had been at war with each other twice since the *Vierdaagse* first happened in 1909.

We trained at school, individually and as a platoon, for months in all weathers, with bleeding blisters and abrasive boots; eventually we were ready for the challenge. I get irritated when people call the Netherlands 'flat'. Our longest march, on the third day, involved a hill that felt like a mountain to climb (it is, in fact, only 350 feet high), and a straight road that took an eternity to descend; a visible church spire did not change in size or proximity for two hours.

We stayed all week in a school, sleeping in makeshift dormitories in the classrooms. We set off before dawn, returning for the afternoon. After food and treatment for blisters, we were meant to sleep, but suffering feet are amazingly resilient when young men from a single sex school find an assembly hall, a rickety record player and not a lot of light. We danced with local girls of our age, singing along with songs that were all in English. For those four nights, my partner was the only girl in Nijmegen, probably the only girl in the Netherlands, who spoke not a word of English. She was pretty and a very good dancer and, in the absence of other means of communication, she taught me how to kiss.

I returned with a military medal and memories of marching on the final day along crowded streets with old men crossing to shake our hands and young girls giving us flowers or chaste kisses of congratulation. Many soldiers failed to finish the full four days, but in 1969 our group of schoolboys completed the 102 miles intact; we felt triumphant and were treated as liberators by many in the crowd, for whom 1944 was a living memory.

Back home, on a rare occasion when Papa was present, I was summoned. Emma stood holding a bamboo cane and waving a letter. A priest at the Nijmegen school had written denouncing the kiss. Emma raged that my offence (of being a teenager) had jeopardised Papa's career. I was too tall and far too fast to be beaten again. It was an unpleasant feature of childhood. That was the last time it was attempted at home.

Papa was intelligent, diligent, charming and invisible. Long before we left Lebanon, Emma had colonised and subjugated him as a stepping-stone to ill-defined ambitions. By the time I began to learn some insight he had, I think, given up hope of liberation and opted for dutiful survival – head down and let's get through this. His eyes lit up in company until even that pleasure was cut short by Emma and the early onset of Alzheimer's.

The Queen and Prince Philip, in the 1960s, were more glamorous than the Kennedys – if you do not believe me, look at photographs of them together at Buckingham Palace in 1961.

In May 1965, Her Majesty attended a gala performance of *Der Rosenkavalier* at the recently rebuilt Opera House in Munich. Local papers showed two photos to mark the visit. The Queen (long white gloves, tiara and sash) next to a Bavarian industrialist's wife (deep in diamonds). The caption read '*altes Gelt*' and '*neues Gelt*' – Old Money v New Money.

Opera is an acquired taste. I acquired it at 14 at a performance of *Der Rosenkavalier*, sitting in the seat occupied by The Queen two years before, between my parents and a very grand lady – the 1967 dress code was black tie and bling. Shortly after the overture began, as the horns blared '*awhoop, awhoop, awhoop, awhooo*!' the grand lady leant towards me and whispered, 'That was the orgasm.' It was the sum of my sex education – deeply embarrassed, I never looked at the grand lady again; let's call her Frau Robinson… *The Graduate* appeared in cinemas at about that time.

Russian tanks rolled into Prague in 1968, 180 miles away from us in Munich. It was a re-run of 1956, when Russians crushed Hungary's uprising.

The first responsibility of the British Consulate General in Munich was the safe passage of British citizens held at the border. Papa went to smooth the evacuation, and we sat in the Café Luitpold, which stayed open until dawn to welcome those fleeing the Russians. Directed by Papa, people in cars and coaches reached Munich after midnight. Hot chocolate is the mainstay of the Luitpold; that night they served it by the tanker load.

Evacuated Britons reached the café with stories and photographs. A young student took pictures through a hole in his coat. He had developed them in Prague and hid them in the lining of his case. They showed tanks ridden by young conscripts, bewildered by the crowd's hostility; the soldiers thought they were on exercises. Road signs pointed in random directions, over-painted in Russian, 'Москба *2000* КМ.' Tanks sank into roadworks, where holes were covered with domestic sheets painted grey to resemble cobbles and trap the Russians.

We heard stories of Czechs resisting with imagination, courage and wit. They paid with blood. Not all the photographs showed humour; more than 100 Czechs were killed, and vastly more were wounded. Twenty-one year-old 'Jan Palach' and 'self-immolation' entered the vocabulary of every language – 20 years later I stood on the haunting spot in Wenceslas Square where he died in a flash of flames. The Prague Spring failed but put another crack in the façade of communism.

Alison and I joined tens of thousands marching through Munich in protest. When we reached Königsplatz, we stood a few feet from the balcony where Hitler presented Mussolini to the serried ranks of Nazi faithful in 1937. Soviet flags were burnt while people waved the Czech red, white and blue. Europe was volatile in 1968, with workers and students fomenting strikes, riots and occupations. The police watched quietly until, without warning, water cannon rumbled into the crowd. The spray was gentle (I have seen worse in Belgium, where water cannon lifted burly miners off the ground), but a voice called, 'Run; don't get wet; they use coloured water.' People ran past, soaked and pink. 'The police go around the cafés and bars picking up anybody with wet, pink clothes.'

We ran.

COLOMBO AND THE TAMIL UPRISING

1970 to 1972

It was still Ceylon when I was there – the change, to Sri Lanka, came in 1972; the 'Blessed Island'. The Portuguese, (the local telephone directory was packed with the names De Sousa, De Silva, Pereira and Fernando) called it Ceilão, hence *Ceylon*. Sri Lanka sits so close to India that, 500 years ago, one could walk along Adam's Bridge from one to the other. Yet this Indian Ocean pearl is light years apart from its larger neighbour.

Papa arrived from Munich as Deputy High Commissioner, never living in his official house but choosing a modest bachelor's bungalow opposite Sirimavo Bandaranaike, Ceylon's Prime Minister. We were exceptionally well guarded during 1971's JVP insurrection and the sharp military clampdown. Emma waited for six months, flew out weeks before I was due to go there, took umbrage at something or nothing and returned to Britain within the week.

The Colombo Club was 100 years old and looked its age; however, with an overnight curfew and civil unrest, it was our refuge. Parties ended after dawn with a big breakfast. We'd sleep at home then go back to the club after lunch. Sri Lanka is so close to the Equator that dawn and dusk arrive at 6 a.m. or p.m. Nightly we witnessed clouds of crows leave en masse for the trees in Victoria (now Viharamahadevi) Park, dislodging the fruit bats, whose sinister black swarms settled where crows had been during the day.

Gambling was forbidden; racing was banned so the

racecourse was where we rode for fun. There is always an appetite for betting; a way can usually be found. A wiry waiter with a big smile was the bookie's runner, his scruffy notebook full of illegible marks recording wagers. He collected cash and ran to a gambling Don to place bets on UK races. Our man was not always lucky, failing to reach the Don and returning bets on horses that had won, 'I am sorry, sir, I was too late to bet. Here is your stake.' We learned not to rely on winners, only to be sure that all losing bets were placed in time.

A curfew was strictly enforced. Like all teenagers, we regarded being grounded as a challenge but soon learnt otherwise. One young American acquaintance tried to dash from one party to another on his motorbike. He was shot and killed at an army roadblock *en route*.

There was a night-club, of sorts, in an old school hall with Ceylon's only rock band, Marci Perera's *Spitfires* – good music but not much fun with a dull room and an early finish. The finest parties were private. Bankers' houses were best, like the Gash home with a snooker room and covered terraces. The two sons, slightly older than me, really knew how to party.

There were many roadblocks and unreasonable demands from fearful soldiers – cars could be seized, and long hair shorn with a bayonet. Soldiers or policeman patrolled in pairs, fixed bayonets making their rifles taller than them, often holding hands as they walked.

For all the weapons, Sri Lanka did not feel dangerous. I met a police chief, shortly after the surprising news that the island's murder rate was higher than New York's. He explained, with gentle patience, 'We are not at all violent people. These men are only killing family members.'

Papa and I toured the island from Colombo and Galle to Kandy, avoiding the dangers of Jaffna and Trincomalee, the root of the civil war. We spent time together but knew each other little better. Sadly, an opportunity passed that would have been a boon for us both.

Inland 8,000-foot mountains rise from flat coastal plains. It is perfect for cultivating tea, as crucial to the mountain economy as fishing and tourism are to the coast. Steep hills are covered in 'lawns' of tea bushes. Newara Eliya (founded by Brits; pronounced 'New Railier') sits at 6,000-feet on a plain with a racecourse. Scottish architecture and clothing influence all: men walked the streets in sarongs and tweed jackets past buildings seemingly transported stone-by-stone from Inverness or Elgin.

Staying at the Hill Club, we played billiards and squash (a big mistake, against a squash pro at that altitude) and visited a tea plantation and drying sheds. 'Two leaves and a bud,' we learned as young women, vast backpacks suspended from their heads, scooped tea leaves from neatly trimmed bushes.

We drove near Kitulgala, where *The Bridge on the River Kwai* was filmed. It was a beautiful, tranquil, green valley with fast water and groups of working elephants hauling wood or being washed. The filming had passed; tourism and white-water rafting had not yet arrived; for that short interlude the valley was a paradise.

Winding roads took us to Kandy, last capital of the island's kings. It was quiet, sleepily huddled on a compact lake with a whitewashed, crenelated balustrade around the waters. The tired, faded elegance of pre-war splendour said, 'This is not a tourist destination'. We had privileged access to the chapel where the Buddha's Tooth is preserved and revered.

That evening we attended the *Perahera* from within the Temple. It was astonishing. The magic does not come from the red and white costumes of bare-chested fire dancers, nor from the hypnotically rhythmic bands of indigenous drummers, nor from the forceful majesty of caparisoned elephants, swaying above the procession. At a time when there were no tourists and when fear of the uprising was real, the heartbeat came from the deep religious significance for tens of thousands watching the Sacred Tooth Relic of Buddha paraded within a dozen carved bells aboard a large tusker; an uninterrupted ritual for almost 2,300 years.

Back on the coast, my age group went to Bentota Beach. In a shack like a weary cricket pavilion we ate curries, fresh from the ocean, washed down with beer or Mateus Rosé! We were the only party each day; now the area is overhung by towering hotels and packed with crowds. A revised Catch 22 might be 'The freedom to travel to places of unspoilt beauty and solitude means that they are no longer places of unspoilt beauty and solitude.'

At home food was simple. Local ingredients and occasional 'treats' such as powdered soups. Once sounds of inconsolable anguish came from the kitchen. We investigated. The devout Hindu kitchen hand wept before a pyre of grey dust, picking out suffocated 'ants'. It took time (and I doubt he believed us) to explain that the 'ants' were chunks of dried mushroom.

One day crowds surged outside the club. A passing Hindu parade surrounded a crane from which a man 'flew' above the ground, casting rose petals over the crowd, suspended with meat hooks through his flesh. He was lowered occasionally to drink. We talked. For years he dreamt of flying, not an uncommon dream, then a voice told him to stop dreaming and fly. He was calm and rational, neither drugged nor, he said, in pain. Faith and hope are powerful tools; a human with belief can have staggering strength and endurance.

Local newspapers showed how protectionist tariffs change behaviour. The social pages told of Nescafé, nylon and Lurex in a country that produces coffee and silk. Vast duties levied on modest imports meant that social status was elevated by expensive lapses in taste.

'MIND THE GAP' — PARIS

1971 and 1972

In the months after finishing A Levels, I worked as a waiter, a stable hand, driving a Bedford TK horsebox to gymkhanas, in a nursery garden, dog-minding and doing any paid work.

Waiting was rewarding. I learned silver service in a pretentious restaurant on the A3 called The Mayflower, which is now closed. The waiters were Italian, Spanish or Portuguese. Management was British. They didn't communicate. It resembled Anthony Bourdain's book, *Kitchen Confidential*, although there were no drugs. Kitchen heat is real, with scratches, cuts and burns. A rude patron would never know how the powerless avenge themselves on the bully.

There were other insights. One Sunday a table celebrated with an inexpensive fixed menu; but they all demanded something expensively different, with shouts and clicked fingers. 'Julian,' said the headwaiter, 'leave them to me. Ask that gentleman what he needs.'

The regular, who lunched alone each Sunday, seemed content, but I asked as I was told.

'Nothing, thank you, but when you have a moment…' His small request was quickly handled; on leaving, he gave me my first large tip.

After service, I added the tip to the pool but was told to keep it 'as a reminder. Julian, that is a gentleman. When we are busy, he asks for nothing; when we are not busy, he demands the best. The others? Huh! They are nobody.' The lesson, he explained, was to deal with silent needs before addressing shouting wants.

Papa suggested teaching at Salem in the gap between not getting into Cambridge and going to King's College London. It seemed rather fluid (no confirmation, instructions, or place to live) but I bubbled with enthusiasm. Salem, founded by Kurt Hahn, was the model for Gordonstoun. It has a strong community ethos, instils independence and, above all, nurtures a sense of belonging. I read about its foundation and its philosophy, and Hahn's escape to Scotland. Although I never reached the converted monastery, Hahn's concept and values appealed, and still do.

Emma and Papa were driving to Germany and offered me a lift. While in Paris, Papa called Salem and found the plan had been 'cancelled'. I was left in Paris. That afternoon I met a family friend, Jean Houillon, a director at Banque Nationale de Paris. He offered me an internship on the foreign exchange counter in a major city-centre branch. Emma discussed accommodation with other Paris friends, the Jugniers, an exchange for when their son had stayed with us. With that I had no further contact with my parents for several months.

Exchange controls restricted me to taking £50 plus £15 in cash; I saved that much for my intended stay in Bavaria. In Paris it was worth 800 francs, two thirds of the monthly minimum wage; *stagiaires* or interns earned 800 francs a month on the assumption that they lived at home.

Emma and Papa had hardly left Paris before Mme Jugnier moved me into the storeroom and, a fortnight later, summoned me to say that the month's rent was 1,500 francs, in line with what American tourists might pay. I offered everything I still had but was told, 'No discussion – pay now or leave'. The conversation that followed on the back stairs as I was supervised packing up in the box room, escalated in volume and intensity. Under her furious verbal assault, I discovered that my time in Paris had already given me a fluent confidence. Instead of sheepishly receiving a scolding, we had a full-on row; Col Jugnier watched in surprise, then shook my hand after his wife turned away.

I spent the night in the entrance to St George's, where I usually went to church. In the morning the vicar helped; Mme Jugnier apparently had something of a bad reputation with the vicar. He found me a place to live: Margaret and Mark Heath (who knew Emma and Papa but not me) drove much of the social life of the OECD HQ in Paris. The Heaths were marvellous. Due to be away for a fortnight, they invited me to live in their *chambre de bonne* and wait at official functions once a month. They were frequent entertainers and would pay for any other work I did. With my remaining cash, I bought a white jacket and a pair of black trousers, a waiter's universal uniform.

A *chambre de bonne* is not attractive at any time of the year. In July and August, with metal-melting heat, it is unbearable. Tucked into the roof above the sixth floor, reached by steep back stairs, the rooms measure less than 80 square feet, with a sloping ceiling and a small window up to 'that little tent of blue which prisoners call the sky'. The shared toilets were regrettably easy to find: two ceramic footplates in the floor above rank water, a single tap and an unmistakable smell. It is now illegal as a dwelling. I tried to meet other residents, but they were a tight community and none spoke English or French. I felt isolated and lonely but lived in a great postcode and had time to read *Lord of the Rings* and numerous books about Napoleon.

At the bank, I arrived early each day to avoid the ritual of walking around to shake everybody's hand and walked all evening, reluctant to return in the stifling heat. I also received my first pay (800 francs in cash) and nervously put half in one pocket and half in another. While I watched marching bands in the Place Vendôme, one pocket was emptied. It was otherwise a remarkable evening: the majesty of the Grenadiers; the Prussian precision of the German Army Band; the skittish scamper of the Bersaglieri who switched off the lights and dashed into the stands to carry the prettiest ladies into the square; the slow step of the *Légion étrangère* for whom victory will wait; an expensive but memorable tattoo!

I have never been as thin as I was then. My money evaporated so I walked to work and ate little, not even every day. While I had the energy to run, I took bread from café tables after the customers left. Not enough to eat until the end of the week is not only the preserve of the idle or the junkie – bad luck strikes where it will, but I knew mine would not last forever.

Eventually the Heaths returned and entertained, I met other interns, life was rebooted, hope rekindled. As a junior waiter I learnt my place: speak only when spoken to, which was usually with curt instructions. Once I recognised a name, the host of a party I'd been at. 'I was there,' I said, and the chef replied, 'Even I was not able to work there, but you did? Respect.' With that I was accepted. I did not dare mention that I had gone as a guest, not as a waiter.

I began to attend parties, weekends away, drinks on the Left Bank and even quiet dinners *à deux*. Returning one evening, I was attacked by two muggers but escaped when a resident emerged to walk his dog. We ducked back in; he fed me brandy and described the violence of recent muggings. I had escaped the hopeless, real world of so many. I was lucky again.

Before leaving Paris, I had one last dinner to thank my mentor, Jean Houillon. He was immensely private, very cultured and successful; he lived with his mother. Not yet a teenager in 1940, he was seized by the Nazis, imprisoned and forced to work in a factory in Germany. He could speak fluent German but never did. Within two decades of his capture, he was already a director of BNP. What caused Jean to thrive when he came back from forced labour camps in Germany whereas my assistant chicken griller in Munich, who was about the same age as Jean, virtually disintegrated on returning from Soviet labour camps in Siberia? Was the cruelty so much greater in Russia? Was it some difference in the two characters? Or was it that Jean returned to a loving family that helped him heal?

In conversation Jean was wary but not bitter, as though he had reached an accommodation with his past but not resolved it. He was both young and old when compared with my parents. He was a survivor. He worked tirelessly and lived with enthusiasm, as though each day might be his last – a distinct possibility, given the way he drove his Porsche.

TURIN AND THE RED BRIGADES

1972 to 1976

Papa's last post was as British Consul in Turin. The job was graded below his ranking at the time, but Emma had insisted on being in Europe with Papa as head of post. Papa had by then stopped fighting. We lived in a large apartment overlooking Corso Galileo Ferraris, at the junction of two glamorous 19th century, tree-lined avenues. La Crocetta is a good neighbourhood. On one corner was an expensive fashion boutique with a sense of humour; one year it displayed a poster with the eye-catching words '*Saldo Porno*,' and, in tiny letters beneath, '*tutti i prezzi sono nudi*' – literally, *Porn Sale – all our prices are stark naked*.

A vast arrangement of flowers appeared with a small, heavily embossed card that read simply *Giovanni Agnelli*. There was also an invitation from Agnelli to meet Arrigo Levi, recently appointed anglophile editor of *La Stampa*. I met l'Avvocato several times. In Turin at the time, indeed for many throughout Italy, he was Caesar.

However, Italy was a country at war with itself, with transient governments struggling to contain violence from terror groups on the far left and far right. Bombs, kidnapping and shootings affected people everywhere; security was obsessive. We frequently saw fast convoys of identical vehicles carrying leading businessmen, bankers or politicians, but in which car? Fabrizia's letters hardly scratched the surface of how terror undermines daily life.

We went to see *La Stampa* being put to bed, with

Arrigo Levi and his wife, Lina. Levi fled Italy after the 1938 Race Laws (*Leggi Razziali*) restricted the rights of Italian Jews, barring him from university, from travelling freely, owning property or working in certain professions. He returned after the war as a journalist, becoming the wise voice of reason in the ears of presidents. *'Memento mori!'* is not always a popular message, he told us.

Creating a newspaper in a pre-digital age was heavy going. Once typesetting was finished and mould-making had started, we dined with Arrigo and Lina, returning to watch the massive presses print and fold the paper. That night's news would have covered *Brigate Rosse* outrages, kneecapping middle managers, murdering executives, waging war against business; the diminutive Arrigo stood tall against the violence, denouncing the terror in print.

We left at about 3 a.m., saying thanks and farewell in the lobby until Arrigo said, 'Let me walk with you to your car.' Lina pleaded with him not to. The police and my parents said, 'No'. He insisted. Before we could move, two cars of Carabinieri checked that the area was safe; armed men formed a shield around us. Arrigo said, 'We cannot allow these men to stop us from the little courtesies that matter.' Not long after our evening with the Levis, his deputy at *La Stampa*, Carlo Casalengo, was ambushed and murdered as he left his home.

A consul's role is doubtless changing, but in the early 1970s it was relatively straightforward, unchanged for centuries: look after travelling Britons and promote British commercial and cultural interests. I spent several weeks as an intern with Papa during my holidays in Turin.

In 1974, we visited Marco Levi in Mondoví. In 1931, the 19-year-old Marco took on a traditional pottery, *Vedova Besio e Figlio*, that his father had rescued from bankruptcy. Monregalese faience (a poor relation of Italian Majolica) are collectors' items and Besio was among the largest of 100 factories, all now closed. Marco was enthusiastic. He led us past traditional racks of unglazed, hand-painted pottery, introducing everybody by name. At lunch he spoke and ate simultaneously for 90 minutes, smiling behind blurry, unwiped spectacles as he cascaded through stories and statistics.

For more than 60 years, he was the only Jewish presence in a city that first provided safety for fleeing Spanish and French Jews in the sixteenth century. Mondoví had a liberal tradition and ignored the papal decree of 1555 requiring that all Jews be confined. The Monregalese ghetto (finally created on paper in 1720) had no gates and was never closed. The family names from Mondoví included Levi, Ottolenghi and Foà.

Marco ignored the 1938 Race Laws and worked openly until the Germans occupied their Italian ally in 1943. The community hid Marco for the rest of WWII. The conspiracy of silence was extraordinary; the penalty for helping him was death. He always escaped capture; when German searches came too close, Marco went out to work in the fields dressed as a peasant, hiding in the open. He managed the factory remotely and observed the festivals, teaching his hosts to make unleavened bread for Passover. After the war, he carried on as before. Besio was the last factory to close; Marco thanked his hometown for their protection by creating and funding a museum marking 300 years of Monregalese faience.

We spent a day with Sergio Pininfarina, visiting his factory and then to his home for lunch. His father, Battista Farina, was nicknamed Pinin. The family name changed to Pininfarina and his logo, 'P' within a shield, is on many of the finest car designs of the last century.

Sergio resembled a playboy with elegance and charm; his wife, Giorgia, had her feet planted firmly on the ground. 'When the children were growing up,' she said, 'I told him we needed a proper family saloon with four doors. He agreed and some weeks later showed me the new car.' Sergio had taken his favourite car to the workshop and, with a massive circular saw, split it and stretched it, adding two extra doors and more seating. Giorgia was apparently unimpressed, 'I did not mean a four-door Ferrari.' He was always ahead of his time.

Turin has a great royal history and rich surrounding countryside. The city's modern focus is commerce and manufacturing. FIAT, by far Italy's largest company, is based there. The region produces some of the world's finest wines and food; one road takes you to the Mediterranean, through the spectacular vineyards of Barolo and past Europe's largest protected area, Gran Paradiso National Park; another takes you across the fertile plains of Lombardy, past paddy fields, towards Milan and the lakes; a third route takes you to the Alps, the road to France, ski resorts and the semi-autonomous region of Val d'Aosta.

Aosta thrives on tourism and a casino in Saint Vincent, run then by Virginia Parma, the mother of my new friend Luigi Mencarelli; however, most of the people in the 1970s lived in traditional frugal communities. Walking through the narrow streets of one village after a day in the mountains, Luigi and I were confronted with a sign reading, '*si prega di spegnere le luci della strada,*' – as you leave, please turn off the streetlights.

One Friday evening Luigi and I went to the casino. There were then only five licensed casinos in Italy, all in the north. The word is a minefield because, pronounced the way we Brits say it, the Italians mean a brothel or a right mess; if you seek 'a place to play games of chance' the emphasis falls on the last syllable, *casinò*. The one in Saint Vincent was Italy's largest, with more than 100 tables.

This is not the glamorous pastime of James Bond; it is soulless. We watched as a car factory worker, still in his overalls, opened the small brown envelope with his week's wages and placed it all on a single number in the high 20s; it won, and he left the original stake and winnings on the same number. It won again, this time with a large audience calling for him to enjoy his good fortune and go home to his family. Again, he left all the money in the same place and for the third time the ball landed on that number. He was hesitating but the casino manager begged him to take the money and go home. Three spins aggregating almost 50,000 to one; he made, in less than five minutes, more than he might have earned in a thousand years. Had it gone another way, his family would not have eaten all week.

With Luigi and other friends, I began to learn Italian. It is easier in Aosta, where the local patois is a hybrid including French. My modest grasp of the language helped when the consulate received a call that a Glaswegian girl was in a ward of the local hospital; there was an issue. The teacher in charge only spoke English; the doctors spoke only Italian and French. I went to unblock the situation which, by the time I arrived, had escalated. 'I'm no letting them touch her; they're no real doctors – they cannae speak English,' was not a good start. I listened to the medics. The girl had peritonitis, the theatre was ready, and the team scrubbed; they dreaded they might be too late. I explained and eventually the teacher reluctantly signed the forms; the operation was a success.

As I waited for the train back to Turin, I saw where St Anselm had been born. Anselm became Archbishop of Canterbury in 1093, aged 60. Reading Theology, I rather liked Anselm. His simple ontological proof of the existence of God defined Him as 'a being than which no greater can be conceived'. However, it suffers the same problem as many algorithms, such as the Black-Scholes pricing model so prevalent in finance. It ultimately depends on subjective human input. 'Rubbish in, rubbish out' is a cautionary tale for the onset of Artificial Intelligence.

Responding to another hospital call, I was joined by a chain-smoking junior Consulate official, Mr Bilotti. We went to Novara, capital of Italy's rice growing region. A British tourist had been in a crash on an autostrada. She was travelling with her daughter and two sons, as well as with her own mother. Bilotti had children of a similar age and could not cope when we were told that the driver had died. It fell to me to tell the injured grandmother that she had lost a daughter and to tell the children that their mother was dead. While I was consoling the family, an official asked for payment for the ambulance; I might have been a bit abrupt, but he did leave us alone. We took the boys to Turin; I spent that night reading them stories and letting them cry. I was studying to be a vicar; only life and death can teach pastoral care.

Back in the office, two British girls reported their passports had been stolen. They had hitch-hiked to Italy for a holiday. One driver gave them a lift across the Alps, stopping for them to photograph a view. As they photographed, he drove off with their clothes, passports, money. I filled in the forms. 'Name as it appears in the passport, please; place and date of birth?' It was standard stuff until I received the same answers for the second girl's form. One mother had said 'No!' to the trip so they used the other girl's birth certificate to obtain a BVP (a temporary passport) at the Post Office. Both IDs contained identical details. As one girl said, innocently, 'Well, it were all OK until summat went wrong.' It was a long day. Travel broadens some minds yet, remarkably, leaves others untouched.

Cavaliere Aldo Bugnone was a market leader. Vast machines with heavy rollers pressed aluminium into sheets: the thickest for car panels; thinner for kitchen tin foil; and the thinnest for Lurex, twinkly threads in cloth. He sold indiscriminately. Everywhere there were photographs of Presidents and PMs, although he showed us how he reversed the photographs when different potential customers visited, so that people from the communist East would see pictures of Bugnone with their Soviet counterparts and people from the West would see Bugnone with their European and North American counterparts.

Bugnone was member *Torino 785* of Propaganda Due

(P2). Silvio Berlusconi was *Milano 625*. Others were unaware of it, because their names had been listed without their knowledge in order to implicate the Establishment. Formed in 1877, P2 became an outlawed Masonic lodge in the 1960s and was linked to Italy's worst 1970s scandals of fraud, organised crime, extremism and at one point involving the Vatican Bank. I met many whose names were listed, including God's Banker (Roberto Calvi, *Milano 519*).

Fashion is big business. I was taught a trick by the international director of Gruppo Finanziario Tessile, the world's largest manufacturer of designer clothing, making outfits for Armani, Dior, Prada and Ralph Lauren. We watched as suits came off the production line to be labelled 'St Michael'. Our host whispered, 'Watch closely,' and randomly an identical suit went to another operator who labelled the sleeve, 'Chester Barrie, Exclusively for Harrods'. 'That is now our secret. Until you earn more, wear an M&S suit with a Hermès tie or jeans with Gucci loafers. Style is a matter of personal taste and confidence, not money.'

Luigi Rossi di Montelera was kidnapped, aged 27, and held for four months before being rescued from a bunker beneath a chicken shed with technical support from the British police and security forces. A friendship was forged with my parents; they attended his wedding, and he came to their official events. I met him at one of those. Although he and I were six years apart in age, he seemed decades older. Luigi became president of Bacardi-Martini, a Deputy (MP) for 16 years and minister for tourism and the arts.

Conversation with Luigi was easy. I insensitively asked how he coped for 120 days in a space where he could neither sit nor see. Luigi explained that he calculated time from sounds and meal deliveries and committed each morning to thinking about a new subject, culminating in an oral dissertation. Later he translated the speech, into French, German and English, and delivered it aloud. Thus, he said, he kept his sanity and humanity. I have often re-run that conversation, thinking, 'How the heck did he survive let alone thrive?'

It was at another such party, celebrating HM The Queen's official birthday, that I met Robin Foà, the son of friends of Emma and Papa. Robin was a young medic, coming to London for two years, to work at Hammersmith Hospital with a team that set out (successfully) to turn the killer tide of leukaemia. He has been a close friend ever since.

Banks were to the 19th and 20th century what cathedrals had been to an earlier age – spaces that told of power and wealth. A charitable institution in Turin was a perfect example. Istituto Bancario San Paolo di Torino was formed in 1563 by a brotherhood to support the poor of Piedmont. Within a century it administered the House of Savoy's finances; by the 20th century it had survived several crashes and crises while feeding hundreds of millions into charity. After WWII, the board decided to renovate using the 'finest interior designers'.

I was taken around by the bank's new chief, Luigi Arcuti, a charming anglophile with a clear mind and wild dress sense. He showed me rooms from derelict chateaux and palaces dating back to the 16th century reassembled as offices and meeting rooms. 'Imagine,' Arcuti said, 'the board demanded an explanation. The architect replied, "You said 'use the best interior designers'; you never said they should be living."' Did the witty Arcuti embellish the story? It was well worth a visit. In 1992, after he left, it became a commercial bank that soon needed to be bailed out. What took more than 400 years to build required only a decade to demolish.

Piedmont, not Paris or Beirut, was where I first learnt about great food – specifically in Turin at Al Gatto Nero, with its simple brick walls, white-jacketed waiters and linen-covered tables. It opened almost 100 years ago and modestly bore two Michelin stars. There, as a teenager, I was served *gli assaggini*. It was magic. Think of *tapas* or a Lebanese *meze*, but this was different; it was not informal. Two dozen fabulous dishes were served, small but perfectly formed, so that we experienced the complete menu. The restaurant is exceptional but not unique, merely part of a culture that prizes food. South of Turin, in Le Langhe, Barolo and Roero, there is a greater density of affordable Michelin one- and two-star restaurants than in any rural district in the world.

In 1974, we attended a banquet at the 18th century Palazzo Madama marking the arrival of Carabinieri Generale Carlo Dalla Chiesa, the scourge of Italian terrorism. He defeated the Red Brigades before his appointment as Prefect for Palermo, to take the fight to the Mafia. The General was a warm man who spoke with us in good English.

Tables groaned with ceremonial silverware. I am no fan of tripe, the first dish, but it was small and delicious, so

I accepted seconds. The lady to my right gave a running commentary of each dish (and second helpings) until I asked, 'How many courses?'

'One for every region of Italy.'

'How many regions?'

'Twenty.'

It was too late to exercise caution, so I ploughed on through the lamb and pork, the fish and spices, pastas, risottos and gnocchi, exotic vegetables, fruits and cheeses. The General's mission covered Italy in all its rich variety.

I felt great sadness when I saw the photographs of his crumpled body with his wife in a modest car after his assassination in Sicily in 1982. Just as he had defeated the Red Brigades, his sacrifice was the turning point that shocked and tamed the warring Mafia.

On three continents, the foundations had been laid for my future. I returned to London without a sense of belonging yet full of hope, to study, work, marry, have a family and live my life.

TO BE (ORDAINED) OR NOT TO BE

1972 to 1975

Old Oundelian Richard Colson is an award-winning contemporary painter. In 1969, obscuring the nine magnificent stained-glass windows by John Piper in the school chapel, Richard painted a colossal triptych. Its powerful black and purple brush strokes were like splodges at close quarters but, at a distance, the three paintings were a compelling vision of the crucifixion, the heads on either side hung low, but the eyes of Jesus looking directly inside the viewer. The eyes challenged, encouraged, and called. My admiration for Albert Schweitzer, a need to be wanted and belong, and the example of people like Ronald all surfaced and yet it was that piercing gaze that was the catalyst for a vocation that, for five years, pulled me towards ordination. Are those good enough reasons?

I applied to read Theology with a view to being ordained, a decision that met with strong opposition at home. Emma announced that I would have to fund myself because I would have no support, nor would they countersign an application that I had completed for a grant. I earned to pay my way.

I sang reasonably well and was persuaded to try for a choral scholarship at Cambridge, to help plug the financial gap. There were 103 candidates and many fewer spaces. We stayed overnight. There were three parts to the day: an academic grilling, a chance to sing in King's College chapel and another interview. As I walked into the first stage, a note sounded on the piano. A semi-circle of tables meant that I could not see all the examiners as questions kept arriving from the periphery of my vision. It was challenging and I was sinking fast.

There was a cull before the final phase. Names were published on a sheet pinned to a college door; we gathered to see where we should report next. I stood for some time, trying to find my name, until a voice said, 'Have you tried looking at the list on the other door?' There I found a page with three names, including mine. It was headed, 'No Longer Required.'

I was offered a place at Durham (but the courses took five years) and at King's College London, where I could take a degree and prepare for ordination in parallel. I chose the latter and lived in the theological hostel in Vincent Square. There was a box room off the library; with no money other than what I could earn, I took that at a lower-than-normal rent, thanks to the thoughtful intervention of the Dean. It was home for three years.

The Dean of King's, Canon Sydney Evans (who had officiated at the wedding of my erstwhile guardian, Ronald Smythe), welcomed us to Vincent Square at Evensong in the chapel. Above the altar, as a powerfully evocative crucifix, was Louis Osman's full-size silver-plated open mantrap: a grizzly jawed and spring-loaded device that could chop the foot off a poacher. Sydney spoke of the services and the community life of the ordinands' residence before closing with his most memorable advice: 'Young people,' he said, 'have sex on the brain. That really is not the most comfortable place to have it.'

General Sir John Hackett was a remarkable man; an artist and academic manqué, he became a soldier, a linguist, an author and the principal of King's College. He welcomed the freshmen in the college chapel. His advice was wide-ranging and witty, a summary of which is simple: be polite; it gives so many more options when the time comes, as it inevitably will, that you need to respond to other people's rudeness. 'Hold the door for the person behind,' he said; 'It might be a friend you're happy to see. But if it is somebody you intensely dislike, you are much better placed to swing the door in their face.'

Every Friday in our first year we volunteered to work in the community or teach. I chose the latter and immediately regretted it. I taught Religion to sixth formers at St Paul's Girls' School, where Alison's godmother was still High Mistress. I was petrified – a 19-year-old faced with some of the most intelligent and confident girls imaginable, a year younger than me in age and a decade older in maturity and worldliness. They politely ran rings around me.

At university I worked tables less frequently and turned instead to a bookshop/publisher. It was not hard to get work if you needed it. Without financial support, I needed it.

SCM publishes theological books. I received generous discounts on textbooks for myself and, for a smaller discount, was allowed to re-sell textbooks to my peer group. I also saw galley proofs of books before publication. Recent books were easier to read and absorb than older texts; I enjoyed citing Siegfried Herrmann's *A History of Israel in Old*

Testament Times in my finals on the day it was published; I have kept the publisher's uncorrected proof.

My first term went well. I began to mix with other students; some are still friends. For Christmas, Alison and I stayed with Emma in Sussex. While there, I spent my first term's savings on riding for several hours each day, learning dressage with Esmé Jacks, and hacking down local roads and tracks. It was very cold and Esmé recommended that I wear sports tights or leggings under my jodhpurs to avoid the discomfort of severely chaffed legs.

Boxing Day (when there was to be a local hunt) took place on a Monday that year. On Sunday, a group of us, including Alison, rode through Coldwaltham Woods and beyond. 'Don't worry,' said Emma, 'I'll set out your clothes, including the leggings, but please don't turn on the lights at 6 in the morning – it'll wake everyone up.'

I dressed in the dark, putting on several layers of clothing ending up with jodhpurs, boots and jacket. Off I went. We were five; one rode Mouse, a full brother of Psalm, on which Ann Moore won a silver medal at the 1972 Munich Olympics. Mouse was a big, strong Grade A show jumper.

It was cold but dry as we left the stable yard some time before the sun rose. Eventually we covered tracks and open country at a good pace, and on a wide path I started to pull alongside Mouse. Without warning, Mouse bucked once, connecting with my right leg and snapping it in two, below the knee. My horse accelerated, the broken leg hanging, held together by my boot. I sat deep and upright, passing the others until I found a steep bank that my horse would not ride up; we slowed and pulled up in a small clearing. I slid to the ground on one foot and lay there for an hour as an ambulance was called. It hurt.

The Land Rover ambulance drove to St Richard's Hospital in Chichester where I lay, by now floating on an agreeable sea of painkillers, in a bay in A&E. A nurse arrived with heavy scissors and began cutting away my right boot and then stopped. Moments later, I saw several smiling nurses at the bottom of the bed. Perhaps not 'smiling' so much as chuckling, because I could feel that the boot and the jodhpurs had been cut off in a sea of blood, exposing the leggings – white, lace, ornately-patterned, Christian Dior ladies' tights. It took six months, in plaster from toe to groin, for my leg to start healing – it took longer to get over the embarrassment of dressing, on trust, in the dark.

My second university term was spent uncomfortably with Emma. After a month, a taxi took me to Chichester each week to sit in the theological college there. Fellow 'theolog' Jeremy Hellier made a carbon copy of all his neat lecture notes and posted them to me each week, and I'd spend a day in the library searching through the texts that matched the lectures. Fr Jeremy is from the West Country, and for decades he has made a difference in churches, schools and the Mission to Seafarers in the Diocese of Bath and Wells. Would that the CofE had more priests like him. Our friendship at university was a huge stroke of luck.

Another stroke of luck was my local vicar, Archdeacon Freddie Kerr-Dineen, who was also my sponsor for ordination. He was rector of St Mary the Virgin in Stopham and also vicar of St Botolph's in the adjacent village of Hardham, where I worshipped after returning from Paris. The church is tiny, with 30 pews. It was built before the Normans arrived, from the rubble and bricks of a Roman military post. Many pews are 15th century: the rest are Victorian copies. St Botolph's walls are richly decorated with some of the oldest Christian images in Britain, every inch taken by 12th century murals illustrating Bible stories or celebrating the heroism of crusaders. It is a miracle that they have survived.

'What is wrong with those portraits of Adam and Eve?' Freddie once asked me. I spluttered aimlessly until he answered his own question, 'They both have belly buttons – they would not have had umbilical cords because they were created, not begotten.' My mentor's mind married immense intellect with kindness and humour. He saw the world from a different perspective (how different is well-illustrated in his book of poems *The Company of Merrymakers*). His were the only sermons I heard that addressed small children and learned adults alike without losing the attention of anybody. Canon Kerr-Dineen had five children of whom Peter is closest to me in age. He is one of the brightest and mildest of City grandees and remains a good friend. Through Peter I met Andrew Barnett, my first Best Man, with whom I studied theology at KCL. He is another theolog who escaped the calling of ordination – he recently retired from the bench after 20 years as a distinguished judge.

By the summer term, I was back in my Vincent Square box room, still plastered from toe to groin but able to attend lectures, St George's Hospital on Hyde Park Corner and exams. After the exams I was summoned by Sydney Evans; he said that he had considered giving me an aegrotat pass to compensate for my medical absences but was happy that I had passed into the second year on my own merits. He gave me great encouragement. I suspect that I only just scraped through, but it was enough.

That summer, with the plaster removed after six months, I hobbled with crutches and required interminable physiotherapy to learn to walk again. I turned to BNP and asked for a desk job in their London office. I worked in Forex settlements where I turned down the offer of a permanent job. It was many years before my salary matched the offer I had refused.

Living in London again, I started to catch up. I did some show jumping, competing against other colleges. I walked all over London, sang in a choir, wrote short stories and started to join in. I mixed very slowly. My 21st birthday passed unnoticed; I had not mentioned it and received no cards from family. It was my life as usual. With so much work at the bookshop and occasionally waiting at tables, I was solvent but did not shine academically or socially.

Usually, I went alone to the Festival Hall (sitting behind the orchestra), to the Royal Albert Hall (standing at the Proms or in the Gallery, lying on the floor to soak in the music), in the gods at the Royal Opera House (there used to be a desk up there where I could follow a score but with a very restricted view… it was years, for example, before I first saw captives emerge onstage while singing the Prisoners' Chorus in *Fidelio*), or standing in the National Theatre or the RSC. Only New York compares with London for the variety and quality of live performances to attend, alone or in company.

I got through years two and three, although parts of the course excited me more than others. St Paul struck me, after trudging through interminable volumes by German theologians among others, as a benign bigot. Before Saul 'saw the light' on the Road to Damascus he was not even benign. Christianity might not exist outside the Jewish faith without him. He opened our religion to the non-Jewish world. He could be read as surprisingly enlightened; he was tireless, courageous, probably admirable and well-liked, but I just didn't get on with Paul.

Ronald Smythe, my guardian for many years, was a big fan of Paul which made me more uncomfortable, as though I had missed something that mattered. Through a close friend, Susan Horsewood-Lee, I met Father Jerome Murphy-O'Connor. He had written more than a dozen books about Paul and was a leading authority. Fr Jerry was a ray of sunshine when he told me, 'It is OK to like the message but not much like the messenger.'

At the heart of Abrahamic faiths is the notion that Man can be redeemed from sin, in much the same way as collateral at a pawn broker can be redeemed… pay the price and everything is OK. However, there are two schools of thought: one is that if you do certain deeds you can earn redemption, while the other postulates that submission to belief in God's mercy and love is all that it takes. I have crudely oversimplified thousands of years of theological discourse. Suffice to say, I could never work out which was the right approach. I was trapped in limbo, not having the experience to comprehend love and yet lacking any confidence in my own work.

I enjoyed comparative religion, studying the Old and New Testaments, reading the Quran, the Bhagavad Gita and other texts. Stripped back, there are extraordinary similarities in most established religions, upon which heaps of differences have been layered. This reading informed my opinion that in debate we should start discussing the topics about which we agree before advancing to the many fewer matters about which we disagree.

People still ask why I was not ordained, which seems reasonable when I've said I might have been; I usually give a flippant answer and move on. It is more common to go from the City to the church than to travel the other way. We all make some decisions without fully knowing why at the time. It took me 50 years to determine why it was right not to proceed.

My faith wobbled in the final year. That is not unusual among ordinands; it is not unknown even among bishops for faith to be challenged and evaporate for a while. My faith, which had been ignited into a calling by an image of the crucifixion, was rocked by a paper about the resurrection that followed. Specifically, my belief was shaken by the very process of textual analysis that was intended to strengthen it.

St Mark's Gospel is recognised as the first to have been written. It was a major source for all that follows. It begins with the words, 'The beginning of the Gospel of Jesus Christ, the Son of God'. But where does it end? Officially St Mark's Gospel ends at chapter 16, verse 20 – 'And they went forth, and preached everywhere, the Lord working with them, and confirming the word with signs following. Amen.'

However, there is a gear shift in the last 12 verses that leads many (most?) scholars to conclude that the last original part of the text is chapter 16 verse 8 – ἐφοβοῦντο γάϱ, 'for they were afraid' – although that is also unsatisfactory; γάϱ or 'because' is unusual as the last word of a sentence and 'fear' makes little sense as the final emotion in a book about hope; surely there must have been more, hence a reason for those extra verses.

On the other hand, what if there should have been less? There are characters and linguistic constructions in later verses that are absent from the earlier text. Did the Gospel perhaps finish with chapter 15 verse 39, when a centurion said, 'Truly this man was the Son of God'? That echoes the opening words. In short, did the story stop before the resurrection? I struggled with this uncertainty. It struck me that if I couldn't make my peace with the religion's central premise then my vocation was a sham; this wasn't the job for me.

Textual analysis does not eliminate faith; brighter minds than mine read the same words and still believe. Hindsight leads me to think that there was another reason, that my calling was in part another siren that an outsider hears when facing a chance to belong. Through ordination, I would have joined a team where I felt comfortable, a team that did the sort of thing I wanted to do and, largely, have done a lot throughout my life. However, as we approached the next stage of commitment, the longed-for sense of belonging faded. The calling may have been right, but the motive and the timing were not. I first told the Dean, Sydney Evans, who asked how he could help. Many of us believed that Sydney should have been a Bishop, combining as he did a rare blend of pastoral ability, academic accomplishment, kindness and wisdom. In 1977 he was appointed Dean of Salisbury Cathedral.

When I told Freddie Kerr-Dineen, my proposer, he was a bit relieved and not surprised. He remained supportive and officiated at my first wedding.

Meanwhile, muddle-headed notions of class remain Britain's greatest divide. In the October 1974 election, there was a polling booth in Vincent Square where I stood as the Liberal 'teller' alongside two chaps with rosettes: one blue, one red. I chatted happily with each but, try as I might, could not ignite a three-way conversation. After an hour, Nanny appeared with a picnic basket for the Tory; she offered a cup of tea to his 'nice Liberal friend.' A Union official arrived a short time later with a flask of tea for the Labour teller, 'and would yer Liberal comrade like a mug?' The country is now no less polarised, but a lot less polite about it.

I left university with a second-class degree (BD) and an ordination qualification (AKC). I needed work. I had worked twice in a bank and seemed competent enough, so I wrote to three companies offering my services. One kindly answered that they were not actually a bank, but good luck. The others each offered me a graduate traineeship; lacking guidance I went unwisely to the one that offered most money, although I never saw the decision not to be ordained as a clash between God and mammon, only a desire to belong.

A TOUR OF BRITAIN

1975

In the weeks before I started my career, my close German friend Martin Bloch and I went in search of my roots, or at least British roots to which I could lay claim. We borrowed his mother's yellow VW Beetle and covered the length and breadth of the country, staying in youth hostels, a rustic B&B or, occasionally, with friends.

I had spent that summer in the consulate in Turin, planning the trip. It was mapped out in a neurotic, pre-internet heap of letters and confirmations. Looking at how things were done then, I remain astonished that anything was… done then. Britain was effectively a foreign country for both of us.

The journey began with a trip to Windsor and then Eton, walking among the buildings and grounds. Many overseas visitors regarded these calm relics of education and entitlement as the HQ of the British Empire, far more important than Whitehall or Oxford Street.

We drove into London to see my patch – Westminster Abbey, St Paul's, the Tower, St James's Park, Somerset House and King's College before walking into the Inns of Court. Although heavily bombed in the 1940s, the whole area (Gray's Inn, Inner and Middle Temple and Lincoln's Inn) retained its character and many of its historic buildings and artefacts. Above all, it retained the serious, privileged tranquillity that, for many who were called to the Bar, had formed an essential ingredient of every stage of their upbringing.

By the time we reached Cambridge, two or three

nights into this homogeneous cultural tour, Martin shook his head as we wandered through colleges and walked along the Backs. 'Let me understand; the people who study and live in these ivory towers are the people who run the country and dispense justice to the man in the street? And this seems normal to the British?' You must admit, superficially the observation is not without merit.

Compare and contrast. We drove north, to my old school and several of the grand houses and beautiful walks *en route*, until we reached Durham, where we had arranged to spend a night in rooms at St Chad's. We had drinks with the Principal, Canon John Fenton; I would have enjoyed studying Theology with him had I chosen to go to St Chad's.

We rose before dawn to arrive at the NCB offices at Seaham Colliery before the sun had fully risen and meet a chaplain who had arranged for us to spend a full shift below ground. Seaham is deep, goes some distance out beneath the North Sea and is best known for the devastating explosion in 1880 that killed 164 men and ripped the heart out of a community.

We stripped alongside the miners and hung our clothes in large wire baskets to be suspended on a locked chain, out of reach. We wore dungarees and lamped helmets with heavy batteries. The cage at a colliery goes down quickly. That drop, at Seaham, was massive; it was one of the deepest mines in Britain. When we clambered out seconds later, we made our way towards a belt to the coalface, dipping our 'hat-lamps' at every corner in order not to blind others. We were briefed and then lay on our stomachs on the damp conveyor until we came to a station where we rose to kneel, grabbed a pillar and pulled ourselves onto the platform. There were loud noises, but everybody had a role and efficiently got on with their work; we observed and admired.

Hours later, after our return from the pitch dark, the miners chatted with us about poetry, marriage, what we had seen, nature, fear and (possibly because of the chaplain) belief. More than one said they'd never spoken together like that; Martin and I learnt much; in particular, one quiet miner's comment, 'Nobody understands miners other than trawlermen. Only they know the power of nature and the fear of God that we experience every day.' For days after that visit, tears of laughter or sorrow left black, coal-dust streaks on our cheeks.

We both admired the decency, commitment and courage of men who daily faced death to support families because there was no choice. I also sensed the immense courage of the very few who left mining, severed their roots and sought a way out for their children; two impossible options. Martin and Martina were with us when we went to see *Billy Elliot the Musical*. Martin and I shuddered at the end, when the miners in orange dropped out of sight in the cage; we both felt that we had shared one tiny step of their journey.

Ten years after our visit, I was saddened by the grotesque mishandling of the miners' strike – employers and unions cornered the miners into an unwinnable conflict and left them to suffer losses and humiliation while employers and union leaders walked away better off. Mines needed to be closed, and new industries needed to be nurtured to keep the hearts of communities beating. Humiliating an opponent provides a short-lived victory.

Continuing north, we were woken by bagpipes played in our room at a YHA hostel, walked along Hadrian's Wall and crossed the border into Scotland. We borrowed a flat just off Princes Street and spent several days going to events at the Edinburgh Festival, dabbling with the Fringe. We climbed to the Castle to see the magnificent Military Tattoo. Further north, we attended the Highland Gathering at Pitlochry and visited much else besides. South of the border and into Wales, we scrambled up Snowdon, visited Britain's coasts and entered Bristol, where we ate our first proper meal in a grand Indian restaurant.

People used to stop in the street, look up and watch as Concorde flew overhead. Roaring like an expensive sports car, it was probably the most beautiful machine ever to fly! We were excited to get inside Filton, near Bristol, where the British Concorde was being built and where the first test flight had taken place. The two of us spent a day being shown around.

As Martin and I walked through the frame of prototype 002, our guide explained every step of its construction. To make it strong enough to fly at Mach 2, it was built from one-foot-thick panels of aluminium; to make it light enough for take-off the panels were hollowed out, leaving cross struts that created a thin sheet with the strength of steel girders. Nature allows itself to be fooled in that way; science is the tool that discovers how to fool nature. The cabin and flight deck were the size of a London Underground carriage but once endowed with supersonic speed, Concorde became a magic carpet for those it carried.

Travelling from south to north, east to west, I was proud of my country and full of hope.

SOME SORT OF BANKER

1975 to 1979

My career choice was Williams & Glyn's, a merger of two old banks and subsidiary of the Royal Bank of Scotland. Each year one graduate trainee was selected as a Glyn Mills Cadet, paid comfortably more than the peer group and rushed through training in half the time. Previous Cadets include Lloyds chairman Sir Jeremy Morse. I was the last Glyn Mills Cadet.

My first branch manager was Philip Izard, who lost as much lending to a Tory MP as he did to a Labour minister. He appears by name in Jeffrey Archer's novel, *Not a Penny More, Not a Penny Less*, as does the very decent Frank Watts, although Archer's novel was largely pure fiction.

For my first week, I counted the cheques that qualified for Town Clearing by 3.10 pm. The exchange of Town cheques with other banks took place nearby and the doors shut precisely – the cheques had to be inside. On my second day, I tripped, and the cheques flew from my hands through the closing door, where they lay inside as I lay outside. The doorman decided that he would rather I picked them up than do it himself, so he reopened the door.

The next day my tally of cheques was £3 million under – a colossal error. On Thursday, I was £3 million over and hard questions were asked. Eventually a petrified young clerk, who started work on the same day as me, put up her hand. At home she'd bragged that she handled cheques worth millions, and her mother slapped her for lying, so she had taken a cheque home to prove it. It was incredibly serious, but nobody could resist the funny side.

My apprenticeship took me into every corner of retail banking. I then joined David Horne at NCDC, the development capital (in modern parlance, private equity) arm of the bank. NCDC invested a small amount of W&G's equity with exceptional success. David had been the youngest director of SG Warburg. He was one of the most remarkable (and unorthodox) bankers and soon after became chairman of Lloyds Merchant Bank. Until then, we were a team of four directors, two secretaries and me, with a lavish Berry Brothers wine account.

Most venture funds have a similar profile: a couple of superstar investments, a couple of complete duds and the majority trudging along. BEC (called variously British Electronic Controls or Ling Dynamic Systems) was our outstanding star. The management team wanted to buy it back but needed funding and, as a listed company, also needed to go through all the hoops of a bid. A competitor had deeper pockets and made a counter bid.

The first leveraged management buyout of a listed company, it looked unlikely to succeed. We put the case to the Monopolies and Mergers Commission, accepting that BEC fell below their threshold. Although the company was small, we explained, the motor and aerospace markets that it served, with vibration test equipment, accounted for a sizable chunk of British GDP. We also drew the MMC's attention to allegations in the magazine *Private Eye* against counterbidder Derritron and its principal shareholder. The other bid was referred, and our side won.

When the three owners reached retirement age, they gave the business to a trust for the benefit of the employees. They were admirably ahead of the trend.

I moved into a compact house in Mortlake with Andrew May, a surgeon at St Thomas' Hospital whom I met through an ad in the *Evening Standard*. Andrew has always blended great kindness and affability with a relentless work ethic, at one stage commuting daily to the south coast. In 1977 Andrew moved to Boston for a long stretch at Massachusetts General, the first building block of Harvard Medical School. I visited him there on my first trip to the USA, in 1978. He is my son Charlie's godfather.

While Andrew was away, I house-shared with Robin Foà from Turin while he worked at Hammersmith Hospital. It was a very happy period at work and personally, although I don't think I fully appreciated how happy at the time.

My sister Alison and I had an opportunity to buy a flat together. It was in the heart of Chelsea, with wonderful views, two good bedrooms, and a roof terrace. However, there was no lift and the lease was short. Between us, with a bank loan, we could afford it. Our offer was accepted. Buying one's first property is exciting.

Shortly before signing, the vendor accepted a marginally higher offer and said she would not now sell to us. The word was not in use in the 1970s, but we had been 'gazumped'. Losing one's first property is disheartening.

Days later Emma announced that she had just bought a flat in Chelsea, the same property. 'You were both so excited – I knew it must be a real bargain, so I bought it for myself!' she explained. I remember seeing it only once after that, for Alison's wedding, snatched over lunch as Tony changed flights between Washington and Zurich while Emma and Papa were in Russia; for much of the time the flat lay empty. Being gazumped on one's first property by a parent is indescribable.

I stayed in Mortlake and joined the Brompton Choral Society (now the London Concert Choir) as a tenor. The conductor and musical director, Donald Cashmore, ran a tight ship, delivering music of an exceptional standard from dedicated amateurs. Monday rehearsals were mandatory; I just managed, dashing from the City on a scooter. The most memorable performance was the *Dream of Gerontius* in Brompton Oratory. It reminded me of Sydney Evans' encouragement to attend Evensong and 'Let the psalms wash over you like a warm bath', completely clearing the mind and rebooting the batteries. Music has that power; the more familiar a piece becomes, the greater its capacity to heal.

I took a motorbike test and gradually shifted from 50cc to 400cc. Some years later I bought a 1000cc monster, a BMW KS100, capable of covering long distances at absurdly high speeds of more than 120 mph. Intense concentration and camaraderie on the open road come with larger bikes.

In the late 1970s I was invited by Adam Lee, a senior colleague, to join the Chelsea Opera Group as Treasurer. Even after the high standard of BCS, this was a musical challenge – being a tenor and treasurer might have made it easier to join. I had heard COG conducted by Colin Davis and

Simon Rattle before I auditioned myself.

COG's finances were not strong. I scoured the pages of *Who's Who* to identify people with whom I had any flimsy connection (school, university, City) and who disclosed an interest in opera. Several sent cheques and things looked marginally better until Chris Patey, a double bass player with COG's orchestra, persuaded his employer, Mobil Oil, to stump up substantial support. Chris's intervention saved the day and, 45 years later, he remains involved as a Trustee of the group's charity.

During the years with COG, we performed works by Berlioz (including *The Trojans*), Bizet, Mozart and Verdi. We sang in the Festival Hall, in Oxford and Cambridge. We were conducted by Roger Norrington and Mark Elder and sat, as the chorus, behind singers who went on to glittering international acclaim. Membership was a privilege.

Soloist Elizabeth Connell had a wonderful, pure mezzo voice. Wherever we performed, she joined the choir after the event to celebrate before returning alone to south-west London. We sang Berlioz's *Damnation of Faust* in Oxford in 1978, and she came on stage in a spectacular outfit. The next week she wore a different dress. Apparently, on reaching London after the concert, she could not reach the zip. Eventually she went to Barnes police station and asked for help. Unzipped, she returned home. 'You can guess I wasn't doing that again in a hurry – I got a new dress,' she explained, in her infectiously cheerful way.

As an encore at the end of a recital in Hastings in 2011, Elizabeth's last ever song in public was 'When I have sung my songs to you, I'll sing no more.' Three months later she died. Shortly after her death, I met Susanna Kemp, the dress maker responsible for the unzippable outfit and, subsequently, many more of Elizabeth's concert clothes.

I met Nicola Bevan one evening at the theatre with Sophia Robinson and other friends. She had great energy and was passionate about family, although she expressed little interest in the arts. Friends deemed the relationship serious when I bought her an early edition of du Maurier's *Rebecca*... and Nicola read it. Eventually, the time came to meet the family. I rode my motorbike to Tyes Place in Sussex for Sunday lunch. I had little experience of families, let alone large ones. Her mother was called the *Ayatollah*; her father was an heir to the Barclays Bank dynasty. It all seemed unnecessarily intimidating, but I was encouraged to stay the course.

NCDC was winding down; success is not always enough to keep the interest of a large organisation. I moved to Orion, a bank where I could travel and use my languages. My first trip overseas began with instructions from the personnel director, Julian Fane, who said, 'When it comes to expenses, I don't much care what you claim, if you don't mind who I show it to!' The threat of complete transparency encourages honesty and caution that could, perhaps, have helped us avoid the periodic scandals of MP's expenses.

Months later I asked Timothy Bevan for his daughter's hand. Being a banker himself, he saw that my career showed promise, although he understood little about the Euromarkets. His only question was, 'Do you earn more than a bummaree?' As it happens, I did... just. Working three minutes from Smithfield Market and happy to talk with everybody, I had been chatting to a porter, or bummaree, the previous week, hearing his complaints about how little he earned as we enjoyed an early drink together (beer for the porter, coffee and a bacon butty for me). Tim approved.

Returning from the City one evening after a moderately sober evening and with a bottle of champagne strapped on the back to mark our engagement, I miscalculated the phasing of traffic lights and braked suddenly. The bike slid one way, and I was thrown the other, under a taxi waiting patiently at the lights. I came to a rest, all but my head and shoulders beneath the cab, and looking up I saw a smiling face looking down, head shaking, who asked, 'Farckin' 'ell, mate! What yer do fer a bleedin' encore?' When I got home, I found that I was in one piece and, more remarkably, so was the champagne – but not for long.

We married in the church in Nicola's home village, and the reception took place in a large marquee in the family garden. Our honeymoon was unusually uneventful. We stayed in the 16th century Quinta das Torres in Azeitão, near Lisbon; it was still largely a family home crumbling under the weight of history. I was ready for life's hopes and promises.

THE INFANCY OF THE EUROMARKETS

1979 to 1982

We settled into Nicola's house in Fulham, a house I had already helped to decorate; I bought my share. Nicola continued working for Mentzendorff, which has imported Bollinger to Britain since 1860. My work was demanding but not excessive; we were comfortable. Weekends were often spent with Nicola's parents, in Sussex at the house she called 'home', sailing or on holiday elsewhere. We explored Kenya together, on safari, in the mountains and on some of the world's most beautiful beaches. We also travelled with friends, particularly Anthony Sharp, whose irresistible sense of humour and kindness have kept us close for decades. We enjoyed the 'best of all possible worlds'.

Petrodollars and Eurobonds were the City's reaction to a massive hike in oil prices in the early 1970s. America printed money to pay for the extra cost of buying energy from the Gulf and elsewhere: that money sought refuge beyond the reach of American regulation. No single bank was big enough handle the flood alone so specialist companies, formed by groups of banks, were the market's response. Orion was one such consortium and it was so successful that five of its six shareholders eventually set up in competition with it.

I started in a pool of aspiring bankers until, having passed the arduous Chase Manhattan Credit Course, I was selected to travel. I covered Italy under the tutelage of William de Gelsey, a polyglot whose energy exhausted two secretaries and numerous assistants while he was on the road for weeks. We ferried cases of paperwork for him to process, and he appointed Signatures to sign on his behalf as he travelled; I practised his squiggle as did others, such as Andrew Large, who became Deputy Governor of the Bank of England.

Chris Chataway, perhaps best known for running a mile in under four minutes in the same race as Roger Bannister, ran the Mergers & Acquisitions department on our floor. He was amusing, modest and frantically hard working.

David Montagu chaired Orion, having left the family business of Samuel Montagu. He brought his favourite doorman with him, Big Cyril, with whom he shared ownership of a successful racehorse. Cyril at the front door and The Hon. David in the overcrowded boardroom made Orion a happy ship.

Decades later I met another Montagu, Elcie, a cheerful, small, determined lady who lived surrounded by paintings, sculptures and beauty. Shortly before she died, I joined her rushing for a train 'to see the Mervyn Peake exhibition at the British Museum.' Thinking of his grizzly Gothic fantasy, *Gormenghast*, I asked what she liked about his dark drawings. 'Well,' she replied, 'I like the ones he gave me – especially his drawings of me as a small girl on holiday.'

However, the City is not about the stars; London was, and remains, a world financial centre because it had the same commitment throughout – the back office, printers, lawyers, accountants and late-night pizzas. I learnt how good in many ways; the Orion print room even helped me create April Fool's telexes in successive years, teasing credit committees as far away as Tokyo and each year appearing the following day in the *Financial Times.*

My new boss, Philip Hubbard, was an academic banker. He spoke slowly, wanting research to cover every utterance. He told me to prove that historically one type of debt cost less than another. It was a laborious task – thousands of calculations taking one hundred hours using a small calculator, all typed by the loyal Esther Tan. The result was inconclusive.

Fifteen years later, I told this story to Andrew Senior, an M&A and computer whizz at Crédit Lyonnais. He leant back, arms stretched, tapping at the keyboard to create a programme. He then hacked into the bank's treasury database to populate his spreadsheets with historic interest rate information. Less than 30 minutes later, he had achieved what it had taken me a long week to calculate before the arrival of personal computers. That is the quantum of change that my generation has experienced. AI may be more dramatic.

Nicola and I watched the royal wedding of Prince Charles and Lady Diana from the window of a Barclays office in Paternoster Square, just over the head of Barbara Walters, broadcasting for ABC. It was a spectacular place to catch arrivals and departures, people crowded along the last leg of the journey to St Paul's, leaning out of windows, hanging atop street signs for a better view. Perhaps the saddest glimpse, in hindsight, was of the open carriage with the newly wed Prince and Fairy Princess: she is waving to the crowds; he is still wearing his gloves, holding his sword with one hand while the other rests in his lap. If ever there was a time to hold hands in public, this was surely it.

In November 1981, Simon Wigg and I were thrown out of Buenos Aires because of my indiscretion about the Falklands. Britons were unaware of Argentine feelings then. At our final meeting of the week, our charming interlocutor took our documents 'To copy, please.' He returned with soldiers and no papers. 'You are on the 6 a.m. flight tomorrow; do not leave your rooms tonight.' Soldiers accompanied us to the Hotel Libertador (an ironic name if you are under 'room arrest'). I tried to leave for dinner, but soldiers with fixed bayonets ushered me back in. The following day we were escorted to the airport for the first plane, eventually flying to Rio, then back to London, with nothing to show for a week's work.

I enjoyed Buenos Aires; official antipathy to Britain was at odds with public opinion; newsstands on every corner offered 200 or more local magazines displaying Lady Di on the front cover. We chatted to people in the streets; some seemed nervous, as well they might with the dictators' spies everywhere, but many were delighted to talk English and discuss Britain and the Queen. We searched for tango dancers at midnight, but chairs were on the tables; 'Too late?' I asked. 'No,' came the reply, 'come back in two hours and it will start.' Argentina should be one of the world's richest countries; incompetence and corruption mean that every few years it crumbles, and poverty is as unequally shared as wealth. While we were there, annual inflation approached 200%; people joked that it was cheaper to travel by taxi (paying at the end of the journey) than by bus (buying a ticket at the start) because your money could earn interest for longer.

Officials had a casual approach to work, regularly postponing meetings or arriving late, so we had a chance to see the town and even to take in *Nutcracker* at the Teatro Colon, one of the world's greatest opera houses. Returning 25 years later, Maria and I went down six stories to where sets and costumes, wigs and shoes are made for use throughout the world. Shrines to Evita with flowers and candles appeared in every room; it is hard to overstate the position she still holds in many Argentine hearts.

Having been 'asked' to leave at short notice, we hit the tourist trail in Rio de Janeiro: *Cristo Redentor*, *Pan de Azúcar,* the works. The last stop before our flight was Copacabana Beach, where we lounged in the sun, discussing how best to explain my failure to conclude the deal. Luck was on our side and our 'wasted' week turned out to be fortunate: the $400 million loan we were working on was not signed by the time Galtieri's men seized the Falklands in April 1982. No money lent meant no money lost. However, by that stage I had been headhunted to join Morgan Grenfell, one of the most prestigious names in the City.

Having seen it being built, I enjoyed the experience of flying on Concorde. There was always 'somebody' on board. And very few passengers, even regulars, were not caught up in the magic to some extent. Perhaps that magic escaped Peter Cook when I sat next to him on a journey to New York. He had arrived in the Concorde lounge at Heathrow long before me; the hospitality was unstinting as, apparently, was his capacity for enjoying it. He was not an easy travelling companion.

There was often a camaraderie on Concorde that is

absent on other business flights. With fewer than 100 passengers and only 30 to 50 people in each of the two cabins, a party atmosphere was possible – as happened when we saw the *aurora borealis* once while returning to the UK. The sky on the port side morphed into a polychrome lava lamp of soft colours for several minutes. Window seat passengers stood to allow others to huddle up to the tiny portholes and experience nature's most marvellous light show, until every passenger had seen the lights; the feelgood factor and champagne consumption were high on that flight.

A few weeks after returning from Latin America, I set off for a month in Calgary. I arrived in Canada in September, at the height of a warm Indian Summer, and had arranged a stopover in Edmonton to track down Uncle Ken, Emma's brother, who was Head of the Alberta College of Art. I had not seen him for decades since our only meeting and Emma gave me no contact details when asked, so I got in a taxi and went to the university campus. After several futile attempts, I discovered that Ken's department was based in Calgary! I finally made (and never again lost) contact with a wonderful character and spent many evenings with him and my cousins during the rest of my stay. When Ken spoke of his sister, Emma, I realised that I was not alone in my discomfort. Ken's measured phrase was that she had 'a very selective memory'.

A Montreal friend, Lynda Luber, tells us Calgary has 'only two seasons, July and Winter'. That month I experienced both. The temperature swung one weekend from plus 25° C to minus 40°. 'Celsius or Fahrenheit?' I asked after a miserable night in the hotel where I'd even used the bath towels to keep from freezing. 'Same darn thing,' came the reply and it turns out that it is. It is also intolerably cold for most.

It was a fiendishly complicated transaction for Bow Valley Industries that took me there yet, as we reached October, the company team attended fewer meetings ('We've already made budget for the year, Julian, so we don't feel any pressure'). That gave me a chance to go up to the Rockies, to see Lake Louise and Banff and to attend an ice hockey game between the Calgary Flames and the New York Rangers, featuring the legendary Phil Esposito, one of the last players to compete in this madly violent sport without a helmet. I even had a weekend back at home in Britain and very happily attended Andrew May's marriage to Vivien.

Eventually I was done and needed to dash back to the office with a dozen heavy boxes of prospectuses printed locally. I missed the flight from Calgary because a predicted dump of snow threatened to close the airport and my flight left early; several of us were stranded, including a tall, good-looking lady in a silver-grey duvet coat with a small chap wrapped in her embrace. We eventually flew to Edmonton, to Winnipeg, to Toronto and New York, changing flights at each airport. I queued to board Concorde for London, and the silver-grey coat was still there. Exhausted back at Heathrow, I waited as my boxes were loaded onto a trolley.

''Ere, guv, yer seen the bloke over there... with the blonde, like – that's Dustin 'ofmann.' I hadn't noticed one of my favourite actors!

I have only missed two flights out of more than 4,000, which surprises anybody familiar with my timekeeping.

In early 1982, I flew to Mexico to conclude a deal. Advising me was David Dickinson, a friend with a sense of humour who became senior partner at Simmons & Simmons. The client's lawyer was Christopher Walford, a partner at Allen and Overy; very decent and serious. Slow progress in negotiations was resolved by deferring to a stuffed toy hippo (for our soon-to-emerge first child) which I placed on the table, shaking or nodding its head so that the other side won the hippo's vote for at least one in three points. Unconventional but successful. Erberto the Hippo helped break the deadlock, maintain honour, and return us to London via New York and a flight on Concorde. Erberto occupied the seat next to Christopher, receiving its own visit from the captain. I took a photo which years later was sent to Christopher as a poster to celebrate his election as Lord Mayor of London.

At some stage every Concorde passenger could enter the cockpit, chat to the captain and see the array of controls banked low above their heads, but it was not always plain sailing. Leaving London in 1993, a tyre burst on the runway and take-off was aborted. Tyres burst a handful of times each year during the 1980s but rarely caused a delay; we stepped off calmly and were ferried back to the Terminal as though nothing had happened, glancing back at the nose wheel flat on the grass at the end of the runway. It was almost the same accident that, seven years later, killed 113 people and eventually grounded Concorde forever. BA Concordes were marginally better protected than those of Air France.

In Europe, work took me regularly to France, Spain and Italy, arranging deals for public and private sector companies. William de Gelsey once asked me to arrange a meeting with

Roberto Calvi at Banco Ambrosiano, but when we arrived, he whispered loudly, 'Why are we meeting this man? This is a mistake. Let's get out.' Such instinct. Not long after, Calvi's body was found, hanged, beneath Blackfriars Bridge.

BUILDING A FAMILY OF MY OWN

1982 to 1988

The time came to move somewhere larger. To make our aspirations and our budget meet, we looked further afield. Stockwell had a pocket of mid-Victorian houses and terraces with massive gardens, excellent transport and easy access to Sussex. But the 1981 headlines were of riots in neighbouring Brixton. A photograph appeared in many newspapers of a Methodist minister, Graham Kent, successfully appealing for calm as police and rioters lined up to clash. I had been at King's with Graham, so we had lunch in the City.

His reassurance was all it took to persuade us to move to a wonderful house in a friendly and diverse street; it was even an unexpected blessing when Antipodean squatters broke in next door and called to introduce themselves with the promise of a crime-free road.

Our house felt huge, on four floors with original Victorian folding shutters and tall ceilings. It needed work, which was fine. We made it ideal for children and got on with our lives.

The expansive kitchen meant I could batch cook for the freezer, not least to use pheasants received from friends who liked to shoot the birds but not to eat them. My cooking worked well until I once mistakenly turned off the full freezer when we went away for a long weekend. There had been news of a housefire caused by an appliance on standby; we soon discovered that a freezer-load can turn putrid in less than a week.

Sophie was born in St Thomas' Hospital during an ancillary workers' strike. Her arrival was a matter of wonder and joy. She was much loved from that day. Nicola's own nanny arrived to help for several weeks, which gave Nicola a taste for a more permanent 'nanny' arrangement although she had no intention of returning to work. Nicola was good at making our curtains, and we had plenty of space so that became her thing.

Much of the income from curtain making is earned from selling fabrics, provided the curtain maker has accounts qualifying for a discount, which involved investment. By chance, Catherine Baldry, wife of a newly elected MP, wanted to sell her curtain business to focus on constituency affairs. I bought Country Furnishings, a shell without customers but with accounts galore. Nicola and Sophie run it successfully to this day, 40 years later.

Getting any small business off the ground requires support, so I learnt to hang curtains, upholster dining room chairs and maintain the books. To reduce pressure, we outsourced the cutting and stitching and set up a separate workshop. The most ambitious project was the design of a set of chambers in Oxford, for which I created the floor plans and elevations so that Nicola could mastermind the building work and soft furnishings. A few hours of commitment every week from each of us gave Nicola financial independence.

As friends married, we went to many weddings in the UK, although Nicola was less keen on going abroad. Martin and Martina's wedding in Germany was large and wonderful; not surprising as Martina is one of five sisters, and the families have extensive networks of friends. I went alone. Nicola came with me when I was a witness at Robin and Rita's wedding in the wine growing area of Le Langhe south of Turin. The ceremony started late as the mayor, who conducted it, had first to deal with emergency road repairs before donning a suit and the flamboyant tricolour sash of office. It was an intimate, wonderful event in a village that Robin has known forever. I have known more members of Martin's family and of Robin's than I do of my own. Three generations of the Foàs and four generations of the Blochs have been my family.

Nicola joined the Italian wedding on the promise of shopping in Florence. She had strong views on clothing. She particularly disliked pink. That Christmas I gave her a wool dress by Emilio Pucci, covered in printed tassels and Pucci's signature, small and clear along the outlines. It was an impulse urged on by a SALE sign. The question, 'What size is your wife, sir?' threw me. I had no idea. The manager lined up her colleagues and asked me to choose the one most like Nicola in size, suggesting that I hug each in turn, to be sure. It was after lunch on Christmas Eve, so I hugged as instructed; the dress was a perfect fit when opened on Christmas day and a firm favourite in her wardrobe. Strangely, it was shocking pink.

Charlie was born 16 months after Sophie arrived, on my 31st birthday. He was a cheerful bruiser of a baby, happy and energetic, and I loved him every bit as much as I loved Sophie.

Driving to Sussex in slow traffic while the children were small, we saw a rocking horse lying in damaged grey gesso paste pieces on the Purley pavement of an antique dealer. We bought it and took the pieces home where, with an instruction book, much equipment from Anthony Dew and more than 200 hours of restoration, Bucephalus rose from the ashes. A grand name for a horse that began life in a 1920s department store, carrying children for a penny ride. Sophie and Charlie loved it in the 1980s, and Maria and I gave Bucephalus to Sophie so that our grandchildren can ride it too.

I continued to sail, as I did for 50 years, sometimes competitively although others deserve the credit for any trophies. The men in Nicola's family were keen sailors, so I joined in. Although I qualified for a licence in Germany, my sailing skills are 'enthusiastic', perhaps 'competent' but far from 'cutting edge'. One skipper, on an overnight race across the English Channel, was so surprised that I had steered for a while in the right direction that he popped up from the chart table to congratulate me. He woke me when he called 'Well done' above the sound of the wind and then realised that I had been fast asleep, my wrists gently draped over the wheel, steering us through the busiest and potentially most dangerous shipping lanes in the world.

The Royal Yacht Squadron in Cowes is the high temple for sailors in Britain. You can watch races from the terrace, just beyond a trophy room that yearns for the return of the America's Cup. You will see the cannon that dictates the progress of Cowes Week and the start line of the Fastnet Race. You might miss two small watercolours by Raoul Dufy, so faded in the sun that you can scarcely see how well he captured the bustle on the Solent.

Few races have the magical draw of the Fastnet. It is the world's largest, most diverse offshore race, over a 700-mile course. It started in 1925 and every other year more than 300 boats take part. The course record is less than 43 hours; when I first raced in 1983 (my father-in-law at the helm of his own boat, *Rushcutter*) we took about a week.

My second foray, in 1985, was very different. Storms whizzed us round; rules introduced after 1979, when 18 people died in the race, meant that no lives were lost although 70 percent of contestants withdrew, and several boats perished. *Rushcutter*'s electrics failed; we rounded the Scillies in pitch black with no instruments, sitting helplessly in the dark, as though being tossed in an industrial washing machine. Largely down to the skipper's skill, we completed the race. Sailing is teamwork, everyone adds something; my main contribution at less dangerous times was in the galley and/or trimming a spinnaker as we scuttled along. I was also tasked with drying the spinnaker in our garden in Stockwell. The vast, coloured sail covered our 60-foot-long garden like a fitted sheet.

BREAKING NEW GROUND

1984 to 1985

George Orwell was right about so much, but not the date. Looking back, 1984/5 may have been the most exciting and successful year of my banking career, with my imagination in full flow for my clients and the children at the centre of my world at home.

We had helped several medium sized US companies to borrow by issuing Eurodollar convertible bonds – loans where the investor had a choice of being repaid in cash or using the investment to buy the issuer's shares at a previously set price.

Esther Tan, who got me through thick and thin for more than a decade, would type the text of pitch letters with a 'modern' golf ball typewriter, leaving large spaces wherever indicated so that I could draw in graphs and charts. I used the children's crayons to colour in the different categories. It was a remarkably successful and novel approach in the days before desktop computers or PowerPoint; we picked up deals that we did not expect to win.

When I approached Moët Hennessy with an idea for a US dollar convertible issue, they were intrigued; it had never been done before by a French company nor, apparently, had it been proposed. Over several meetings with Patrick Houël, the idea and structure evolved.

My pitch was simple. A growing proportion of Moët's income was in dollars, so it made sense to have liabilities in dollars, and rapid growth needs capital which can be cheaper using convertible debt. Patrick agreed. So did Michel Baillon, finance director of ACCOR, the world's largest hotel group. Patrick and Michel seemed uncannily well prepared until they explained that they compared notes by phone while I travelled between their offices.

Both deals took months, working with Charles Clark at Linklaters in Paris. Charles is generous, adventurous yet very measured, with surely one of the finest brains of his generation. He is exceptionally good company and remains a very good friend.

Moët Hennessy was the first to launch. The transaction was named a Deal of the Year by the finance magazine, *Institutional Investor.* Successful in the markets, it annoyed traditional French banks. Accidentally attached to a congratulatory letter from one of Moët's leading financiers was an internal memo: 'It is only a combination of snobbery and ignorance that led to the selection of an English merchant bank to lead the issue'. The French bank in question no longer exists while LVMH is one of the world's most successful companies and its principal shareholder vies to be the world's richest man.

I was appointed as *Représentant de la Masse* in both cases – it is a distinctly French role, tasked with 'defending the interests of the creditors' and I relished the title of this sinecure.

An arbitrage trade exploits temporary price discrepancies between markets. Back in London a Morgan Grenfell colleague, David Hoblyn, saw a similar opportunity if assets were repackaged to appeal to new classes of investors. The word 'Securitisation' did not exist in Europe in 1985 – together we used his idea twice, with great success, repackaging a government guaranteed loan to Brazil and a portfolio of domestic mortgages. However, an arbitrage moves swiftly from 'opportunity' to 'hazard' when done too often. Other banks created securitised deals on an industrial scale, long after the discrepancy vanished. A tsunami of 'securitisation' deals, far more complex than we had created, contributed to the collapse of the banking system in 2008!

Texaco was an important banking client for Morgan Grenfell, but their requirement for one operation seemed impossible; it involved multiple leases to finance a massive catalytic cracker in Wales and Texaco wanted to change the way it was repaid. It seemed too great a challenge and their lead US banks told them so.

That weekend I built a pyramid with the children using their vast collection of Lego bricks. Suddenly the construction triggered an idea to solve Texaco's issue. It was a ridiculously simple idea that required absurdly complex calculations to prove its worth. Three of us, with differing skill sets, created a financial model to match the Lego one. It took three weeks and, when done, directors and dealers looked at it and, to our surprise, approved.

Executing the deals, worth almost £1 billion in today's money, involved several disciplines working together in a single dealing room on a single day. It was impeccably planned and was being meticulously carried out when a rumour emerged of another assassination attempt on President Reagan. Silently the strategy was adjusted. It was soon done. It had been, apparently, one of the bank's most profitable single transactions to date.

At the end of this considerable run of profitable creativity, Nicola and I were invited to sit at the top table at that year's Christmas dinner – a very grand affair in Park Lane. Nicola preferred not to go, which took the edge off my celebration.

Early in 1985 I had a meeting with Stephen O'Brien, a decade after we first met in a church hall. Stephen 'invited' me to mentor recipients of the Prince's Trust grants. One does not say 'No' to this extraordinary man – now Sir Stephen O'Brien, CBE, co-founder of Business in the Community and architect of the Prince's Trust Youth Business.

THE PRINCE'S TRUST

1985 to 1989

Stephen O'Brien is an inspiration and has been for me since we first met when I was a teenager. He seemed very certain of life in a way that I could scarcely imagine. Some years later, after I had gone into the City, I turned to him for advice. He was Chairman of money-brokers Charles Fulton, ordained as a deacon and co-founder of Project Fullemploy.

Fullemploy gave disadvantaged youngsters employment skills. Most were from ethnic minorities and, equipped with a CV, a purpose and some understanding of money, the majority found work. Having introduced me to Fullemploy in the late 1970s, Stephen persuaded me to be a Prince's Trust volunteer in the 1980s. My role was to mentor incredible young people who, with nothing, sought to create businesses and improve their lives.

At about that time, Robert Maxwell told his son Ian to volunteer with the Prince's Trust. Ian commuted between Paris and London as often as I did at that point. We enjoyed time together on the Prince's Trust; I went to a major family birthday party at Headington Hill Hall – jazz band playing in the drive on arrival and a vast family portrait watching the celebrations.

Ian called, 'Are you in Paris next week? We've got a book launch for the Russians; it could be fun.' Maxwell had published some Politburo speeches with an initial print run of six million – a must-have for Party officials. Ian is charming and great company, so I joined him at the Russian

Embassy in Paris. Our host was the aristocratic ambassador, H.E. Yuli Vorontsov.

Vorontsov was elegant, with flawless English; 'You can't possibly drink cheap vodka.' He led us to a distinguished side room, where drinks were delicious and intoxicating. 'You chaps remind me of my son, who is in our foreign service,' said Vorontsov.

'Is he serving overseas?' I asked.

'Better than that,' he replied, 'He is in Washington, behind enemy lines.'

I mentored six young businesses. Three survived and three didn't, close to the average outcome for venture capital investments in the City. I enjoyed mentoring. It gives hope and shares good fortune.

When I met Jane McAdam, a medal maker and sculptor, she was pleasant, quiet, took no notes and asked no questions. Nothing fazed her. A remarkable talent, she had already cast a prize-winning, asymmetrical medal in 1981 to mark Picasso's centenary. For a French client, I commissioned a medal from her, and it was brilliant. We lost touch as soon as she was no longer obliged to have a mentor; she had never needed me anyway.

I heard nothing further until I read Lucian Freud's obituary, naming his children. Jane McAdam Freud was a very successful sculptor who was finally reconciled with her father. I was sad to learn that she had died in 2022, at such a young age.

The two Steves required more time. They set up as couriers and almost lost the business with a drink-driving offence celebrating their grant. They nearly lost it again when the start-up newspaper, *The Sunday Correspondent,* collapsed after less than a year in business, leaving a heap of unpaid debts. They stuck with it and built a steady business. Sounding like twins, they identified themselves by their parental heritage: 'it's English Steve,' or 'it's Asian Steve.'

Decades later I received a call. 'Hi, it's Steve, English Steve, remember me? I found you online. I was telling my kids how I got started. Well, I employ 75 people now and realize I never thanked you.' Steve's success is what the Prince's Trust has done for hundreds of thousands, more than any government scheme has achieved.

Annie Noble traded as *Bonelle*, designing and making clever clothes to order for children's shops. Often deliveries were rejected, apparently because of her Jamaican parentage. I had difficulty believing such racism until I spoke to the shopkeepers; it still shocks me. Rather than confront it, as I should have done, we set up Young Classics Limited together, using Annie's middle name: *Young Classics – Designed by Caroline Noble*, traditional children's clothes by mail order.

The range included sailor suits and dresses, smocked frocks, shirts, shorts and jackets; Annie had an instinct for colour and design. A friend, Janet Harris, volunteered to join us.

We built the business, with a catalogue every second season printed by City contacts. Professional photographers (such as Clive Boursnell), volunteer models (our children and their friends) and a press list for PR (lent by a Tie Rack director) resulted in a full-page article in the *Glasgow Herald* and another in *Harper's Bazaar* which led to orders from housing estates and grand estates; some clothes reached Kensington Palace for Princes William and Harry.

We made mistakes and learnt lessons. Entrepreneurs differ from employees in one major respect. When something inevitably goes wrong, a company executive or government official sends a memo to land the blame on a colleague's desk. An entrepreneur studies the error to learn lessons. The difference is huge and touches everything… if it goes wrong I lose my own money, not the fruit of the Money Tree or OPM, Other People's Money!

We made enough to pay the bills, especially Annie's salary. Just as it was getting too large to cope, Annie was recruited to help young Brixton entrepreneurs. She is still helping others.

A FINANCIAL REVOLUTION

1986 to 1988

The Antipodeans made good on their pledge to keep our Stockwell street safe, although there were break-ins, muggings and even murders in neighbouring streets. Time to move.

The search took us gradually further west, away from easy public transport and towards parks and open spaces. Between Wandsworth and Clapham Commons, we found a house in need of much renovation, and it took time to gut and reconstruct with the no-expense-spared attitude of two people preparing their forever home. An Aga in the Mark Wilkinson bespoke kitchen and Manuel Canova fabrics in the living room! We were unlucky with builders, with delays and overruns, but eventually we moved in.

Fortunately, by then we had bought the Red House, a Grade II Listed cottage in south Norfolk, with a vast Wellingtonia, a small bridge onto the village green and a large garden. I papered the walls and repaired and repainted everything else while Nicola made soft furnishings. It was a perfect retreat in a village that welcomed us warmly.

Meanwhile work took me further afield. In the mid-1980s, Pittsburgh reeked of collapsing industry; parts of the city were forbidding. One evening I passed the shadows of its proud history, the birthplace H J Heinz, Mellon and Carnegie, and in my ignorance strayed into Sixth Avenue; within minutes an anxious man approached, ‘Excuse me, sir, you must be from out of town; this is not a safe place to walk – may I lead you somewhere safer?' Sixth Avenue was then known for despair and violence. Now it is the city's cultural district.

I was covering two regions, managing a team in Europe, especially France, and supporting a team in the USA. On one trip, two weeks spent flying to 20 US cities was as tough for the programme as it was for my colleague's insatiable appetite for burgers – Wendy's, Arby's, McDonalds, Burger King, Dairy Queen. Our last stop was Toys 'R' Us head office in Wayne, New Jersey. I was desperate for joined-up-meat with a knife and fork.

Our motel had a sandwich machine with a flickering light, that was empty. We searched for an hour until we were led to a truck stop. Outside were 18-wheelers, polished chrome and Wild West images; inside, a large screen, Rock 'n' Roll and well-inked men in denim jackets.

Our waitress resembled a clichéd caricature of a blowsy barmaid: 'Hi, my name's Mindy. What is your pleasure today?' She was in a hurry.

Weary of burgers, I replied flippantly, 'Ideally lobster washed down with champagne, followed by fillet steaks with a good bottle of claret, please.'

Mindy turned; the truckers regarded us as aliens.

We waited. I was ready to admit my mistake when Mindy returned. She set two places, put down two plates of micro-waved Lobster thermidor and began pouring a fizzy drink saying, 'This is Domaine Chandon, made in the Napa Valley by the méthode champenoise. Enjoy.' It was delicious.

Mindy came again with filet mignon steaks, green beans and French fries, perfectly cooked. 'This is a Cabernet

Sauvignon, the same grape varietal as a Bordeaux, or claret as you Brits call it; this comes from Sonoma Valley and 1984 was a great year – have a nice meal!'

Game, set and match to the charming Mindy, and a vivid reminder about not judging a book by its cover.

I loved travelling around the USA. My first visit was in 1978, to New York to stay in the apartment that Stephen Funnell shared with his future wife, Suzi; and New England to stay with Andrew May in Boston. Countering that first visit, I soon learned that America has few walking cities and a vast majority of driving cities. It also has many of my favourite museums, such as the Metropolitan and the Cloisters, MoMA, the Frick, Isabella Stewart Gardner, Chicago's Art Institute and San Francisco's Legion of Honor. I always found time for a visit.

Back home, the City changed forever with Big Bang. In late 1984, retail and merchant banks alike were getting ready to acquire brokers and jobbers so they could participate in the liberalisation of the City, that some saw as the opening of the casino doors.

The 1986 Financial Services Act was a game changer. In 1984, finance represented 3.1% of UK exports. By 2008 that figure had risen to 34.1% of all UK exports. Here, in part, were the seeds of 2008's crash and bailout.

The merry-go-round was exciting; everyone jockeyed for position. Liberalisation meant the end of the rule that a firm could either trade in shares for a client (a stockbroker) or trade on its own account (a jobber). Large financial institutions bought broking and jobbing partnerships. MG acquired

Pinchin Denny & Co (a jobber whose partners included the French equities wizard Chris Hipkins) and Pember & Boyle (a stockbroker whose partners included Tim's older brother, Robin Bevan). I already knew Chris and Robin well.

Partnerships had unlimited liability; losses were funded by partners, even if that meant losing everything. However, that constraint was lifted, and the temptation of 'risk-free' bonuses grew. Rana Foroohar, in her 2016 book *Makers and Takers*, captures the shift perfectly as the 'Too Big to Fail problem, or at least the part of it involving the socialisation of risk and the privatisation of profit'. Much the same misallocation of risk and reward as in Derek Lamb's rendition of the folk song, 'She was poor, but she was honest':

It's the same the whole world over
It's a shame, a wretched shame
It's the rich who get the pleasure
And the poor who get the blame.

The pace was so frantic that systems and programmes were introduced to minimise the time in which decisions were made. Trading programmes, an early version of Artificial Intelligence, had few manual overrides or circuit breakers. Programmed protective selling triggers waves of additional protective selling over which nobody exercised control. This builds extreme volatility into the increasingly fragile architecture of financial markets.

In late 1987, after 18 months of building works, we settled into a house with everything we wanted. That winter I was invited to St Moritz, staying in a crowded chalet with Nicola's brother Hugh and his chums and travelling with her parents. We went for the Cresta Run.

The Cresta Run is a head-first dash on a bladed tray (called, ominously, a 'skeleton') down a sinuous, walled ice slope at high speeds. It is terrifyingly good fun and potentially lethal. Lt Col Digby Willoughby drilled non-members, like me, on the Supplementary List at the St Moritz Tobogganing Club. He woke us up with a Death Talk, illustrated with X-rated X-rays of previously damaged limbs.

On the Cresta Run, a skeleton would naturally 'pop out of Shuttlecock Corner, like the pips out of an orange', unless properly steered by the rider. Steering is achieved with slight shifts in body position or movements of the head. In practice, one in every dozen rides ends in hay bales off the course, always with bruises, often with broken bones.

Shuttlecock injects a madness into us all. Falling at this corner earns membership of the Shuttlecock Club, with its own tie adorned with a badminton birdie. Why do it? It is unlike anything else; the rider is at once in control and potentially out of control. The thrill of moving at more than 50 mph with your nose six inches from the ice is indescribable. Why do it? Why on earth not, if you get the chance? Above all, it teaches a balance between risk and reward.

On Friday 16 October 1987, we left a dance in Hammersmith at 1 a.m. into 80 mph winds. Others were blown off their feet. After a disturbed night, I went to work before 7 and found roads blocked by fallen trees and masonry. I drove across Clapham Common on the grass away from roads and trees, then spent the day preparing for a meeting in Scotland.

On Black Monday, 19 October 1987, I flew to Glasgow as planned. The market had been weak on Friday but far from unusual, apart from the storm damage and the number of empty desks. As I reached my meeting, I was whisked into their dealing room. It was crowded and cowed. Every number on every screen was red. In part, the crash was triggered by expectations of higher inflation and a weaker economy, although that had been the case for several months before October. Primarily, however, the uncontrollable ferocity of the one day fall in share prices was driven by programme trading; structures introduced so recently already had the capability to wipe out fortunes and savings.

The world had changed, and old financial solutions did not seem relevant. I returned to London empty-handed.

The engine room of Morgan Grenfell's corporate finance department no longer whirred. Activity, highly dependent on the health of the stock market, almost ceased. However, institutions still had money to invest, and companies still had needs. I was asked to give a talk to the bank about capital markets options in a collapsing corporate finance world. There was only one presentation software, Harvard Graphics, and that only had two stock images, a donkey and an elephant, symbols of the main American political parties.

I created a story using these images to identify two imaginary companies and to illustrate different ways to meet the needs of an imagined transaction. The room was full, probably because Robin Bevan insisted that everybody attended 'my nephew's talk'. It helped pull two divergent sides of the bank together for a while. However, the merchant bankers seemed uncomfortable, explained by the first question: 'How did you know that Donkey was our code name for Dunlop?' Until that question, I hadn't known.

Perhaps because of the talk, David Douglas-Home called 'for a chat'. He projected easy charm but was very purposeful; I suspect he never called just 'for a chat'. Eventually, he asked if I would go to Edinburgh to learn the ropes and, in a year, run the private bank there. It would be an interesting promotion, removing me from the snake pit of the capital markets and providing more family time. I knew the team and love the city, so I said 'maybe'. I knew what the job required and how I could make a difference. I told Nicola what was proposed and how a few years there could benefit us and the children. I asked how she felt about the idea. It was a short conversation: 'I'm not moving.'

That autumn, I was headhunted from my job at Morgan Grenfell. As Nicola would not move to Edinburgh, I changed job. We went on holiday and enjoyed our newly refurbished house, spending weekends at the Red House, which was looking at its best. The children were happy and starting the great adventure of education. It seemed that we had almost everything we could want as a couple.

A NEW JOB, A NEW EVERYTHING

1988 to 1999

The week before I started the new job, I was formally notified that Nicola wanted a 'trial separation'. It was a shock that was never discussed or explained. Initially, I lived in the otherwise empty London house of Nicola's parents, hoping that everything would work out. It's hard to address a problem when nobody will say what the problem is, if indeed there was a problem. Then good friends helped. Less than a decade after learning to have a family for the first time, my family vanished. Apparently while the marriage was existential for me, it was merely transactional for Nicola's family. That became clearer and relentlessly more bruising over the following decade.

It was not a good foundation on which to build a substantial department for a major bank.

Val Le Grice rang. He was a family friend who became an eminent QC specialising in family law. We regularly sailed together on Tim's boat; during the children's first summers we would stay in one of his cottages near Newlyn. His grandparents had been close to Nicola's grandparents and so on through the generations. Val called to say that Tim had sought advice about divorce solicitors and was looking for the toughest available. Val, concerned for me by the negative tone of Tim's enquiry, advised that I needed somebody in the same league, like Fiona Shackleton, a newish partner at Farrer & Co who greatly impressed Val's fellow barristers. So much for trial separation.

The divorce took place at breakneck, heart-break speed, with no reasoning and no conversation about the children's needs. Both sets of lawyers were baffled; the process was precipitous and angry. The London house we had just refurbished was sold. The house in Norfolk was sold. I rented a large pantechnicon one Friday night and reached Shelfanger at 3 a.m. Two hours and much coffee later, I single-handedly loaded it with all our furniture and possessions – beds, chests of drawers, boxes of kitchen utensils and all our gardening equipment, everything. By Sunday evening, I had delivered everything to the correct destination and the lorry was returned to the yard.

Knowing the indefatigable support I've had from many long-standing friends, I surprisingly did it alone. At the time I felt unable to ask; I felt alone, financially broken, and ashamed, not of anything I had done but of the unexplained failure of my marriage, into which I thought I had put more than heart and soul. I felt as I had as a child – that if I had only worked harder, I might have been loved. It just doesn't work that way. The second great commandment is 'Thou shalt love thy neighbour as thyself.' The problem there is, how to proceed if you do not love yourself?

I regret the years when I did not spend more time with those friends. Friends are the family we chose, and mine are spread across the world. In my wish to belong, I looked in the wrong direction.

Staying with me in London one night, Sophie crawled into my bed as I slept, woke me and whispered, 'You won't forget me, Daddy, will you?' All illusion of family evaporated.

The Red House had been a particularly happy place for all of us, or so I thought. In 1988, I was invited to chair the Shelfanger Village Quiz, a great feeling that overcame the burden of setting all the questions. Remember, this was the year before Tim Berners-Lee invented things we now know as WWW, HTML, URLs and HTTP – this was long before popular access to the internet. Putting together a quiz was a real bind!

The evening was a success. Even after we sold the house during our divorce, I was invited back each year to set and chair the quiz. I was thrilled and remarked, 'You make me feel like an insider'.

'No Julian,' came the reply, in the languidly earnest tones of Norfolk, 'you're not an insider; howsomever, you are an outsider we can trust.' The story of any wanderer's life but at least 'I weren't a vister.'

I was hired to set up an International Capital Markets team at Credit Lyonnais Securities (CLS) that would enable its parent company Crédit Lyonnais (CL) to capitalise on its position as one of the world's largest banks. I worked hand in glove with a very bright CL executive, a graduate of one of France's *grandes écoles*, on the inside track but with no former experience of the business. I would drive into the City before 7 a.m., swim a mile and be fresh at my desk as the day began. It was an adventure or a distraction.

A few weeks after I arrived, Morgan Grenfell stopped its stock market and trading operations, and 450 MG Securities staff were laid off. I phoned a friend, Chris Hipkins, well-known as London's best trader in French equities. Chris and

I assembled a strong team covering trading, sales and research for European stocks catapulting CL into a strong position.

Working with Chris and people I already knew helped me to cope. It was tough to handle the unpleasantness of separation and then the nastiness of divorce at the same time as trying to navigate the commercial ineptitude of an over-politicised French bank. The department grew and had many successes, although it never fulfilled its potential.

I enjoyed regular business trips to Dublin. I ate grandly with the future billionaires of the Celtic Tiger boom or drank Guinness and ate smoked salmon in pubs with similarly interesting Dubliners. Everywhere there was great wit and conversation. However, that stopped whenever the boys in black berets appeared with buckets. I would be told briskly not to say a word with my give-away accent. That tide turned in the mid-90s and, as they entered, the IRA's collectors were greeted with jeers of 'Why don't yer feck off!'

Often terrorism is theft masquerading as revolution. Behind many movements lies a trade in drugs, protection, modern-day slaves and weapons; criminals shapeshifting in the shadow of real issues. When an economy works for everyone, when there is real hope, then people confidently shout at gangsters, 'Why don't yer feck off!' Until then, in a climate of hopelessness, the terrorists' actions obscure the real needs, and issues are not resolved.

Dermot Desmond is one of Ireland's richest men. At the time, he was a flamboyant Dublin financier, and CL was his main shareholder. Once at lunch in Chelsea to discuss his car leasing business, the conversation revolved around repossessions (especially of Rolls-Royces) and racing. I mentioned a horse running that afternoon and he said, 'My driver can take you to Ladbrokes if you like.'

I stepped from his Rolls into a smoke-filled bookie's and put £5 on the 100 to one outsider. It started slowly; I was leaving when the commentary tone changed. In a gripping race, the horse clawed its way to a win. Jealous eyes watched me walk out with a big win and surprisingly the car was waiting. One hardened gambler called out, 'He must know what he's doin'; you should see his feckin' car.' If only! My life was restless and unsettled.

I had a favourite restaurant, Le Caprice, where I could eat an inexpensive meal and still be made to feel like the master of the house. Although I was a modest spender, I got to know the front of house team well; indeed, when I finally settled and married for the last time, in 2008, the legendary Jesus Adorno was at our wedding with his wife.

I have only been on one blind date – it was not a success. I collected her and asked, 'Where would you like to eat after the play?'

The passive-aggressive answer was, 'There's only one place, the Caprice; but if you haven't booked, don't bother.'

I phoned as we drove and asked. The reply was 'I'm very sorry, sir, we are fully booked; perhaps another evening.'

'Good evening, Angelo; how are you?'

'Ah, Mr Morton; of course, I have a table for you; at what time?'

It was a good play and a good meal but with little conversation and we never met again.

There was a pan-European wave of telecoms privatisations in the early 1990s. Keith Sykes (the top UK analyst in the sector and a dear friend) and I proposed that CLS should organise a Telecoms conference, supported by his ground-breaking research, to position the bank for a major role in the transactions. Keith wrote a definitive encyclopaedia of specific and comparative data about every European company in the sector. It was immediately hailed as The Telephone Directory.

The conference, at CL's Paris HQ over two days, attracted the chair of every European telecom operator, leading telecoms investors and regulators, with the relevant EU Director General as a keynote speaker. They assembled in the conference theatre on the first day.

While they waited, CL chairman Jean-Yves Haberer stood outside debating whether it was worth his while to open the event. In the end, we started late, with a curt welcome, and the chair's swift departure. It was typical of the bank's culture. Sometimes an organisation's failure is inevitable, as with Haberer's inexpert 'leadership' at CL.

Some good resulted. Keith and I pitched to advise *ÖPTV*, Austrian Post and Telecoms, on privatisation; we won the business against top league competition.

Before long we hit a problem. On a flight back from Vienna, with a cold, my left ear went 'pop!' and began to bleed. The pain was indescribable. An ambulance rushed me to hospital from the airport and, with a perforated eardrum, I was grounded for three months. Visits to Vienna were by ferry and sleeper train.

On the first journey, I met a delightful diplomat. He had been 'our man in the Christmas Islands and on Tristan

Da Cunha'. Not surprisingly, he had appeared on Desert Island Discs, and he chose another eight records when his mother appeared in her own right, explaining that 'she only recognised one tune, the National Anthem, because everybody stood up'. We discussed his choices, and he asked mine. Faced with the choice, I would want musical dialogue between voices or instruments. On a desert island, I would most miss conversation; I largely grew up without it, but I have learned to enjoy it so much.

Without tights there would have been no miniskirts. On another Vienna visit I met Wolford, the world's leading manufacturer of expensive tights. Wolford was founded by two families whose interests had diverged but neither could afford to buy out the other. I was called on for ideas to unblock the impasse. The assumption was that we'd find a passive investor, but that would only postpone the argument, so I proposed listing the company's shares in Wien, Paris, London, the three city names in Wolford's logo.

Dealings with the Finance Director were refreshingly straightforward. Fritz Humer, the marketing-obsessed CEO, was more complicated. The date for the deal drifted, and discussions about price become hopelessly unrealistic. Pricing can be as much an art as a science, so I proposed that we launch on St Valentine's Day and offer shares to the public, to be called *Damen Aktien* or Lady's Shares with the same price as Wolford's flagship tights, *Fatal*. It was higher than we had discussed but after the launch investors were happy to pay far more in the market. It was the best performing share in Europe for the next two years.

There have been many milestone art events, like the Great Japan Exhibition in 1981 or Tutankhamun a decade earlier. My moment of marvel was at the Mauritshuis in 1996, when a meeting was postponed, and I saw a queue. 'It's the Vermeer, sir,' said my taxi driver. 'It's sold out, but people always hope.' With little hope I joined the queue at 8.30 a.m. and soon heard a French tourist calling, '*J'ai deux billets à vendre*,' so, without seeing him, I shouted, '*J'achète*' and bought two tickets for 9 a.m. I gave the spare to a queueing art student.

Twenty-three of Vermeer's works were on display, at the time the largest number ever in a single place: most of his iconic masterpieces, two thirds of his attributed output. Many were painted from one spot: the window on the left, often the heavy chair with lion's head carvings. With growing financial security, stained glass appears and then a skirting board of Delft tiles; the checker-board floor gains sophistication, reinforcing perspective. The characters, mostly women, evolve as he returns to a subject. His genius with light is there from the outset. It was a stroke of luck, and the grateful art student was a well-informed guide.

In the mid-1990s flying between European countries became easier. Several low-cost airlines stepped in to take advantage, of which only easyJet and Ryanair remain. I met Franco Mancassola, founder of Debonair and in need of funding. Having been international chairman of Continental and set up a low-cost carrier in Hawaii, Franco saw an opportunity for innovation in Europe. Debonair was a low-cost airline with extra legroom, European hubs, Affordable Business Class and the first iteration of dynamic pricing, which Franco called Buckets. It was a very clever system.

Franco understood the US model, where funding for start-up airlines was readily available. The phenomenon was new in Europe, where most airlines had been state-owned and where independents (such as Virgin) depended on trans-atlantic business. We had to identify new funding sources. Franco enjoyed the process as I worked every angle, eventually selecting a new European stock exchange on which to float his shares. He described the analysis as 'imagination; that's intelligence having fun'. He was a large character and passionate. We introduced him to many people before the final decision.

People may be tempted when first meeting Sir Richard Branson to assume his diffidence means that he does not understand. They explain their ideas in detail, often in more detail than was intended. When we took Franco to meet Sir Richard at his home/HQ in Holland Park, it was a fascinating master class in information gathering.

Without having secured Virgin's support, we undertook a trip around Europe to meet potential institutional investors during a week set aside for Sophie to have work experience with me. Franco agreed that she join the roadshow and help. Starting with lunch in London on Monday, we flew to Hamburg, Paris and Madrid, changed planes in Basel for Copenhagen and finally to Stockholm. Sophie's work experience was in Club class and top hotels all the way! Aged 15, Sophie soon showed that she had the ability to make people do as she wished without appearing bossy. By the time we reached Scandinavia, the '*trainee*' was in charge.

I liked Debonair and thought it might thrive when

an opportunity occurred in 1999 to merge it with a similar operator. Unfortunately, the talks faltered; the wrong sort of aircraft (the BAe 146 was notoriously expensive to run), two big personalities, growing competition… too many obstacles. Both airlines disappeared but they shaped the way we all travel.

Apart from the first three years of being single, I spent Christmas each year with Andrew and Vivien May in Colchester. It was a welcome refuge for me and a home from home for the children if they were with me for Christmas.

If I was not able to see the children at weekends, I frequently went to Munich. It is a small town and easy to get around. Shops shut at midday on Saturday and reopened on Monday, so there was no retail distraction. I almost always stayed with the Moutiers. Bernard was an art dealer, known for sourcing impressionist and post-Impressionist paintings of exceptional quality. I'd known them and their daughter, Evelyne, since she was a child. 'My' room in Munich was filled with masterpieces, including two mesmerising works of dark-eyed ladies by Berthe Morisot. Visits to Munich were relaxed and welcoming, with occasional museum visits or parties; I was always rested on my return.

LONDON'S HOMELESS

1988 to 2000

Without my children, I would not spend Christmas on my own. In this country alone, hundreds of thousands of fathers and mothers must feel such desolation every year. I remembered it from the other end of the telescope when I was younger and Papa was not with us, or I was not with my family; it is not a new phenomenon caused by divorce.

I volunteered to serve lunch at a drop-in centre for the homeless in Aldgate.

People confuse the homeless and rough sleepers. The latter live 24/7 in the open, sleeping in doorways or tunnels, and used to number about 500 on any given night in London; numbers have possibly more than doubled since. 10,000 people sleep rough at some stage in London in a year. Homelessness is a bigger issue affecting more than 50,000 households in London throughout the year, rising to more than twice that figure when totally inadequate and de-humanised accommodation is included. The homeless live in condemnable flats with damp and rot, in hostels or on somebody's sofa or floor. The homeless live in fear and discomfort. More than one per cent of London families are without a 'home'.

I am warm and dry in my study, with a radiator and good lighting, hail crashing against the window. Even now, more than 30 years after I first engaged with homelessness, I cannot begin to understand the despair of sleeping outside in these conditions with no prospect of anything improving. Equally I cannot fully grasp the courage of a person whose life is so desperate and abusive that living rough appears to offer more hope. It is no comfort to know that 'ye have the poor with you always,' although the quotation continues, 'and whenever ye will ye may do them good;' the problem should surely be shrinking, not growing.

My experience of sleeping rough was one night in June 1989; Bejay wanted to share his world with me at the start of a highly valued and rewarding relationship.

Back to lunch on Christmas Day, 1988. The volunteers arrived early, and we stood peeling and prepping for 300 to 400 people; there are no bookings or tickets so you are never quite sure, and it is one day when you cannot go short. The menu offered the full Christmas works: turkey with all its trimmings and heaps of vegetables, roast and mashed potatoes and several gallons of gravy. There were vegetarian options and salads to be prepped as well. And puddings – the whole range of Christmas puds, with creams and custards.

Each person has their own reason to volunteer. One girl hitchhiked from The Hague, having failed to find an option in the Netherlands. There were committed Christians and decided don't-knows. One family popped in for an hour, as they had done for many years; the oldest daughter explained that it was their tradition and she couldn't imagine lunch, presents and the Queen's speech at home unless she had first served food at St Botolph's.

In a corner Bejay sat, with Naomi's tired head on his lap. I was carrying a half gallon pot of tea with plastic beakers in a stack under one arm when a voice called, 'Yer ain't got a little espresso for me, 'ave yer? It'd be jus' right after a meal like that. Yer know, I always 'ad espresso after dinner when I lived in the Sarth of France.' We chatted and he helped clear the tables, with a capacity for non-stop banter.

In the 25 years that I knew Bejay, we talked most weeks. To this day I do not know where his reality began or where the real world ended. It didn't matter. History, especially a personal history like his, belongs to the person telling the story and there is rarely one single '*truth*'. What I do know as '*truth*' was that, over the next quarter century, the warmth and strength of Bejay's friendship to me outweighed mine to him ten-fold.

For almost 10 years, I popped into St Botolph's every Thursday evening and stayed until late, sometimes ending with a hospital run and into the small hours in A&E. Doris Boyd MBE was the lifeblood of the crypt. Look up in the City, you see history and financial excess; look down and you see need. Doris served a full career in accounts. Why do this in retirement? 'Julian, there's no bloomin' point in goin' to Church an' talkin' abaht God all day Sunday if yer don't get off yer you-know-what an' do some'at abaht it fer the rest of the week.' Her whisper is often in my ear although I rarely do it justice as she would.

Once I watched Doris stepping between two dossers in a knife fight near the crypt; there was a crowd, blood and the risk of worse. Raising a hand to each chest, she said, 'Come on, boys; I'll have them knives, please;' they meekly obeyed. I admired her courage; she saw it differently: 'It was one against one but if they'd laid a finger on me, they'd have bin lynched by that lot.'

There are many characters in drop-in centres. Charlie

was six feet tall, rake thin with a shock of red hair and a ready smile. He was a Glaswegian whose conversation was littered with 'f***ing this' and 'c***ing that'. He beckoned; 'Hey, Julian, y' gonna gimme me a game o' f***king Scraable,' was his irresistible invitation; we played. Charlie was very good company.

Not long after we started, I realised my mistake; I had taken on a Scrabble master with a vocabulary beyond the F-word and the C-word. I was being trounced. Suddenly Charlie warned 'Dinna turn roond an' dinna f***ing look,' as a disturbance behind me grew louder. Charlie had just cleared his rack, with a ridiculously high score, when he reached across the board and pushed me to one side; a heavy metal chair crashed down where I was sitting.

Charlie leapt at the man who was about to flatten me and pushed him roughly against the wall; the brief silence was broken by a menacing growl – 'You f***ing leave mah mon alone when I'm f***king beatin' him at Scraable.'

There are many reasons, other than addiction or illness, for people to be excluded. A quiet, well-spoken man never gave his name. We met each week for six months, then he vanished; back, I hope, to a good life. In the latter weeks, he confided that he had been a supermarket manager and went through a messy divorce. He bought a bedsit and was rebuilding his life when a fire destroyed everything. Issues with insurance left him with a burnt-out shell, a mortgage and an unscalable mountain of debt. One day he gave me a copy of Boswell's *A Tour in the Hebrides with Dr Johnson*. 'I've enjoyed this,' he said, 'and I am sure you will too.' I did enjoy it, and I still have the book; I have never seen him since.

Bejay challenged me one evening: 'Come 'n see my part o' town 'cos it ain't the same as what yours is.' He was right of course and asked for 24 hours of my life.

We met on the steps of St Martin's at 6.30 one morning. Bejay's rules were: one sleeping bag, a simple waterproof jacket, an ounce of tobacco and £3 in cash, but on no account was I to carry ID, credit cards or a season ticket. We walked and chatted, as we always did for the rest of Bejay's life, about anything and nothing.

In St James's Park, he teased me about the crowds going to work, 'booted 'n suited, like what you is most days,' We reached Victoria Passage in time to join the queue for the 'best breakfast in town, 'n it's only 70p.' It was a feast.

There had been a murder at the Waterloo Bullring that morning, making it all 'a bit difficult, like' so we moved on. Bejay had lived in a 'bash' near the Festival Hall, and the new occupant was persuaded to 'gimme a tour'. It was the size of a cardboard bed with a recycled door bearing a padlock, 'to keep the squatters aht.' Bejay's name was etched on the scrap walls, a dosser's equivalent of a Blue Plaque.

We returned to St Martin's and stood in the sombre queue for a numbered ticket for lunch; the quota is limited. From volunteering at weekends, I knew the social worker giving out tickets and spoke to him by name – he made no eye contact and gave no sign of recognition; sadly, for him this had become a job. £1 bought a pleasant two-course meal but no welcome.

In the City, Bejay and I stood incongruously in front of Louis Vuitton at the Royal Exchange. Pointing at a large leather suitcase in the window, he said, 'I bet that must cost £100. I know 'cos the copies in the market cost £30 or £40.' I didn't have the courage then, or ever, to suggest that the case then cost £3,000. It seemed an obscene argument to have, while we prepared to sleep on a pavement, as he had done most nights of his life.

There was an awkward moment when a drunk poked me in the chest and asked, 'Who's this?'

'He's my friend – he's a dosser with L-plates,' Bejay replied; and after a bit of very physical unpleasantness, we moved on. We walked more than 15 miles that day, saying 'wotcher' to dozens of people along the way. 'Wotcher' can mean many things.

At Lincoln's Inn Fields, somebody said, 'You can sleep over there, mate; it's a good spot,' pointing at a bald patch beneath a tree where a rat waited patiently for us amid the discarded rubbish.

Bejay replied before I could say a word, 'No, thanks mate, we'd better push orf. We gotta long way ter go. Wotcher.' It was an extraordinary camp; there was a commonly held view among those living there that the gardens had a seventeenth-century covenant offering newcomers to London the right to squat in camps while they settled. It resembled the photographs of the refugee camp at Sangatte, the 'Jungle', and this shadow of dislocation fell for many years across a most affluent part of London.

There is little safety, sleeping rough overnight. Some sleep away from the crowds, hoping for the safety of being invisible although, when the worst does happen, their bodies can lie unfound for weeks. Others opt for broad daylight with possible witnesses to protect them. Bejay chose the Post Office doorway in Kingsway; shuttered off now, it was then a Dossers' Dorchester and much sought after, although nowhere is truly safe. People urinate on rough sleepers, or set them alight, kick them or steal their bags and boots. I slept well, too tired to worry, and woke rested, unaware that Bejay had arranged a rota of his pals to stand watch all night and let nobody disturb me, apart from the Sally Army who appeared at 1 a.m., waking me to offer tea and Jesus.

At one point I smoked 40 cigarettes a day. Nothing becomes smoking as much as the quitting, but it had a positive side: I could sit on the pavement and share a cigarette, perhaps with an ex-serviceman for whom conversation and a laugh may briefly defer the yearning to obliterate consciousness. Acknowledging a fellow human is often worth more than cash.

Many former soldiers cannot cope with their nightmares, having been discharged after a lifetime of structure and support into a world that neither understands nor takes the time to listen. Schizophrenia and bipolar disorder are two of London's other exposed nerves, as so many sufferers cannot bear to calm themselves with the debilitating medical cosh and hopelessness that make them zombies.

Violence is a way of life; beggars are controlled by 'taxmen' who extort a cut. Prostitution and drugs are found everywhere – most often one pays for the other. At St Botolph's, I regularly met a dozen members of one family in which, for generation after generation, mothers were said to have pimped their under-age daughters in Brick Lane, as grannies had pimped them. They were a close family, apparently loving and intelligent; they helped others to complete complex benefits forms (for a fee) and any of the women might have succeeded at university and in life beyond. Neither police nor social workers felt they had enough information to charge them.

Male prostitution is rife; as they age, some rent-boys openly discussed plans to transition, to retain a job where women have a longer shelf life than boys. Drunkenness, drugs and despair – where is hope?

Rabbi Hugo Gryn recorded his father's words when, together, they were forced to march from Auschwitz to Lieberose concentration camp in 1944: 'We know that you can live three weeks without food, and you can live for three days without water, but you cannot live for three minutes without hope.'

Some weeks later, I took Bejay and Naomi to supper at Joe Allen. It sounds a strange decision, but it was perfect. Bejay loved everything about the place, but Naomi was initially very uncomfortable; the waiter sensed it. He squatted next to her, put the menu to one side and engaged her in conversation about what she would like to eat, until she had disclosed all her favourite things, not one of which was on the menu. Didn't matter; the waiter and kitchen constructed a meal that met her wishes, and she was soon smiling and talking – it was perhaps the happiest I ever saw her.

Shortly after I met him, Bejay moved with Naomi into a one-bedroom flat on the Old Kent Road. When Zeus was born, Bejay created a bedroom for the baby by removing the doors from the hall cupboard. Bejay was an ingenious DIY addict and boasted of being a 'skip diver', rescuing discarded scraps from building sites and crafting them into shelves and basic furniture. I had never heard the phrase until years later, when Maria and I visited Highgrove. A guide said that a large stone, on which a statue stood, had been rescued from a building site (*en route* from Windsor). She called the future king 'a great skip diver'.

My friendship with Bejay remained strong. We saw each other frequently, spoke every week for the rest of his life and enjoyed each other's company. The early years were a golden period in Bejay's life. He and Naomi flourished, Zeus was born, and the family moved to a two-bedroom flat near Tower Bridge, close to a great nursery school; Bejay got his first job in decades, as a storeman at Viking, and was rapidly promoted to forklift truck driver and then to team leader. Bejay and Naomi married in Peckham.

Bejay's happiness was infectious, and I was thrilled to be his best man. Naomi was reticent, bright but crippled by anxiety and, as it turned out, many other severe problems. They were great together and Naomi relished being a mother as much as Bejay loved being a dad.

Zeus was almost four, and at school, when Conan was born. But a day later, Naomi went into a severe catatonic state, a depression at the extreme end of postpartum psychosis. She was sectioned, at the instigation of the hospital, for her safety and that of the new-born child.

Bejay looked after Zeus, and we visited Naomi regularly but saw no recognition or change, locked into those bleak surroundings. One day, some weeks into this dreadful process, Bejay rang in great distress; Naomi had disappeared and somehow taken Conan. Bejay ran to the school and arrived too late – Naomi had already persuaded the school to release Zeus early. The three of them had disappeared.

For several days Bejay chased the police, trying to get them to put out a Missing Person notice, calling family and hospitals and getting nowhere. Eventually Bejay surmised that the police were not really interested. I phoned to ask about progress; a young PC bluffed and stumbled until I asked for the officer in charge. Within minutes the matter escalated; I was given a name and a mobile number.

The inspector immediately answered the call; surprisingly, as he explained that he was on a golf course. It was a short conversation, and he called back within minutes, having set a search in progress. Naomi was traced to Norwich in less than a day. Why I got the red-carpet treatment puzzles me – does a certain voice and manner really carry disproportionate weight in our supposedly classless society?

The battle now began to regain access to the children. Weeks passed, causing Bejay untold grief. In a period of distraction, he had an accident at Viking: a pile of laden pallets fell on him, and his back was broken. We fought on while Bejay was being prepared in hospital for life in a wheelchair, which is how he was until he died.

Much as I respect the rule of law, I don't much enjoy going to court – as a plaintiff, respondent or witness. Perhaps the strangest appearance was in this fight for access to Zeus and Conan in the Central Family Court in High Holborn.

Bejay's solicitor went out of business on the eve of the hearing, and the administrator refused to release the papers, arguing the files were assets in a liquidation and could not go anywhere.

The judge allowed me to ask questions of the lawyers for Norfolk County Council as they argued a case to deny Bejay access to his children. The social workers had done little or no homework or chose to ignore important details. We made very good progress. The judge granted Bejay access, initially supervised and then without limit. This was the law at its wisest, ignoring niceties in favour of the main question. I ensured that Bejay could go to Norwich at least fortnightly. Before he was 10, Zeus looked after his mother and brother knowing that his father was a phone call away. The children were never put into care or separated. They grew up as principled adults and still look after their mother.

THE *COMITÉ D'ENTREPRISE*

1989 to 1997

For several years at CL, I rubbed shoulders with the essence of the French establishment, the politically plugged-in graduates of the *grandes écoles*, an élite battalion with jobs for life jogging in the murky treacle of power at the heart of the French administration. They can be fearsomely intelligent, not always very commercial and with no notion of *égalité*. France can only be understood through exposure to these *inspecteurs de n'importe quoi*. They know no *win-win*, only a *zero-sum game* where one person's gain is another's loss; despite their inalienable job security, they are programmed to fight for the whole prize and stop every other person from getting anything. That attitude is reflected in all that they do.

Rather than focus on business, CL went through a power change, as graduates of the École Polytechnique (the *X*) were dislodged by similarly inappropriately qualified graduates of the École Nationale d'Administration (the *énarques*), laying foundations for their future careers in politics or public administration.

So that the bank could fulfil its legal obligations, I was asked to serve on the *comité d'entreprise* or workers' council representing UK employees. It involved an annual two-day meeting with the bank's main board in Paris and regular correspondence otherwise. I sat with shop stewards from *Force Ouvrière*, CGT, CFDT and other far left unions in *bleu de travail* and was the only executive in their number. There was mistrust when we met – not just a *suit* but a *rosbif* as well – but it soon faded. We agreed that we had similar goals for the staff we represented. We had much to discuss whenever we met and between times.

At formal meetings, the board sat opposite us, avoiding eye contact, let alone attempting to meet the workforce or pretending to listen. The structure was a dispiriting gesture, a nonsensical sham. Of course, the workforce should be respected; they are the people whose work helps create the wealth of the business; they are part of the team and, not surprisingly, they deliver better results when given even modest respect. At CL (and many other places) an inadequate management team thrived on a mistaken sense of entitlement until the business collapsed.

Through CL, I met 28-year-old Jean-Christophe Iseux von Pfetten, a French diplomat in London accumulating qualifications from both Oxford and Cambridge. He was also joint Master of Fox Hounds in the New Forest and persuaded me to have a go. It is a genteel, respectful hunt. Two police officers accompanied us on foot, with breath enough to chat with everybody. A car window displayed an elaborate embroidery sampler, politely asking the hunt to desist.

All sorts hunt. In much of the country, it is highly inclusive. I rode beside nurses, factory workers, mothers, farm labourers, students, pensioners, bankers, garage mechanics and landowners – on a horse, everyone looks everyone else straight in the eye. Although I had to hire a horse, a day's hunting cost no more than a ticket to a football match or a seat at a popular musical. Hunting involves long pauses and short dashes. The dashes are exhilarating and unpredictable. During the pauses you sit, chat and, in those days, I would join others having a cigarette.

Life evolves. I no longer hunt or smoke, and I am sure that I will never do either again. I would not enjoy it as I did, but I would not stand in anybody's way if that were their choice.

I spent plenty of time in Asia, travelling to Hong Kong, Indonesia and Singapore to close improbable deals. In a different context, I went once to the Philippines. President Aquino was to address the 1991 ASEAN conference in Manila. CL needed somebody there and I went, leaving on Saturday for Mumbai, Hong Kong and then Manila.

When I met President Aquino, I wore a yellow tie to honour her peaceful revolution. We spoke briefly; she was small, polite and business-like. As she moved, I spoke with her security detail. Days before, soldiers had entered her bedroom at the Presidential Palace, the guard said; they found Aquino kneeling in prayer. Pointing a gun at her, the rebellious captain sneered, 'That's right; pray for your soul.'

She rose, faced him and said, 'I am not praying for my soul; I am praying for yours,' and with that the guns were lowered. True or not, the story reflects the courage that her troops believed in.

Walking around Manila, there is a vast collapsing conference centre built under President Marcos with sub-standard concrete and a massive budget overrun, rumoured to have enriched the Marcos accounts. I watched the garish Jeepneys ply their taxi trade and learned to appreciate the adage that 'the Philippines have spent 350 years in a convent and 50 years in Hollywood.' There is a lot more history than that in this large country.

The banquet that evening was filmed for the national TV news. Dancers performed and, possibly as the only delegate who had arrived directly from Europe, I was invited onstage to dance the *tinikling*, hopping in waltz time with heavy bamboo poles snapping at my ankles. Cameras whirred; my dance partner said, 'Look in my eyes and, whatever you do, don't look down.' The rhythmic 'bang-bang-clack' and clapping are like folk dancing anywhere. On that day's news headlines, I jumped in time with the rhythm; amazingly, I was never hit.

The following morning, I left for Tokyo and saw the vast spume of smoke and pumice hanging over Mount Pinatubo, the source of the largest volcanic eruption since Krakatoa in 1883. After a few hours in Tokyo, I took a flight across the International Date Line to California. Then, after meetings in Anaheim, near Los Angeles, I returned to London on Sunday. It was not unreasonable to deflect the question 'What do you do for a living?' by saying, 'I test seats for airlines.'

Before the flight from LA back to London, I went to church in Yorba Linda with my client, co-owner of a Detroit-based company that was buying a quick print franchise in the UK. Yorba Linda was California's fastest growing town, the birthplace of Richard Nixon.

Yorba Linda residents go to church *en masse* every Sunday. I was taken to a Catholic church, a semi-circle around the altar accommodating 1,200 plus a choir; it was packed. That morning, Sunday school teachers stood with heads bowed, awaiting anointment with oil. A voice soared beautifully, and the whole congregation joined her singing 'Glorious Things of Thee are Spoken, Zion City of Our God', to the tune of the German national hymn. We think of it as '*Deutschland, Deutschland über alles*', although that version of the *Deutschlandlied* has not officially been sung in my lifetime. Members of the congregation raised their right arms 'in benediction' until everybody stood, singing and saluting. It felt uncomfortable, but I said nothing to my host – his surname was Kaiser.

Why does this minor domestic scene matter? Because, more than almost any other aspect of life in the United States, religion and particularly a robust Christianity is the driving force. We cannot understand the world's largest economy and most powerful nation without understanding this about what makes people in its heartlands tick.

On other occasions, I went to Tokyo twice to transact business with Yamanouchi Pharmaceutical in a room with a very dull painting by Georges Rouault and a wonderfully fresh and massive painting by Matisse. It was my bad luck to have spent the first week opposite the Rouault. It was difficult to get around a city where nobody could understand a word I said; however, most Japanese are naturally courteous, and I explored parks and temples. On my last night, I set out at 2 a.m. to visit the 57-acre Tsukiji wholesale fish market, where I took hundreds of photographs in black and white.

Tsukiji was a working market, not a tourist spot. I was certainly the only *gaijin* there that night. Stalls sold every imaginable fish and sea food in vast quantities; trollies of ice were delivered throughout the night to keep the produce fresh; outside the covered market, bonfires were built of discarded packaging; the shouts of tuna auctions drowned out other sounds. Traders all wore baseball caps and on each there was a prominently displayed licence plaque, identifying the bidder to the auctioneer's minders. The auctioneers stand on a small platform, hollering at remarkable speeds, surrounded by the bodies of hundreds of tuna, the tail removed, and a small cut made to show the quality of the meat. I stood back and observed, unimpeded as I photographed from a corner. I breakfasted on the freshest sashimi and tea at a bar surrounded by traders at the end of their day.

RESTLESS

1989 to 1995

Divorce is almost always horrible – mine was no exception. Few easily survive the aftermath of an angry divorce. The two worst affected victims are usually truth and the children. Noël Coward wrote in *Blithe Spirit*: 'It's discouraging to think how many people are shocked by honesty and how few by deceit.' The unpleasantness lasted until my former father-in-law's death, and the fall out continued after that. We all deserved better.

Without Fiona Shackleton's kindness and that of old friends and new, I do not know how I would have coped. As it was, I left the marriage with nothing, in debt, deprived of the family that had been the centre of my existence and bewildered by the absence of reasons or an explanation. I had to begin again. I drew on huge reserves of hope.

My first focus was the children and then work. Life settled into an uneasy pattern, dividing time between building a successful team at the office, business travel, the children and the joy of fatherhood and, finally, lawyers and the disheartening squabbling.

At weekends, with or without the children, I became a regular churchgoer at St Mark's on Battersea Rise. It was a new relationship with the church, one where I could teach in the children's church and occasionally preach at early morning services on Sunday without feeling the need to 'belong'. On most Sundays, for several years, I would drive Florence Burnell to church. She loved the children and her 'goodbye' to them, when she was well over 100 and a few hours before she died, was moving for her, me and the children. Before that Sunday, she had always said 'See you next week;' it was the only time she ever said 'goodbye'.

Florence grew up in poverty in the final decade of Queen Victoria's reign and yet, asked how she was, she would always say 'blooming and flourishing… that's what Florence means'. Her indomitable strength came from her ability and desire to give. Florence's stories from Victorian Britain encouraged Sophie to read history at university.

Emma did not tell Papa about the divorce or talk to me about his health. It was deteriorating. I would regularly take Sunday lunch down to them near Pulborough or see one or both parents in London; Papa and I lunched in the City or near Aldwych. He seemed physically fit, but each time I saw him the impact of Alzheimer's had worsened. We arranged periodic respite care in a specialist home in Midhurst; when I took or collected him, he seemed content but not communicative. I had not seen him for a few weeks when, one summer, Emma said that she was going on a big holiday and would I 'keep an eye on him'.

I went to Sussex and was shocked by the speed of his deterioration. In four or five weeks, he had become non-verbal and visibly distressed. He had lost weight, and his room was locked off from the rest of the house and musty. I took him to London and organised care for the hours when I could not be with him. Washing him, it became clear that his body was badly burned and bruised, that he was doubly incontinent, and two hernias bulged against his skin. My GP came immediately to examine him and provide medication.

On a previous visit, I had seen a box of cine films; Emma was 'about to throw those out. What would you want with them?' I had seen no pictures of my childhood, so I had them converted into two long videos, which arrived with an infinitely irritating Muzak soundtrack days before I brought Papa to stay. It was the best medicine. He recognised times and places. The videos and Disney's *Fantasia* kept him happy for hours each day.

When I took him back to Sussex, it was to the care home and from there to the cottage hospital where, in January 1994, he died of pneumonia. He was cremated in Chichester, on a day when flooding meant that he was transported to the crematorium by a police boat. He would have liked that.

My principal legacy from my mother is an enduring interest in the arts, paintings, sculpture, performances and buildings – museums are the only places where I can remember consistently being happy with her, the salvage from my childhood.

My oldest school friend, Benjamin Rhodes, is a successful dealer in contemporary art. He is also one of my close family of friends. When I spend time with him, I realise how little I really know about his world. He and Carol, his late wife, took me to an exhibition of work by Yoko Ono; two exhibits remain in my mind. One is, *White Chess Set (Chess set for playing as long as you remember where all your pieces are)*. All the squares and pieces are white, representing chess as non-adversarial in an anti-war statement. There is a copy in MoMA in New York.

The second is *Painting to Hammer a Nail In / Cross Version*. There was a large wooden cruciform with a hammer and a bucket of nails. Pinned beside it was an invitation to climb a ladder and hammer a nail into the wood. The day changes the moment you first drive a nail into that cross – it marks you, like few other things I have done. Designed as a remembrance of martyrs, it was a raw expression of art, a clattering experience of guilt.

In 1989, the Moutiers invited me to join a trip to Russia at a time when I had no access to the children. I had known the intermarried French and German couples in the group since the 1960s, albeit some better than others.

St Petersburg, before the fall of the Berlin Wall and still Leningrad, was emerging from decades of neglect and being renovated, restored, re-gilded. There was little traffic and few Western tourists. Residents wavered publicly between 'wary' and 'polite'.

The Hermitage was inevitably a highlight. With a collection of three to four million items, only a fraction can be displayed at any time. Impressionist and post-impressionist paintings form one of the museum's proudest collections; they were shown in a small mezzanine gallery, and no items of great note were on display during our visit.

One of our group, Barbara Lambrecht, collects art. Gentle and soft-spoken, she and her brother inherited a brewery. She enjoyed Bernard Moutier's company and his advice with her collection. In the Hermitage, she left the impressionist gallery and Bernard whispered in my ear, 'Barbara wishes to see the Canova statues; she says she has more pleasure from the impressionists she has at home. They are better than these.'

In 2017, almost 30 years after that preposterous throwaway line, Barbara sold several works from her private collection at Christie's. It was to help fund her contemporary art museum in Siegen. Barbara's works included Picasso, Berthe Morisot, Renoir, Boudin, Monet, Dufy, Corot, Kees van Dongen, and raised millions. It dawned on me that Bernard was right to say, that day in the Hermitage, 'her impressionists are better than these.'

I wrote about Leningrad at the time: 'We experienced an exciting, reawakening giant of a country emerging from 70 years as a slow, communist caterpillar into a future as a beautiful butterfly or a mangy moth – who knows which? Contrast is everywhere – the aspirations of Perestroika against the empty reality of a declining Third World power, the beauty of a restored past and the stark reality of recent history, the glorious views of Leningrad and the bleak lives of its people. But they remain ordinary people, just like us in the West, and for all the contrasts we have so much more in common.'

On the train to Moscow, a Russian with excellent German joined us; his father had been a doctor with the occupying Soviet forces in East Germany. He gave us vodka and coupons for chai – tea, soap and sugar were rationed in *Piotr*, as he called it, but not in the capital.

Standing in the lobby of the Cosmos Hotel in Moscow, I watched the 'unfree' world walk past: Chinese in grey Mao suits, Africans with coloured hats and long robes, Yemenis in white dishdasha and keffiyeh, Palestinians and Cubans in military fatigues. The assembled stereotypes boasted the global reach of Soviet power. On a landing between floors, American teenagers were joshing and jostling to the despair of a dowdy teacher. She tapped a biro on the stair rail and there followed the divine sound of choral music. Suddenly the world in the lobby fell silent. Music is the greatest natural diplomacy in the world.

I was lucky to have Fiona Shackleton in my corner, a brilliant, diligent and empathetic terrier.

Through Fiona, I met Lucinda Prior-Palmer, who is determined, committed and instinctively intelligent although she is very diffident about her education. Above all she is kind and great fun. Before I ever met her, I had been at both Badminton and Burghley when she won three-day equestrian events and, after watching her final win, I avidly read her press articles about eventing and competition.

I quote her frequently. In the late 1980s, fatalities increased in her sport. Officials sought to reduce the risk, accepting the common view that courses had become too dangerous. Lucinda demurred. For her the problem lay with over-coached horses, training out their instinct for self-preservation so they would no longer avoid accidents without a rider's instructions, when the rider could least well instruct. I have never doubted that she was right.

This 'process overriding common sense' exists everywhere, so that now 'the means justifies the end'; so long as you follow due process, the outcome is immaterial. Such nonsense.

Sylvia Darley, Malcolm Sargent's unofficial manager, marked her friend's memory by founding the Malcolm Sargent Cancer Fund for Children. Sargent and its successor charity now raises £25 million each year to support families. I became involved through a friend, Tod Barton. At a fundraiser at Burghley House in Stamford, I was handed a letter as I was about to address the guests. It was written to the parents of a young cancer victim who, some weeks before her death, had presented a bouquet to the Princess of Wales at the Albert Hall.

Diana wrote, in her big round hand, that she could not conceive of the pain; like losing a limb, it would change them forever. She added touching details of each encounter, including private visits to a hospice, and ended with, 'you will never get over her loss, but one day I hope you may learn how to live with it.' Diana, Princess of Wales, touched and improved the lives of ordinary people by her simple understanding of grief.

The charity held an event at No. 10 Downing Street, hosted by John Major (Prime Minister at the time). He is a taller, more charismatic presence that his press image would suggest. He has a sincerity and charm that leave a lasting impression and intentionally put his listener at ease. He spoke with wonder at the pleasure of writing at the same desk as Pitt the Younger. At about the same time I met Margaret Thatcher, whose presence was more intimidating; she spoke about Benjamin Franklin with a depth of knowledge that impressed the experts present. Her greatest kindness was reserved for those who worked for her, rather than those who worked with her.

Queen Elizabeth, the Queen Mother, was ageless. She was in her early 90s on the only occasion I met her. Gently engaging, amusing, interested and a mallow-coated steel girder. Mary Lesley (working with the luxury interior design studio Nina Campbell) invited me to go around her latest project, The Duke and Duchess of York's new-build property Sunninghill Park, on the day that the Queen Mother was making her first visit to her grandson's new house. We were close.

When Mary called me, the construction was far from finished. Prince Andrew had invited 'Granny' to tour, and Mary and I accompanied them with an architect and a bodyguard.

We toured the ground floor, destined to be decorated by Mary at Nina Campbell with some rooms by American design legend, Sister Parish. We then waited at the bottom of a 20 feet ladder to the first floor. 'Has none of you ever been on a submarine? Do you know nothing of the protocol?' asked Queen Elizabeth. We climbed; watching her follow unaided was unnerving.

Prince Andrew showed passion; he studied soundproofing and brickwork, security and plumbing. He was eager to share his knowledge, after his grandmother left. He gave a demo in the Portakabin. 'This is the bullet-proof glass for the safe room,' he explained as he was about to smash a glass square on the corner of a metal filing cabinet. 'It's strong enough to withstand a rocket propelled grenade.' Crash, bang, shatter and scatter! The Duke of York swore as shards exploded in all directions – 'Wrong bloody piece of glass!'

Weeks later I spent a day alone at Sunninghill Park, 48 hours before the Yorks moved in. The house was more attractive than the press allowed. I created a portfolio of photographs from every angle. Each dining chair had a dark blue seat embroidered with different flowers. Prince Andrew's dressing room was a riot of tartans. The secure room was claustrophobic in the extreme but a place of comfort. The tiny baldachin above their bed was fun to photograph on my back, between the pillows. The house was intimate, homely and grand. I photographed every corner. The next day I delivered more than 20 rolls of film to the Royal developer at Wallace Heaton in New Bond Street and never saw them again.

Months passed until Mary was invited to the housewarming – I was her guest. As we approached, paparazzi surrounded the car with cameras poised. It is humbling to be the only unknowns at a party; the cameras were lowered without a single flash as we passed. We recognised everyone, although it took time to identify a clean-shaven Billy Connelly until he spoke. After dinner, we moved towards the dancefloor in an adjacent marquee. Prince Andrew was set to say a few words when a keyboard was wheeled in. Change of plan. The Yorks sat on stage and another of the guests, Elton John, played and sang. Unforgettable.

Early the following morning, on our way back from the amazing party, we went to Victoria Station and picked up the Sunday papers. All had the story of the party, without any photos of us obviously. The reporting in every paper was a work of fiction, from the menu to the music and everything in between. It was a compelling witness for the saying, 'believe nothing of what you hear and only half of what you see'.

I have danced or reeled since childhood; it is a fixture in every city where more than a handful of Scots live and possibly the best, most enjoyable aerobic exercise. It is also inexpensive, although there are formal balls such as the Royal Caledonian, the world's oldest charity ball, where I danced a few steps holding the hand of Princess Margaret, while her hand still held a lit cigarette. The ball raises a lot for charity, but my experience suggests the wholesalers at New Covent Garden raise more at their Christmas bash each year in a less formal setting; very effective, albeit more blue jokes than blue blood.

Perhaps Papa's greatest gift, facing challenges as we grew up, was the love of music. I discovered later that he had played in an orchestra at university. He introduced me to opera when we lived in Munich and, although he never talked about it or indeed about much, I became aware of its importance as he was dying. It is a rewarding and wonderful legacy.

I share that love of music with two friends above all: Charles Clark and Anthony Sharp. I was immensely happy to be Anthony's Best Man at his and Sarah's wedding, eclipsed in the speeches by Sarah's daughter Daisy.

In the late 1980s, I became one of Fifty Ladies and Gentlemen of the Opera, Wasfi Kani's imaginative initial funding for Pimlico Opera. Since 1987, she has put on popular musicals in high security prisons; professionals sing the lead roles and prisoners play the rest. At an early performance in the Victorian-era gym at HM Prison Wandsworth, we were instructed by a nervous warder: 'Ladies and Gentlemen, please remain in your seats while we lock up the cast.' We still go whenever possible; the performances change the lives of prisoners and audiences alike.

After the divorce, I continued to enjoy opera whenever I could afford to go. Tickets were almost always worth the price, especially when something remarkable happened. In September 1993, I heard Marilyn Horne perform *L'Italiana in Algieri*. She was 'the greatest Rossini singer in the World'. The audience roared with delight. After several curtain calls, Miss Horne called for silence. 'Rossini quit writing opera when he was 37; I have been singing his work on stage for the exact same length of time. Tonight, you have witnessed my last Rossini role performed.' She went on to praise Rossini's work, although she was not heard above the emotion.

Opera tickets are expensive; however, when Covent Garden was refurbished in the late 1990s, the seats were sold and I bought one to use at home; it cost less to buy than it ever cost to rent for an evening, albeit at home there are neither sets nor singers.

I'd known Elizabeth since the 1970s when she married a friend of mine from whom she had since divorced, and we saw a very great deal of each other in the 1990s. Intelligent, feisty and generous, she had little time for the barriers of social convention. Among many adventures, we went to Covent Garden whenever possible.

Elizabeth and I were in the Crush Bar during the interval of *Die Frau Ohne Schatten* at the Opera House in 1992. I had watched Bernard Haitink at rehearsal that day and was loving the production with its dramatic set created by David Hockney using characteristically strong colours and bold shapes. Grabbing an extra glass, Elizabeth said, 'Let's say hello to Hockney.'

Some events have been chronicled in my mind by one man's images more than any other's. Hockney captured his parents, his relationships and himself with an unvarnished honesty, without all the status props that were once essential in portraiture. He captured 'ageing' with that gentleness and insight that Alan Bennett achieves with words.

Hockney is warm and modest, and welcomed being approached by strangers. After a while we said, 'You doubtless have other people to talk to,' and he replied, 'No, not really.' We chatted until the bell for the second act. Nobody had approached. As we parted company, that gentle voice repeated, 'Thank you, nobody usually talks to me at these things.'

In 1993, when the Vatican's greatest treasure was undergoing massive restoration, I was in Rome with Elizabeth; she was in John Major's Cabinet Office at the time. After our respective work was done, we joined David Davis, Minister of State for Europe, and our ambassador to the Holy See, for a private tour. We were led through a hidden door into the Sistine Chapel, beneath Michelangelo's *Last Judgement*. The fresco was clad in nine stories of scaffolding, right to the ceiling. In 450 years, since Michelangelo had finished his work, the ceiling had grown dark with candle smoke. I remembered it coated in a film of black when I lay there as a child, looking through binoculars; the transformation was astounding.

The Chapel was closed to the public and Gianluigi Colalucci, the chief restorer, guided us to the ceiling, alluding to the controversy about the restoration. He is rightly proud of his work, which enables a new generation to experience the impact of Michelangelo's original masterpiece as the artist himself would have seen it. Colalucci carried a photograph of a 1549 painting by Venusti in the Capodimonte Museum in Naples, that preserved the strong colours from before the 'touch up' demanded by Biagio da Cesena. Da Cesena objected to widespread nudity in religious works and insisted that naked flesh be 'painted over'. Instead, because that goes against the nature of 'fresco', offending areas of the painting were hacked out and fresh plaster applied to absorb the new colours of fabrics, some during Michelangelo's lifetime, most after his death. Michelangelo's revenge was to portray da Cesena in the *Last Judgement* as Minos, with ass's ears and a snake biting his genitalia.

When it was time to leave the ceiling, the lift operator said, '*Ah ben, a l'Inferno*' ('Ah well, down to hell') and the others descended. I remained chatting with Professor Colalucci. At his invitation, before our own descent, I placed a hand on the ceiling and, with Colalucci's insights at every step, I touched the hem of Jesus' flimsy garment. I saw humility in Michelangelo's self-portrait as the flayed skin of St Bartholomew, contrasting with his confident indignation when ravaging da Cesena, and I looked into the eyes of the saints.

Standing one foot from *The Last Judgement*, almost five centuries since it was painted, you can still clearly see peg marks where finely pricked cartoons were attached, and charcoal dust was used to create outlines. Marks were visible where offending images had been hacked out and new plaster inserted to satisfy da Cesena. You see the bold, crude brush strokes, distorted but essential to convey an image from an angle at a distance. The flesh tones were alive, and contorted shapes at close quarters seemed normal from the ground.

I imagine that fewer people may have touched the ceiling of the Sistine Chapel than the number who have reached the summit of Everest (6,338 at the last count, apparently).

Holidays with the children were an oasis of calm enjoyment amid the restlessness. Being a father allowed me to breathe and admire. We had wonderful adventures, driving across France and Italy to explore, see friends, and have fun – including taking a ferry up to Hamburg to drive into Denmark and the original Legoland. However, holidays were difficult to plan when there were tiresome arguments about dates or when handovers took place in random places (such as a marina in the South of France, an airport in Corsica), tacked onto an exhausting holiday with their maternal grandparents. These handover skirmishes continued for years, but the children and I still managed to visit many of Europe's great cities and sites. Sophie stayed awake throughout a performance of *Otello* at the Verona arena, while Charlie eventually slept on an inflatable lilo on the stone steps.

LEAPING IN AGAIN

1995 to 1997

In the mid 1990s, still restless, unsettled by the relentless on-going conflict of divorce and wanting to provide the best environment for Sophie and Charles, I remarried. My new wife was a good physiotherapist, of my own age and with an appetite for theatre, clothes and good living. It was her first marriage. In the evening or at weekends, I drove her to see patients. From the outset everybody, other than we two protagonists, recognised the pitfalls of such a hasty union.

As the 'designated driver' I met her patients, a distinguished and interesting group. One took us to the first night of the 1995 revival of *Rosencrantz and Guildenstern Are Dead*. In the Green Room during the interval, Tom Stoppard stood, holding two lit cigarettes, and randomly asked 'Is it still any good?'

'It's still brilliant,' did little to resolve his anxiety.

For two years, we accompanied a patient to Jamaica and in particular to Jamaica Inn, an idyllic hotel where Marilyn Monroe and Arthur Miller honeymooned, Winston Churchill often stayed, Noel Coward and Ian Fleming drank.

The guests at Jamaica Inn included the powerful and the rich; the stars were the staff – Rupert, Teddy, Arthur and many others whose lives were dedicated to this little paradise. Arthur ran the beach, as he had for more than 40 years. Most nights, he slept in a straw hut on the sands. Guests tried to persuade him to travel, if only to visit his children in Manhattan. His answer never changed: 'If people come to my beach to rest or celebrate with their families and for the best moments in their lives, well, why would I leave my paradise?'

Jamaica Inn sits on a small sandy bay between two promontories. The sea can be dangerous; Arthur earned two Royal Humane Society certificates for pulling people from the ocean in time. Few people rescue one life, but Arthur was exceptional.

Having enjoyed the underwater sights in Jamaica, I learnt to dive, taking the PADI course in London, qualifying with the open water test in the Maldives – swimming 30 metres below the surface, thrilled by the weightlessness and colours. Priscilla, my examiner, asked if I'd enjoyed diving. Absolutely. So why, she asked, had I chewed through the regulator, the mouthpiece of the breathing apparatus? She had never seen that before. Whatever had happened to the infant in Beirut, obviously I was still nervous of salt water.

On one trip to Jamaica, I walked to the back of the plane for a cigarette. Two young people, casually dressed, began a surreal conversation with me. In time I realised that they were undercover police watching potential drug dealers and they realised that I was not their senior colleague. Am I more impressed that we do such surveillance or more appalled at how ham-fisted it appeared to be? Dunno!

We went to the glamorous New York wedding of a couple we met in Jamaica. At the reception, the band leader was Lester Lanin, legendary East Coast musician of choice for socialites since the 1920s. He had played at seven White House Inaugural Balls and at the wedding of the bride's parents. The bride's family reached America in the 1640s; the groom's family arrived 300 plus years later. It was a sadly doomed marriage of history and the American Dream.

I spent a large part of my childhood in museums where I could wallow in looking at many of the world's greatest paintings. At home, the only painting was a fine copy of Reynolds' portrait of *Kitty Fisher* painted by Uncle Ken at the Slade. I have enjoyed accumulating paintings and drawings, each one with a story and a connection with the artist. Lisa Sainsbury once told us, 'Don't buy paintings if you can't afford them,' kindly adding, 'but buy the best you can afford when you buy.' I ignored part one of her injunction and have stuck with part two.

As my wife's driver, I often went to Robert and Lisa Sainsbury's Dulwich house, with floor to ceiling doors and monastic elegance. At the time, their new interest in Oriental work adorned the walls and bookshelves, easels and lecterns. Their collection, housed at the University of East Anglia, is not about strong colours or images but offers subtler insights. They were absorbed in their interests and in each other. They were generous and supportive of some of the greatest artists and architects of the 20th century, commissioning them as unknowns. Many of them were at a landmark anniversary dinner at the museum that we attended.

David Attenborough talked that night. He could talk about anything and retain his audience's awe-struck focus. After dinner that evening it was about a small carving, bought decades before, on a Pacific Ocean island. The story was as exciting, as he told it, as an encounter with a pride of hungry lions or the mating rituals of an endangered species. I sat next to his daughter, Susan, who said how he valued it. There is an earnest, almost boyish, enthusiasm in his voice and a scholarly authority in his words that, together, are irresistible.

I have lived my adult life in a democracy, and I am very glad of it. No matter how well-intentioned and benign a dictator appears at the outset, abuse of absolute power is inevitable. Winston Churchill said 'democracy is the worst form of Government except for all those other forms that have been tried from time to time...' which is surely true.

Dudley Heesom was an institution at Oundle – a history teacher who had taught generations. He taught in PowerPoint, before the word existed… headings, bullet points and sub-groups of text were used to muster our thoughts and reasoning. However, Dudley was no fan of democracy, valuing expertise above the vote. He was aware of Napoleon's failings but greatly admired the Emperor's civic achievements, his focus on education, administration, sound finance, law and infrastructure. I also admire Napoleon but was glad of his defeat. Until the 1990s, I had not met a dictator.

My second wife treated Augusto Pinochet for several years. I met him often. No topic was off-limits. We talked of Chile's condition when, during a family party, military chiefs barged in to announce their coup – a coup he claimed to be reluctant to join but willing to lead. I believe he saw parallels between his role and that of his idol, Napoleon. Pinochet talked knowledgeably of the Emperor's civic achievements as his inspiration. He frequently explained his ambitions for health care, education, economic growth, pensions. He may have achieved some of what he set out to do, but any dictatorship lacks the essential checks and balances and the road to hell is paved with good intentions.

Reviewing the third volume of Charles Moore's book, *Margaret Thatcher, The Authorized Biography: Herself Alone*, Mat Youkee wrote in *The Guardian*, published on 4 October 2019, 'Although they never met in power, Thatcher was impressed by the success of Chile's neoliberal economic program and Pinochet's bloody stance against communism in Latin America. Above all she felt a "great debt for [Pinochet's] secret actions during the Falklands war", according to Moore.'

Once both had left power, Thatcher and Pinochet spent time together whenever he was in London, or so the latter told me when he described their friendship.

In 1997, we celebrated *Semana Nacional* in Santiago, when every building displays the Chilean flag. Accompanied by a charming Colonel, Julio Soto Silva, we visited Valparaiso and the Pacific coast; the Teatro Municipal, a dull name for a beautiful Garnier-designed building; and a ski resort. That journey was hairier than mere hairpin bends; at a roadblock, a young conscript nervously pointed his gun while our host reached for his ID. Our army driver swung open his door to explain and his pistol fell to the tarmac. The driver's reactions were faster than the youngster's and a crisis was averted.

That week we watched the *Parada Militar*, a glorious tattoo with all Latin America's armies marching past President Frey and, next to him, Generalissimo Pinochet. We met the head of the Argentine army, General Martín Balza, who joked about his incarceration by the British in 1982, living on a diet of cornflakes and tinned potatoes. Some minutes later, he reappeared to give me a memento of his time on the Falklands: a pottery boot bearing the Argentine army insignia, its toecap lifting off the sole.

In late 1998, Pinochet was arrested in a London hospital and spent 18 months under house arrest in Virginia Water. Driving his physio, I saw him twice a week and our lively discussions and polite disagreements continued. Studying Shakespeare's *Julius Caesar* at school, I remember these words about that Roman dictator: 'The evil that men do lives after them; the good is oft interred with their bones'; no matter how well-intentioned a dictator's first steps to power, history is rightly not kind to the memory of dictators of the right or left.

Communists and Nazis, National Socialists, resemble identical twins espousing the same lousy bigotry save that the former involves the middle class mobilising the workers to dislodge the establishment while the latter is the establishment mobilising the workers to curtail the middle class. In time, of course, a successful communist state becomes fascist – look at Russia or China – when communists become the establishment and inevitably seek to stymie the new middle class.

LOSING AT SNAKES AND LADDERS

1997 to 2001

A banker typically measures success by how well he has done for himself rather than how he does the job. On that measure I did not score highly. I soon learned the truth of a wise saying, that 'success has many fathers while failure is an orphan'. Many claim credit, few deserve credit, and none accepts responsibility. I enjoyed finding solutions and doing so profitably for the bank, priorities that earned warm words from many clients but modest bonuses.

In the run up to Christmas 1997, I was told that the department I'd helped to create and build would be moved to Paris, and none of the London team would be part of its future. It was a recipe for an unhappy Christmas. Two other conversations made it worse.

My former father-in-law, Tim, appeared, demanding my redundancy cheque and a lien over my house, with threats of court action. It was the start of a bitter, baseless and futile chapter for us all, but above all for Tim.

My second wife, late one evening, demanded a divorce, because I was 'no longer a pension provider'. I had perhaps anticipated it when I found yellow Post-Its 'owning' food in the fridge, like a student flat share. To be fair, we surely both had the wrong reasons for marrying. We sat with John Cornwell as mediator and rapidly reached an equitable solution that restored her previous financial standing and independence. John was an example of fairness and intelligence, an antidote to conflict. John could not be bullied – he brushed pressures aside in a measured, courteous and unanswerable way. His work, (and I don't doubt his legacy after his tragically early death) has improved many lives.

Over the next 18 months, many of Tim's letters were spiteful and foul with fiction. Death does not make a person a saint or a devil, theologically or biographically; it merely denies them the right of reply. I therefore write nothing about him that I did not, with cause, write or say to him.

We ended up in court twice after my redundancy. The result included a court order imposing limits on Tim's actions; I am confident that he ignored the order. The nastiness rumbled on.

Meanwhile, Norman Tebbit's words ringing in my ears, I 'got on my bike and looked for work'. It is a 1940s bike with no gears, a basket on the handlebars and an astonishing top speed. I discovered the speed one morning cycling across Battersea Park to see a client in Spitalfields; a blue light flashed; a siren gave a single '*whoop*'. 'Well sir, which is it to be? Should I give you a ticket for cycling on a pedestrian footpath or a ticket for breaking the speed limit?' I begged the motorcycle cop to give me the latter (so that I could frame it) but in the end he gave me neither.

New clients appeared; new business relationships formed.

My worst moment in broad daylight was being hit by a car whose driver wasn't looking as she joined Hyde Park Corner. My helmet was split, the front wheel crumpled, and I lay on the road near my broken specs as the driver paused, looked down and said, 'Well, you're alive' before driving off.

I limped home, carrying my damaged bike in the freezing cold and remembering Irving Stone's words in *The Agony and the Ecstasy* when Michelangelo was asked how he kept warm in his winter exile – 'Indignation. Best fuel I know. Never burns out.'

As we eased into a new century, life was challenging but navigable. I was not alone. There was a new person in my life, and she has been at its heart ever since.

In June 2000, Emma returned from a cruise that reached Singapore. A few days later she fell and was taken to hospital in Guildford; I visited regularly with little interaction. In early July, I was called in urgently. 'She's delirious; keeps murmuring about Ulan Bator. We do not think she has long.' I showed her Mongolian itinerary; on the day she died, she was due at an audience with President Bagabandi in gratitude for work she had done for Mongolians in London. Too late, they rushed her to a side room for resuscitation. Her last words, to a nurse adjusting her pillow as she was pumped full of adrenaline, were a whispered 'Thank you.' She was full of contradictions.

Alison and I cleared her house after Emma died. The place was full of 'stuff'. In a locked cabinet with no key, we found photographs that we had never seen. Most were so badly out of focus that we could not tell who or where was depicted. There were scrap books of paper cuttings about my ex-wife's family but no mementoes of Alison or me; presents we had given her over the previous 20 years were in a cupboard – kept but never unwrapped.

She left no will. She left, instead, boxes of spiral-bound shorthand notebooks, hundreds of them, in which she recorded everything she did, said, heard or read. She wrote out, verbatim, calls that Alison or I had as teenagers, presumably overheard on an extension; the text of letters to us, steamed open and resealed, or recorded as destroyed: her letters to Papa deciding who we could meet; letters to schools to dictate what we could not do (such as acting, joining a trip or studying certain subjects); letters to family to explain why they never saw us; notes about my university grant that she received but I did not. She was our own Stasi, our own secret police, intervening in every step of our lives to coerce, subjugate and exercise control.

The latest notebook covered her Saga cruise, weeks before; confined to her cabin while ill in the Indian Ocean, she wrote poems from memory. I knew all but one, the most telling: Emma wrote Philip Larkin's 'This Be The Verse' in full. It starts:

> They f***k you up, your mum and dad.
> They may not mean to, but they do.
> They fill you with the faults they had
> And add some extra, just for you.

I remembered a phone conversation with Emma some years before. She was struggling to breathe, and I was trying to keep her alert until the arrival of an ambulance that I had called on a separate line from the office. She spoke to me, for the only time in my life, about *her* family.

Emma was born on 14 December 1918, the first time

that women exercised the right to vote in Britain. The law arose in part through pressure from *suffragists* (the peaceful ones) and *suffragettes* (the ones who made great physical sacrifices to state their claim). Grandma, a committed suffragist, was denied the opportunity to vote that day because she was at home giving birth to my mother. Emma claimed they were never reconciled. Our conversation was interrupted by the ambulance and never resumed. Shortly after she had open heart surgery to fix a valve at Hammersmith Hospital, a ward I shall return to, and lived for another decade.

When the dull burgundy plastic urn of ashes arrived from the crematorium, I looked for happy memories of Emma as places to scatter her ashes. She was not meaningfully a mother and could not love her children. We could still celebrate her strengths – she was passionate about art and history and a diligent friend to many. She is scattered in the gardens of 40 museums around the world, mostly places we visited with her as children. The story of her scattering deserves a book of its own. We take her with us, in discreet containers; her ashes rest in the Frick Collection and Metropolitan Museum; the Louvre and Versailles; the Villa Borghese and the Vatican (including the German Cemetery); the Getty Museum in Los Angeles and the Grand Canyon (where she took her only helicopter flight); the V&A and Tate Britain. The list goes on.

Maria bought the little opaque plastic bottles in which her ashes are transported with dignity. The lids, I noticed recently, bear the words *Body Shop*.

The children were both away boarding and now in their teens. I took Sophie to Rome so that we could walk again around this glorious city. There is always some new wonder to see. The journalist Silvio Negro wrote, '*Roma, non basta una vita*'; no matter how often I go, nor how long I live, there will always be more to see in Rome. It was in the early months of the new millennium; boards outside St Peter's displayed a tariff of special indulgences for the afterlife, an aspect of religion that leaves me unmoved. We saw Pope John Paul II preside over a Sunday service from the steps of St Peter's. He was immensely fragile.

I took Charlie to Paris. We were there for several days, including the final section of the Tour de France – we watched from atop the Arc de Triomphe as the peloton repeatedly rocked their way up the Champs-Elysées and rocketed their way back to the Place de la Concorde; after several circuits we went down and walked among the crowds. It was one of Lance Armstrong's 'wins' that have since been erased from the record books. Although few thought it then, his reputation was also immensely fragile.

NEW HORIZONS

1998 to 2004

Having been made redundant by the French, I was offered a desk in a mews house in Marylebone and became a partner in a small financial services boutique.

We developed our business focus on media and events, restructuring and funding a futuristic TV company (its technology remains more advanced than Sky+, proving that marketing, management and timing are often more important than having the best ideas); and arranging the successful merger of CSS (a leading events management business) and Stellar Management (a top talent manager in motor sports, golf and entertainment).

In time, I added travel, food and associated supply chains to our skill sets. I joined the boards of two successful travel agencies (one business, one retail) and worked with a brilliant, unorthodox French entrepreneur whose food traceability solutions were streets ahead of what we have now but too far advanced for the main supermarkets; timing again. Through this engagement we met an outstanding and delightful businessmen, Nicholas Saphir, of whom more later.

Advising an American with radio stations throughout eastern Europe, I met Maria at the *Daily Mail*, where she was Marketing Director for cable TV channels. We met again when DMGT shut her part of the business and she joined our boutique, adding serious sector experience. I felt sympathy when she studied for her FSA exams and the right to give corporate finance advice – even as a seasoned banker, I would probably have failed.

Maria and I held, between us, a minority position in a partnership of four. We spent an increasing amount of time together and it became clear that the foursome would not last. One morning, our senior partner removed the mezuzah from the lintel of my office door, a strangely ritualistic way of declaring me an outcast.

Maria and I set up our own advisory firm, The Rushton Partnership, where we continued to work with our existing clients and attracted more. We also created an international network (Concilio) with partner firms in Athens, Barcelona, Copenhagen, Frankfurt, Milan, Moscow, New York and Paris. It was a joyous alliance of like-minded people, sharing ideas and connections, pitching together for business and delivering well above our individual capacity. In New York I found a wonderful kindred spirit in Michael Lyall, a principal with our US partner, a friendship that was cut short by his shocking death in his 60s.

Michael introduced us to Jean-Marc Beaujolin and Giulio Severini, two profoundly decent and successful Africa hands who wanted to make a positive difference in the world by creating a portal called Humanitarian World. The story of Michael's link with Jean-Marc is gripping enough to merit its own book, covering their respective parents' WWII secret heroism and close connection.

HumWorld, as we called it, appealed to two British character traits – charity and chance. It aimed to create a full range of online gambling, giving 20% of gross gaming revenue to global charities and a humanitarian portal. Put in context, existing players spent 40% of GGR on advertising. We started to assemble a team, write a business plan and devise an approach to raise funds. First on board, as chairman, was Tim Holley, retired Chief Executive of Camelot who had rolled out the Lottery. We brought together charities and humanitarian partners.

Our first approach was Johann Olav Koss, a legendary medal-winning speed skater from a ridiculously early age who had qualified as a doctor with an MBA. Having won triple gold at the 1994 Winter Olympics, he asked that cash given to celebrate his medals go to charity.

Koss told us his story. With those donations, he flew to Eritrea with 10 tonnes of sports kit and was criticised for not taking food or medicine. However, the Eritrean president called it 'The greatest gift... For the first time we are being treated as human beings – not just something to be kept alive.' For more than 1.5 million children worldwide each year, Right to Play provides medicine, education and a living as part of playing football.

At our next stop, RNIB, we met the chairman, blind from birth, and the sighted CEO. The CEO's questions were gritty, aimed at protecting the charity's purpose and reputation. I explained software designed to enable the blind to play bridge or poker online on level terms with sighted players. The CEO rejected the idea bluntly; 'But' interrupted the chairman, clearly irritated, 'why should I not be allowed to have fun like anybody else, just because I am blind?'

The project raised its initial target funding and employed, on paper, first-class management. However, when a fiscal structure and incentivisation schemes were in place, surveys, market research and reports were written, and consultants had been consulted, the opportunity and funds had gone. It was a colossal disappointment. An entrepreneur is nothing like an employee – one creates while, no matter how good the CV, the other generally manages.

It is, perhaps, human nature to gravitate towards the most exciting topic in the room, like moths to a flame. I have repeatedly encountered companies, clubs or institutions that experience unexpected crises that should have been predictable. The trigger is always the most 'glamorous' item on the agenda, an acquisition, listing, major funding or massive building project. The format is always the same… management at all levels want to be a part of the project and neglect the business. The outcome is always the same… the project may or may not be completed but the business suffers badly from the neglect.

Rushton advised many entrepreneurial small companies. One, John Rose, came with a plan to adapt trawlers for HNW tourists to search the ocean's floor for historical sunken vessels. We developed the idea into a business, Treasure Leisure, and set out to fund it.

In 2004, we asked for an overdue invoice to be paid; Rose responded by suing us for £150,000. It was baseless and intentionally intimidating. Nor could I tell Maria the extent of the issue – her mother, Mary, lay in hospital in a coma from which she never recovered.

The case was heard in Norwich Crown Court. Christian Birchley-Titmus, our solicitor, was imperturbable, diligent and persistent; we were well guided and supported. The attempt to bully us with spurious counterclaims is apparently 'part of the game' but he shielded us well.

I was in the witness box for four hours of cross-examination as Rose's QC tried every approach. Finally, he asked: 'Are you familiar with the Public Offers of Securities Regulations 1995?'

'I am, your Honour,' and so it went on and on. Did I know what they were, what they meant, how they applied? I mentioned a book, *Regulatory Issues for Capital Markets Transactions*, with a chapter about the POS Regs that had led me to research the rules.

The QC mocked, 'You expect this court to believe that, just because you read a chapter in a book, you did this additional reading?'

'Your Honour, I did not read that book… I wrote it.' We won our claim and, dwarfing the claim, we won our costs in full.

A memory returned of graffiti I had seen in the 1970s, on a wall in Cowes. It read 'Justice, like a Rolls-Royce, is available for all'. John Rose drove a Rolls-Royce; we had justice.

I don't play golf, although we've had several clients whose business is golf. One client sponsored a charity foursome at Stoke Park. 'Come on,' it's founder Dennis Garrison said, 'let's caddy these four around the course.' During the day I carried the bags of Jasper Carrott, Bob Wilson, David Seaman and Nick Faldo.

Nick chatted as we walked. His phone rang several times, to rebukes from Jasper Carrott. 'Answer *your* phone,'

Nick said to me, knowing full well that it was his own phone, not mine, that was ringing. I therefore answered his phone, and it was the European Tour urgently trying to reach Mr Faldo. I passed the phone to Nick. There was a short conversation, air punches and, with a big smile, Nick announced that he had just been selected as Ryder Cup Captain for Europe's defence of the Cup in 2008. I put his phone back in the bag and the moment felt quite historic.

Bob was inspiring. While we walked, he talked freely of losing his daughter, Anna, just before her 32nd birthday; there was no self-pity or bitterness although I cannot imagine the pain of permanently losing a child. He asked, 'How many fathers have the opportunity to know their daughters as close friends in adulthood?' and talked of his admiration for Anna. That day informed my thoughts when Sophie lost a child, at ten days, and bore the grief with fortitude and courage that I still find humbling. I wonder if Bob has any idea how much he touches people's lives; I suspect he just thinks, 'How lucky I am to have had Anna's inspiration.'

ACTING A LITTLE

1998 to 2014

Among the notes that Alison and I found after Emma died, were Emma's letters to schools instructing that I was 'not to be allowed to appear on stage'. It may explain why I was not cast in school plays when I was keen; in a way I have been acting all my life.

In 1997 I joined The Hurlingham Club, an anachronistically privileged haven in south-west London. Two ageless ladies, Deborah Williams and Jane Rawlins, asked if I acted or sang; I said 'no' to the former and 'almost a tenor' to the latter. They dragooned me into the Players.

Within months I was cast as Maxim de Winter in *Rebecca*. It was a challenge and great fun, intensifying my love of theatre. Shortly after I was Garry Essendine, a part Coward wrote for himself in *Present Laughter*.

With delightful predictability, I was cast as Sir Robert Morton in *The Winslow Boy* and as Dr Julian Winston in *The Cactus Flower*. What satisfaction in both cases.

I was cast disproportionately as a butler, culminating in the title role of *The Admirable Crichton*. Getting the balance between work and drama also meant I missed some productions such as Peter Jamieson's direction of *Titanic the Musical*. It felt sad to be in the audience and not on stage.

The hardest role was as John Clarke in *The Calendar Girls*. Wheeled on, shortly before the character dies, I appeared bald and exhausted. Acting, I drew on the last weeks that Marilyn Johnson's husband, Ahmed, was alive. His dignity, hope and physical emptiness were painful to watch as he ebbed away; he was an inspiration and a poignant memory.

By 2006, I was almost ready to direct. Maria suggested Ayckbourn's *Small Family Business* – a difficult piece to produce in an amateur setting, because the set is a two-story house with several active rooms on each floor. We managed using clever lighting, a contraption designed by fellow member Derek Power and scaffolding poles to imply walls and doors.

The costumes were mostly conventional, but Maria went to *Ann Summers* for one outfit, encountering a shocked acquaintance as she emerged with a package!.

The largely amateur cast learnt lines with varying degrees of success and delivered a wonderful result. However, one line trumped us; we could not understand it. 'You'll have the heavy women after you.' Elizabeth Bell originally spoke the line as the sex kitten Anita McCracken at the National Theatre. Fellow member Peter Benson had been a NT trustee; he reached out to Ayckbourn without much hope of a response. A call from Scarborough was a surprise – 'Alan can't remember what he meant so we've had a word with Elizabeth, and she could never make it out either; she thought it might have been a printing mistake.'

Maria and I were together 24/7 – work, drama and at home; I had arrived where I belong. Maria is my other half in every sense. The last line of a Nat King Cole song, 'Nature Boy', captures her place in my life: 'The greatest thing you'll ever learn, is just to love and be loved in return.' Without her I would be incomplete; my book would have no purpose.

My second production, in 2009, was altogether more risqué. *Feelgood* is a hilarious political comedy by Alistair Beaton. The 'excessive' use of the F-word caused the Hurlingham Committee concern, and trigger warnings appeared on tickets. A paragraph in *The Times* gossip column, 'People', read 'Distinguished members of the exclusive Hurlingham Club beware. The latest theatrical production, *Feelgood,* "is the first play to have a language warning, given that the F-word is spoken for the first time on the Mulgrave stage"!'

'It ain't the first time,' said Bob, the craftsman helping me to create a set, 'I 'it me thumb on stage with an 'ammer last year and I used the F-word quite a lot, as I recall.'

We had taken soundings from our target audience. Nobody was shocked, some expressed disappointment 'but that's how things are'. Jean, a debutante in her time, simply said, 'Julian, I really don't mind if people say f**k, but I draw the line at blasphemy.' I spent several hours that night replacing the names of the Holy Trinity with expletives.

There was a wonderful, ambulant production of *Wind in the Willows* in which I was a humble boatman, tasked with rowing Toad across the lake at Hurlingham. Each day, as I made my way to the boat, I was stopped by a gang of weasels demanding a forfeit; each day I wrote a new nonsense verse as my price of passage. I can still recite one of the poems, 'The Frog':

The young girl held the creature in the palm of her hand –
A moment she's regretted ever since,

For then there was a rumour in that dim and distant land
That if you kissed a frog, you'd find a prince.

Two bulbous eyes looked up at her from that small lump of green.
She puckered up, her heart set to explode,
But too soon she had discovered that the truth has always been
That if you kiss a toad, it's still a toad.

The 1991 Olivier Award winning *Out of Order* is one of Ray Cooney's wonderfully complicated farces, involving a cheating MP and a body caught in a sash window. It was my next chance to direct. We met David Warwick, the *body* in the original production. He guided us, which was great fun and endlessly instructive. He taught me that farce only works when actors play it straight. Through David we met Ray himself, at the Menier Chocolate Factory, performing in an earlier version of the play featuring the same characters. After the curtain call, Ray met each member of *my* cast and left them inspired and uplifted. It was, perhaps, the happiest production in my amateur dramatic 'career'.

In 2010, I was invited to join Croydon Operatic and Dramatic Association's production of Michael Frayn's *Noises Off* at the Fairfield Halls. CODA is a strong company. I was Lloyd Dallas, a 'Director' who instructs the cast on-stage from the audience. We rehearsed in school halls and gyms without access to the theatre or set until 24 hours before opening.

Each evening, I briefed the ushers that I'd start in the auditorium then go on stage. On Saturday, two ushers missed the briefing. The curtain rose, Dotty began, and I called from the gallery, 'You leave the sardines, and you hang the phone up.'

An usher shone a torch at me and said, 'Please sit down, sir, there's a play going on.'

I explained and continued, and his attempts to silence me grew louder. Then comes a line, starting softly and building to an enraged yell, 'Thank you, Garry, I'm very touched. Now will you GET OFF THE F***ING STAGE!'

Behind me, the shocked usher matched my volume, 'There's no need for that sort of language, sir. I'M CALLING SECURITY!'

By then, I was running down to the stalls. I was asked for my ticket, and tried to explain before bellowing, 'SARDINES,' over a new usher's shoulder.

'Keep your voice down; there's still time to get a ticket, yer know.'

'SARDINES,' I repeated and again was rebuked. Saying 'Excuse me' politely, I walked to the stage, calling out my lines with the usher's voice loudly behind me –

'Hey, you, stop. I don't know – there's always one tries to get in without a ticket.'

When told of our dramas, Michael Frayn wrote: 'Many Dallases have been shushed by the audience, but I've never heard of the staff of the theatre trying to throw one out before'.

Jane Jamieson helped me to believe that I could still sing; she has a kind and infectious enthusiasm. Over the years we had fun with an idea of Martin Bishop's – waiting on tables and singing. I was in productions in English, French and Italian.

I enjoyed them all, especially the latter which was my final appearance. I sang *Funiculì Funiculà* written by Luigi Denza. The lyrics are fiendishly tricky, written in Neapolitan patois, and Denza's great-grandson, Paul, was in the audience that night.

AROUND THE WORLD IN 80 MONTHS

2002 to 2008

Maria and I had plans to go to South Africa; everything was booked for five of us (Charlie was bringing a school friend). Suddenly the situation changed; it was no longer safe for us to go. Sophie and Charlie opted to spend Christmas with Nicola, so we decided to flop in South Beach Miami for a week. We went around Miami on public transport, drove down towards Key West and saw in the New Year at Nikki Beach, feeling very out of place.

After a week we had a farewell brunch with a friend at News Café, where we had eaten almost every day. Our waiter was a patrician young actor. He stood, arms crossed, listening as we ordered. 'We'll have one granola with fruit, no blueberries, yoghurt and nuts but no hazel nuts, French toast with Canadian Maple syrup, not the other stuff, and on the side, please; a cappuccino with only a half shot, another with an extra shot…' and the order went on and on.

Suddenly Maria said, 'Why aren't you writing this down?' and he smiled.

A few minutes later our waiter returned. 'I just want to get it right for you; so, you want one granola with blueberries, no yoghurt but extra hazel nuts, French toast with syrup on top, but not Maple syrup, and two flat whites with a single shot…' Steam was coming out of Maria's ears as he repeated the entire order incorrectly. Eventually, he placed a hand gently on her forearm and smiled, 'My dear, even Americans can have a sense of irony'. The order was perfect, his smile charming.

Service throughout America is an art form. From other waiters we learnt about tipping, which always strikes non-Americans as ridiculously expensive. The US has two levels of minimum wage – one for the vast majority and another, just 30% of the first, for waiters and 'employees who receive tips'. Most restaurants and bars do not pay their waiters but send the minimum wage to the tax authorities to cover income tax payable on tips.

I was a director of two travel companies so opportunities to travel were plentiful, and technology already allowed us to conduct business from around the world. We were in our fifties and spent time in Africa, America (North and South), Asia, Australasia and Europe. In brief, we touched on every continent except Antarctica. Having already travelled much myself, as a child and for work, I loved sharing that with Maria – a chance to show my roots, develop a tapestry of shared experience and create roots together.

A new restaurant, Latium, became another favourite haunt. It had a brilliant chef, Maurizio Morelli, and talented Maitre d'/sommelier, Antonio Cerilli. Unfortunately, Maurizio and Antonio were strong willed and fell out irreconcilably. As a friend of the family, I was invited to resolve matters for them and their silent partner, Claudio Pulze, who has owned Michelin starred restaurants from Aubergine to Zafferano.

I asked Claudio the secret of a good restaurant: 'Julian, that is easy; good food in the category, a warm welcome and a fair price.'

'If it's that easy, Claudio, why do so many fail?'

'That's also easy. We all know the ingredients, but we don't know the right proportions.'

We were invited to the christening near Rome of Esme, Antonio's first child. Forty people, mostly family, sat at a trestle table overlooking a historic town and valley. A dozen delicious courses had been made by the older women of the family using produce, including chicken and pork, from the gardens around the half-finished house.

Later we visited Certosa di Trisulti in Abruzzo, a monastery in a barracks clinging to the Apennine mountains and furnished like a stately home. It was consecrated in 1211, carved imperfectly above the door as MCC XI. We sat in the chapel as a priest recounted its history, when two boisterous infants scurried forwards, tugging at the lace altar cloth to reach the cross and candlesticks. An anxious mother ran to stop them, but the priest softly intervened, '*Lasciali; non hanno mai peccati*' ('Let them be, they have never sinned'). Without a murmur, the children returned to their seats, and the priest continued, unperturbed.

We went to Berlin with Helen and Ami Weinstock; only Maria had previously been there. A friend recommended Dieter as our driver; they had met him at Masada in Israel. Dieter took us around *Jewish* Berlin with insights that exceeded our hopes. Ami's father, who had recently died, came from pre-war Berlin, escaping to Jerusalem and settling in Australia; Ami inherited his father's determination and built a business empire.

Ami comes across as 'one tough dude' and yet he felt

unable to visit Berlin while his father lived. In one small residential square, there is a bronze sculpture of an abandoned breakfast table, overlooked by a black wall bearing the chilling words, *'Es ist nur eine Frage der Zeit'* – it is just a matter of time. Ami stood at a nearby corner with tears in his eyes. 'I don't know where Dad lived; we never talked about Berlin – it was too painful for him. I wish I knew if he lived on this street or that one or where he grew up as a kid.' Today, more than at any time in my life, we see the wholesale severance of roots for millions around the world.

Helen stood quietly by him. Her mother was Polish; all her mother's siblings were murdered in Auschwitz. We met Helen's mother in Sydney, defiant in old age and thrilled that she had so many grandchildren to 'replace our lost generation'. There is a growing generation of great-grandchildren.

There are thought-provoking memorials in many places in Berlin, some seldom visited. There are also bland plaques from the 1950s.

Gleis 17 at Grunewald Station shows where Jews were deported in plain sight of leafy suburbia. The deportees would have been herded into cattle trucks attached to the same commuter trains they had once used, possibly seen by former colleagues as they were transported to certain death.

At the corner with Jagowstraße, a 1950s plaque casually 'regrets the misfortune that befell so many who lived in Germany'. A few steps away, bundles of rags (actually, it was a white marble sculpture of victims, tied together in blocks) are loaded onto the rusting structure of a train on the pavement where Berlin's largest (2,000-seat) synagogue had been destroyed in Levetzowstraße.

Throughout Berlin, bronze cobbles (*Stolpersteine* or stumbling stones) in the street mark houses from which Jewish families were taken to the camps. Cigarette butts on the pavement, casually lying by the bronze markers, mean no disrespect but show that people stop to read them, to contemplate what happened seven decades ago.

Dieter drove past the Eisenman and Buro-designed Memorial to the Murdered Jews of Europe on our left and a small, new grey concrete hut in the woods of the Tiergarten Park on our right. 'I may not be Jewish,' observed Dieter pointing to the right, 'but I think I understand. The only memorial to my kind is this one and nobody knows it is there.' It is the *Denkmal für die im Nationalsozialismus verfolgten Homosexuellen*. Through a window, like a gun loop in a blockhouse, is a permanent showing of film of a same sex couple kissing. Dieter was an inspired choice of guide.

We went to the house on Wannsee where the annihilation of European Jewry was planned in January 1942. Among items in a permanent exhibition is a typewriter from the period. As we might have keys for £, $ or €, this typewriter has one specifically for ϟϟ, the hateful symbol of the notorious Schutzstaffel. Maps showed the Jewish population of Europe at the time, with numbers marked for each country. It totalled almost 10 million. By the end of the war, more than 60% of them had been murdered. That is the meaning of *genocide*.

Maria and I took advantage of Ryanair's £1 flights. We flew to Barcelona, Paris, Rome, Venice and beyond on early evening flights to enjoy dinner and a late-night walk. A dawn *vaporetto* in Venice is shared with some of the 50,000 residents on their way to work, watching the early market, rubbish collection and workings of a living city, not a museum.

In 2006, Robin invited me to say a few words at Bruno's funeral; I had read a poem, selected by Bruno, at Mildred's funeral some time before. Bruno and Mildred were good friends of Emma and Papa. On the eve of the funeral, I slept in Bruno's Turin study, contemplating the mosaic of paintings and dipping into books on his shelves. Bruno was an architect of immense and gentle intellect. He read in several languages, making dated notes in the margins, his comments in the language of the book. He was witty, quiet and kind.

Roberto Foà had three children: Bruno, Mauro, who died young, and Paola. Roberto was a very successful Turin broker in the early 20th century who acquired, on behalf of the National University Library in Turin, a collection of manuscripts by Antonio Vivaldi including 300 concertos, dozens of sacred works and 19 'lost' operas; the gift triggered the revival of the forgotten Red Priest's popularity.

The offer to finance this exceptional purchase was originally rejected, apparently because of the antisemitic tone of Mussolini's rise to power in the 1920s. In 1927, Roberto eventually succeeded in having his generous offer accepted with help from two others, Alberto Gentili and Renzo Giordano; ironically all three were Jewish, but the legacy was too good to miss. Roberto was later blocked from funding a second, smaller purchase. A letter from a government department in Rome advised that, 'It is not considered convenient, for obvious reasons, to approach Roberto Foà in the context. Clearly the government considers that pecunia olet[3], since it comes from an anti-fascist who has been on the watchlist of OVRA [Mussolini's secret police equivalent of the Gestapo]. It would be best not to have a debt of gratitude to him in case it becomes necessary for him to be arrested.'

Roberto wrote to Renzo at the time of the gift in 1927: 'Someday, Paola and Bruno will see how their parents tried, through an unselfish act, to show them that wealth and the possibilities that life brings should not represent the aim of existence but be a means of effecting good and worthy deeds.'

Bruno's life reflected his father's uplifting philosophy, and Bruno in turn passed that on to Robin, and from Robin and Rita it passed to their sons, Stefano and Alberto.

That year, Maria and I went to Oman over Christmas. The country's tourism was just about to take off, with the infrastructure broadly in place but none of the inconvenience of crowds. The coast and the mountains are sensational. In the old capital of Nizwa, we were among a handful of tourists. From the clothing, setting and practices, it feels as though history has stopped in the time of Christ, with few changes apart from ubiquitous rifles and mobile phones. Oman seemed to be a country with exceptional wealth and natural beauty but little real ambition for most of its citizens.

With the prospect of Artificial Intelligence growing, there is an argument that this new technology can fund a Universal

3 Normally the expression is '*pecunia non olet*' meaning that money does not smell. Apparently it does when the donor is an anti-fascist.

Income, even a Universal High Income (UHI). Such an income is already in place in many parts of the world, including Oman. As we were to witness in Uluru and can see in multi-generational unemployment in the UK, handouts do not solve human problems. When Jesus said, in his 40-day trial in the desert, 'Man does not live by bread alone', he was quoting Deuteronomy, written more than 2,500 years ago and still relevant today. Worldwide, people have four compelling motivations, which I simplify as 'fear, greed, pride and need'. Others have a different list, largely down to semantics: 'addiction', 'desire', 'obsession' are among suggested additions although I think all are bound up in 'need'. UHI cannot improve the human condition unless people also have a purpose or motivation. Without hope or purpose, money is nothing.

The following spring, we sailed down the Nile to Cairo with Simon and Jayni Beecroft. It was a spectacular cruise. The crew of the new Zahra was exemplary: thoughtful, attentive to detail, welcoming and fun. During quiet moments on deck, we could watch children herding goats as though transported from the time of the pharaohs. When docked, we had private visits to some of the most glorious temples and tombs. We then spent a few days in a well-known Cairo hotel. We experienced the best and then the worst of hospitality. The wealth of exquisite antiquity along the Nile contrasts uncomfortably with the modern squalor in Cairo.

Before flying home, we sat in the Executive Lounge with only two other occupants, Archbishop Desmond Tutu and a tough nun. Maria stood by him before we boarded and softly said what a shame it was that a person of his universal moral authority had not felt able to speak out against atrocities committed in Zimbabwe in the name of President Robert Mugabe. The next day, at a conference in London, Tutu made an unambiguous, unscripted public criticism of Mugabe for the first time. A coincidence? Perhaps, but I'd be less surprised if he just needed a nudge from an unexpected source.

On our way to Australia in 2007, we stopped in Bangkok, left our cases at the airport with a man in an Oriental Hotel blazer and flew directly to Siem Riep with hand baggage. Early morning visits to Angkor Wat avoided the crowds. Alone we enjoyed the friezes, temples and wild fig trees encroaching on history. There are images of battles by land and sea, religious festivals and royal progressions, dancing and trading caravans. It is a vast and fascinating complex with an ideal light for photography just after dawn and before dusk. One incongruous carving adorned the Bayon Temple, contrasting with the great themes of tradition and war: a young Vietnamese trader weighs goods for a Khmer girl, their fathers looking on. The boy is distracted by the girl's bare bosom (customary in Cambodia until the 20th century) and does not see her toe tipping the scales. Both fathers smile, one has a finger to his lips to urge silence. A modern moment captured 800 years ago.

Returning, the airline warned of a scam: thieves imitate hotel porters to steal luggage. It was an uncomfortable wait until a man in a familiar blazer approached with the words, 'Your luggage is already in your suite.' The service throughout our stay was instinctive and impeccable. Kurt

Wachtveitl was long regarded as the best General Manager in the world. Modestly he told us it was easier in some countries, such as Thailand; his concern was that so many luxury hotels are opening, requiring tens of thousands of staff worldwide, which poses an impossible challenge in countries with no culture of service.

We stayed with Ami and Helen in Sydney before exploring a continent. You could fit a map of Europe inside Australia without even touching the coasts, and yet the Australian population is scarcely as numerous as the unofficial population of Istanbul or a dozen other cities.

We holidayed in Noosa Heads and sailed among the mangroves in the inlets. We trekked in the Daintree Rainforest, sat on the soft sands at Cape Tribulation, 'scuba' dived at the Great Barrier Reef. The diving was amazing – a sense of weightlessness and brilliant colours and areas so deep that no light entered them. After a suitable 36 hours pause, we flew to Uluru, stopping briefly in Alice.

Uluru changes colour throughout the day, but mostly it is a rusty red. More people saw *Blood Swept Lands and Seas of Red* at the Tower of London during a few months in 2014 than visited Uluru in the first 125 years since the Rock was 'found' by a surveyor and named Ayers' Rock after a politician. We saw the sun fall through its folds, which changed to deep purples and oranges, and returned to our tented hotel to prepare for a meal under the stars. The area had suffered almost no rainfall in six years, so we were surprised by a smattering of raindrops and then thunder and lightning forking in from all angles towards the ferrous Rock. A decade of rain in eight hours of darkness, and the following day flora had appeared overnight, several inches of fresh green shoots and unhoped for blossom, as well as waterfalls cascading down the grooves that Europeans call The Skull.

We flew from Uluru to Perth sitting with Bridget, who had worked with Aboriginal Australians in Uluru for 25 years. Her view was, 'you really can't rush things; we all need to evolve'.

Bridget described the evolutionary process thus: for 80,000 years men gathered food and water all day, leaving governance to older men. Women spent their waking hours preparing food, using hostile ingredients, and bringing up children, teaching the Dreamtime spiritual stories until they became adults around puberty. There were then decades of abuse by the invaders and suddenly a remorseful nation gave handouts and participation in democracy. Bridget explained that a very hard life should have improved.

However, she said that in practice, in the absence of social evolution, the indigenous way of life and purpose were destroyed with nothing to take their place except, for a tragically large number, drugs and drink; hence my thoughts about UHI. We can create a greater '*wrong*', using an easy option to right an earlier wrong. Communication and respect heal souls and minds more than anonymous, easily diverted heaps of money with no human touch.

We saw few Aboriginal Australians in Sydney. I walked from Rushcutters Bay through Kings Cross to Woolloomooloo Finger Wharf, where excellent restaurants cluster, into the Art Gallery of NSW, across the park, around the harbour to the opera house. Had we been younger, we might have moved there. The parks, the public buildings, the Victorian houses are almost like home, but always with an exotic twist, such as fruit bats hanging from the branches. Chris and Judy have been there for decades, now living between Haymarket and the Rocks, weathering the storms and thriving on the other side. They have been an inspiration, and thanks to modern communications we can talk regularly, although we seldom see each other more than once a year.

Maria and I travelled throughout the USA. During the leaf peeping season, we flew up to Buffalo to see Niagara and drove past the Finger Lakes, Ithaca, New England and Boston. Marking the anniversary of the death of Maria's mother, Mary, we went to Glendale (Little Armenia in LA) and visited Death Valley, Vegas, Yosemite and the Grand Canyon. We cruised up the West coast to Alaska and watched as glaciers calved and whales did their thing. We went to New York often and to Florida. No wonder so few Americans have passports – the country has it all.

We were back in the UK for Jane and Jeremy Scott's country house wedding. I read a piece during the ceremony; my first thought (a passage from Khalil Gibran's *The Prophet*) was rejected by the Registrar because 'the title has religious connotations'.

Another reader, Jeremy's Washington-based cousin Sandy Greenberg, had an even harder time. 'I need to read your speech before we can proceed,' said the Registrar.

'That seems a bit unfair as I cannot read it,' said the blind Sandy, 'but I can recite it for you,' and he delivered an anodyne 10 minutes of waffle, holding up the bride and her little bridesmaids who were eager to scatter rose petals where she was to walk.

When Sandy spoke at the ceremony, it was a fervent discourse about marriage as a sacrament, its importance within the Jewish faith and much of significance; occasionally he remarked that he could hear the Registrar moving her chair to stand and reprimand him.

Sandy Greenberg was born in Buffalo and received a full scholarship to attend Columbia University in Manhattan, where his roommates were Arthur and Jerry. He dropped out of college when misdiagnosed glaucoma caused his eyesight to fail. Arthur persuaded him to return to his studies and for the following years, Arthur read all their textbooks and notes out loud. It was the foundation of a life-long friendship.

Sandy got a First in his initial degree, went on to Harvard to read for a master's and PhD, and then went to Oxford as a Marshall Scholar. By then, he had married his childhood sweetheart, Sue, to whom he is still very happily married and whom he has not seen clearly since January 1961. While moving from one centre of academic excellence to another, Sandy was called by Arthur with a request for a loan to cut a demo disc, which starts with the words, 'Hello Darkness, my old friend'. *Darkness* was Arthur's affectionately ironic nickname for Sandy when he went blind. Sandy has had a hugely successful career as an inventor, entrepreneur and philanthropist, and he is one of the most delightful and important men I have met. When talking, Sandy still calls Art Garfunkel, his old roommate 'Arthur', and he should know – they remain closer than brothers. Jerry, the third roommate, is Jerry Speyer, owner of the Rockefeller Centre and a huge backer of Sandy and Art's charitable search to defeat avoidable blindness.

In Buffalo, we were soaked in the mist of Niagara Falls. We flew to Iguassu that winter, to be soaked in the spray of the Devil's Throat, watched by soaring condors; then from Buenos Aires to Rio, pausing at the millionaire's playground of Punta del Este. There we visited the Gaudi-esque Casapueblo of Carlos Páez Vilaró, one of Uruguay's leading artistic figures. We went to buy two prints but were refused: 'This one has a dirty mark on the sun, and it is the only copy we have'. After pleading, the artist himself was disturbed to opine on 'to sell or not to sell'. Thirty minutes later the prints returned, one signed '*A Maria con carino*' and the other, with a flock of felt tip birds scuttling across the blemished sun, signed '*A Julian con un abraz*'. In 2022, I gave the felt-tip amended print to Charlie's Uruguayan partner, Lula, a happy new owner of the story.

News of our property sale and purchase arrived as we entered the harbour at Rio. We celebrated by buying a ring at H. Stern, possibly for more than I calculated. Together with new friends, Bill and Lynda Luber, we were offered a car and guide with whom to tour the city. The guide remained in the car for all the main sights until we reached Ipanema Beach, where she joined us, unwrapping the boxed ring and passing it to me with the words, 'It's best if you carry the engagement ring in your pocket.' Unprompted, a Rio shop assistant had proposed on my behalf!

We returned to London to gut and refurbish a new home,

looking for deals as ever. A friend recommended a new workshop in Acton ('great quality, cheaper than IKEA'), so we went.

The workshop's owner, Khushal Ahmed, created a business from nothing since arriving in Britain as a 21-year-old refugee. As a child, in Afghanistan, he worked for his father, a tailor with a market stall. He had a talent, essential in tailoring, for making fabric bend around the contours of a body. Some dangerous years later, he told us, via Russia and the back of a lorry through Europe, he reached Britain with £20 and no work. Watching an upholsterer in a shop window, he reckoned it was like tailoring – making fabric curve around shapes. He asked for a job.

We happily spent time with him and, shortly after he set up The Sofa & Chair Company, we bought several pieces for the new flat. He is a quiet, determined, warm individual with a commitment to quality. Maria tells me he is a very good-looking man. Employing more than 100 designers and craftsmen in a gleaming new factory, Khushal can claim to be Britain's leading manufacturer of bespoke furniture, servicing the best international interior designers.

Something about Khushal's story touches me, as do the stories of friends whose families, over centuries, have been able to make their lives in this country. There are few places where successful immigration happens, and my hometown can be a refuge for people from all three faiths of The Book, and from other religions or none. This is not a new phenomenon; Voltaire praised England's toleration of religious refugees in *Letters on the English* (1733) and again in *Treatise on*

Toleration (1763).

However, it is more personal than that. Maria is wholly Armenian. Her mother, Mary was driven, feisty, loving, fierce, stubborn, hard-working and loyal. More than 100 years ago, Maria's grandparents fled the Turkish genocide in their homeland. From their refuge in Persia, some migrated to India, many went to Glendale in Los Angeles. Later, many settled peacefully and securely in Britain, refugees for the third time in two generations.

Armenians form a great diaspora, along with Lebanese and Jews. There are 11 million Armenians globally, fewer than three million of whom live in Armenia; 15 million Jews worldwide but only six million in Israel; and 18 million Lebanese but fewer than four million in their homeland. These three peoples have much in common: an escape from violence, pride in their heritage, love of food and, frequently, portable skills. All three have also added immeasurably to the culture and wealth of the countries in which these diasporas have settled. As I write, all three homelands are at war, as so many nations are in a world that is more unstable than at any time in my memory.

It is generally acknowledged that the Ottoman government systematically killed 1.5 million Armenians, more than a third of those alive in the early 20th century. I write 'generally acknowledged' because Turkey's government denies genocide, notwithstanding the evidence. It is said that when we forget history, we are condemned to repeat it. The real lesson that history teaches us is that the lessons of history are not learnt. Historical amnesia can be deliberate. In Obersalzberg in August 1939, justifying his brutal invasion of

Poland and policy of eliminating 'all of Polish derivation and language', Adolf Hitler said, 'Who, after all, speaks today of the annihilation of the Armenians?'

In 2008 in Westminster Abbey, commemorating the centenary of the Armenian Genocide in the presence of the Armenian President and Prince Charles, Bishop of London Richard Chartres said reconciliation might be possible but not forgiveness because, 'what has not been confessed cannot be forgiven,' a theological view fitting many commonplace situations.

I am privileged that Mary called me her 'son-in-law', although sadly she had died before we married. Names matter. Stephen, her hairdresser for decades, shut the salon for her funeral. While she was in a coma in hospital, he did her hair every week: 'I can't let anybody else touch Mrs Petro's hair.' Formality can be intimate when every call centre uses first names. One of Maria's longest standing friends, Elena, was a teenager when she met Mary. They loved each other dearly, and yet Elena only ever called Mary 'Mrs Petro,' even on a wreath of flowers at her funeral.

Meanwhile, the marriage proposal made to Maria (by that H. Stern shop assistant on Ipanema Beach) had not achieved the desired result. I tried myself this time. Britain's Sunday papers have pages of car registrations for sale. Flicking through, one caught my eye – K999 MSM. We were buying a second car; the number was inexpensive; I bought it. 'Would you like this number plate on your new car?' met with an indifferent, 'It's OK, but those are not my initials.' 'But they could be,' I replied… and, now that we are married, they are.

CITY FOOD CENTRES AND BEING A BIT OF A 'FOODIE'

2004 to 2012

What do my childhood homes – Lebanon, France and Italy – have in common? Great food. It would be a bit surprising if I didn't like food, both in the kitchen and on the plate. The whole food industry is a natural habitat for migrants and transmigrants.

I worked in restaurants and kitchens as a teenager and learned to appreciate the role of different stations: the quiet concentration of prep; the drudging loneliness of the plongeur; the frenzy of the finish and the pressure of the pass. The finest food and the best restaurants are a hard world, where 'haves' and 'have nots' interact but never meet. Orwell's masterpiece, *Down and out in Paris and London*, was written 90 years ago – how much progress can we claim to have made?

In the early 1990s I took the children to Ravello, surely one of the most beautiful places on earth. It overlooks the Mediterranean, south of Naples and the Terrace of Infinity at Villa Cimbrone is the backdrop of many people's dreams.

All day, good food is served at Cumpa' Cosimo, just off the main square and with Netta Bettone as the third generation in charge.

'Is there anything else you would like?' she asked one evening.

'Yes, I would love to see the kitchen where this food was prepared.'

'Then be here before 7 tomorrow morning and you will see.'

The next day, having arranged a 'babysitter', I worked in her ancient kitchen, with cave-like walls and volcanic bursts of flame. Netta tasked me with the day's production of ragù ('put celery in with onion, to sweat; leave garlic until the end or it becomes bitter'), peperonata, melanzane alla parmigiana and the patient folding of risotto. I then had lunch with the children, watching 'my food' being served to the public.

In 2006, El Bullí was rated the 'best restaurant in the world' and we were there. It had been a long journey – Maria tried to book two years running but having had no response we arranged instead to celebrate the *quatorze juillet* with Jon and Sally Butler in France.

Then, flights booked for France, we received a (pre-Google Translate) email from Spain: 'Dear Gentle Lady, we have a solution to your petition'– an irresistible table for four at El Bullí on a Saturday evening in mid-July. Having watched the fireworks in France, we flew to Roses in Jon's Beechcraft. We arrived at the restaurant early (just after 8 pm!) and sat on a terrace above an idyllic bay, where a guitarist led his friends in song around a fire on the sand.

Jon asked for champagne; the waiter urged that, with the adventures in store, we opt for an inexpensive cava and then led us into the kitchen to meet Ferran Adrià, one of the most influential chefs of the 20th century, who calmly showed us his alchemist's laboratory.

Jon was passionate about food and wine. Two hours later, 15 courses from the start of a sensational meal with several dishes to go, he paused and said, 'I'd kill for a Big Mac.'

We ate 26 courses. A culinary Cirque du Soleil performed on our tongues. The Master of Ceremonies (our waiter) guided us through the spectacle. We dipped bone spoons into small tins of caviar; the appearance and texture were perfect, yet we ate droplets of melon. We had strawberries that tasted of olives, or was it the other way around? Each plate was a surprise. We never did get Jon's Big Mac.

With El Bulli as a catalyst, Northern Spain became the Mecca for fine dining in the early 2000s. In 2008, we went with the Weinstocks to San Sebastian with their wonderful 8-year-old son Nathan in tow. We ate affordably at the world's great restaurants including Asador Etxebarri, where Victor Arguizoniz and a young Mancunian grilled everything, even risotto, in a tiny, over-heated space using two baker's ovens, four grills and 20 types of wood.

At each place, Nathan asked for spaghetti with a tomato sauce and each celebrity chef obliged, emerging to the chagrin of regulars to solicit Nathan's approval. At Akelarre, a three Michelin star restaurant overlooking the horseshoe bay of San Sebastian, chef Pedro Subijana, emerged seeking a thumbs-up from Nathan, but the sleepy lad politely cut him off: 'Thank you – it was nice enough, but I had better at Mugaritz.'

My godson Jack Sharp was an excellent cook at 12, devouring cookbooks and programmes with the determination that he brings to everything. I suggested a visit to New Covent Garden, shortly after 6 one morning, to get a feel for where food comes from. He was ready, eager and full of interesting questions when we reached the bustling wholesale market. Jack wanted to know everything; his insatiable curiosity is one of the joys of time spent in his company.

After leaving the Market, we drove to Arlington Place, behind The Ritz, to arrive before 9. For 50 years, Le Caprice was a leading address in fashionable London for discretion, power lunches and affordable comfort food. As I have written, it was my favourite haunt. Courtesy of our friend, *Maitre d'* Jesus Adorno, we met the head chef, changed into whites, and set to work.

Jack and I chopped salads for the day, peeled prawns and prepped the Thai sea bass fillets. Jack baked the day's blueberry muffins and dipped the chocolate biscuits.

We stopped for lunch and chatted with the chefs, all impressed by Jack's proficiency and enthusiasm. 'Do you want to be a chef, Jack?' He was politely non-committal. 'Well, are you thinking of going to Westminster?'

'Mummy and Daddy have looked at Westminster, but I think I'll go to Winchester.'

'Yeah, that's good too,' and I'll never know if Jack realised that the chefs meant Westminster Kingsway Catering College or if the chefs knew that Jack meant Westminster School. Sitting at the bar for lunch, Jack surveyed Le Caprice celebrities eating food he'd prepared. It was a proud morning.

With all this and much else in mind, I leapt at the invitation from Nicholas Saphir to attend a meeting at New Covent Garden with the traders who make up the committee of the Covent Garden Tenants Association. It marked the start of the most compelling, exciting, enriching and frustrating eight years; it colours how I see everything about the way Britain functions.

Nicholas wrote the 2002 *Review of London Wholesale Markets*, an excellent and radical report with both insight and foresight that was commissioned, accepted and largely shelved by successive governments. Among the conclusions of his research was the startling proportion of London traffic dedicated to moving food and ingredients in vans. His recommendations were wise commercially, socially and ecologically. Nicholas has a barrister's incisive mind, several generations of links to the Covent Garden Market, acumen and experience from a very successful business career, the inclination of a farmer and a limitless address book. He is also profoundly decent and great fun. I was so lucky that he invited me to join his adventure.

We were asked by the tenants to advise and develop ideas and relationships that would do much more than just protect the future of the Larder of London and the Southeast. We worked hard and well; his ideas, our ideas, would undoubtedly have changed the development for the better. Because of Nicholas, City Food Centres (the business that he created and took me into as a junior partner) was also invited to advise on the future of Digbeth Market in Birmingham. During that process, we met Andy Street at the HQ of John Lewis in Victoria. He is easy to talk with and impressive to watch in action. Above all, he is passionate about getting things done right. The resulting development was not what we originally proposed but, with our input, it revitalised that wholesale market.

Convent Garden was developed in the 12th century, on a site controlled by Westminster Abbey that had been planted in the 7th century as Lundenwic (which translates roughly as the London Trading Zone). It has survived for more than 1,000 years for good reasons; a major city needs an efficient means of receiving and distributing food – it cannot rely on a near monopsony of suppliers such as a handful of supermarkets.

Since the early days of chartered markets, new wholesalers have flourished; many were recent immigrants. Anybody could set up a business with no capital, sharp wits and a good reputation. Deals are settled at the end of the day; a trader buys stock during the night, sells it and is paid when he needs to pay. If he fails to pay, he is out of business almost immediately; if he pays, he builds a reputation and, possibly, a fortune. I worked with many traders who comfortably earned more than my well-dressed City colleagues.

Our work took eight years, with regular meetings in the market. When traders like Gary Marshall, Peter Fowler and Jason Tanner say, 'Let's have lunch,' they mean a meeting before 7 a.m. to iron things out. Traders are entrepreneurial, risk-takers, hard workers and a community with a few simple rules. They have no time for fellow traders who go bankrupt and make no effort to pay their debts; one or two well-known names excite fury.

Our ideas developed, at first in conversation with the tenants and possible development partners, then on paper, in writing and in architects' sketches (through iterations of the giant SOM – Skidmore, Owings and Merrill; the small, award-winning practice of Ash Sakula; and international innovators, Grimshaw Architects) until finally each idea evolved into 3-D CGI and real-life models. We needed well-funded partners for the tenants, so that we could develop the ideas and, in time, realistically bid for the chance to realise the vision.

Gosh! Developers come in all shapes and sizes and make extraordinary claims. We met great institutions, which we had no reason to mistrust, and ambitious individuals, one or two of whom we had no reason to trust. We chose to work with one of the world's largest construction and development companies, Bouygues. It was an excellent choice; they completely understood and supported the ambitious scope of our proposals.

At the heart of our City Food Centres philosophy is the creation of destinations in key areas of major cities with a primary focus on food – it's sourcing, production, enjoyment, distribution and all the research, educational, commercial, archival and working opportunities associated with food and hospitality. The concept is ambitious, comprehensive and commercially viable. It creates a centre of excellence and a hub for the community and enhances surrounding values. Food City London was designed for the 57-acre Nine Elms complex where London's leading wholesale market for fresh produce has been since the early 1970s.

Food was a big news story for several contrasting reasons: at one end, London had become the culinary capital of Europe;

at the other, childhood obesity doubled between 1995 and 2005. *Jamie Oliver and the Dinner Ladies*, broadcast in 2005, triggered a debate, shifting the focus from Health to Education. The School Food Trust (SFT) was launched that year to support new school kitchens and sound food.

Prue Leith became chair of SFT in 2006. Her wisdom and no-nonsense approach mobilised decision makers. She invited 100 such people to lunch in a marquee in the Market car park. Lord Adonis, Education Minister, was a typical guest. I was also there. School meals in 2006 involved tired kitchens, under-staffing and an ingredients budget of 40p per child. Children preferred junk food. Prue pressed for an ingredient budget of 75p and other improvements. The budget for ingredients for lunch for 100 adults that day was £75. The meal was delicious.

Sadly, the government did not follow through. After a flurry of activity, SFT ran out of money and closed in 2017. New inquiries and initiatives replaced it. Childhood obesity is at crisis levels. There was an opportunity to crack the problem through education, but obesity has reverted to being a health issue, costing billions more and adding to the woes of the NHS.

Research included a visit to Poundbury, hosted by HRH The Prince of Wales and addressed by the Luxembourg-born architectural theorist and urban planner Léon Krier, who speaks like a cult leader.

In the 1980s, Prince Charles was asked to sell land to Dorchester Council for development and offered instead to develop it himself. In delivering this promise he largely adopted Krier's philosophy, tempered with his own thoughts on putting people at the heart of the process. Love it or loathe it (and some of the architecture can be quite twee), few can argue against Poundbury's success; it works for the residents, the environment, and the developers.

Our small group listened to Krier preach and heard HRH speak with passion and knowledge – an example of the student becoming the better teacher. We toured the town on foot, returning to Brownsword Hall for lunch. Most took a slow coach; I walked, arriving ten minutes before the rest to stand alone with Prince Charles and his advisor on rainforests. King Charles III, as he is now, is interested, witty, studious and engaging.

We discussed Poundbury and the Nine Elms development, the importance of planning serving people within a community and Le Corbusier's notion that 'a city does not come to life until the cemetery is full.' Tea was brought for the Prince, who earnestly sniffed it.

'No food taster, Sir?'

He smiled, 'No, sadly, we must all make economies.' He has always tried to make a difference and has achieved more than most politicians.

I sat for lunch that day with Andrew and Christina Brownsword, after whom the hall is named. From nothing, they built a fortune making greetings cards. Andrew enthused about restoring 1 Royal Crescent, Bath, a time capsule of Jane Austen's era, displaying many of the Brownsword collection of paintings. They share what they have created in the spirit of Roberto Foà's gift of Vivaldi manuscripts to the National Library in Italy or Andrew Carnegie's dictum that, 'the man who dies thus rich dies disgraced'.

We spent more than two years going through the various stages of the NCG bid until we were in the final two. The bidding document ran to thousands of pages and weighed several kilos. In that, there were hundreds of pages about Food City London and its component ambitions and supporters, with oodles of commitments and references, illustrations and spreadsheets proving our case. A building is just a building until it has a purpose – its value depends on its location and its use. Food City demonstrated the use and the value. It read well and it scored very highly in the objective evaluation.

The decision, when announced, was a travesty: we won the bid, only to have the maximum subjective deduction from our winning score resulting in the contract being awarded by a whisker to the other bidder. The decision was subject to Judicial Review, at which I understood that an accommodation was reached, money changed hands, and the QUANGO saved face by not being forced to correct (reverse) the contract award. Things did not go well for the winning bidder – property changed hands, construction fell way behind schedule and at one stage we were asked what we would suggest, 'but, sorry, there's no budget left!' There will be a new market although the story is yet another of the untold scandals of public procurement incompetence. It was emotional.

QUANGOs are not a good vehicle for innovation and when a QUANGO engages inadequate executives, whose pay flatters their performance and ability, it cannot be entrusted with a vision. Entrepreneurs and thinkers create while armies of consultants are paid by the hour, partially to provide mitigation for mediocrity as things go wrong. Result? Innovation is expensively strangled by those entrusted to nurture it. It was a sad process and a squandered opportunity that had the potential to show Britain's imagination at its best. Tragically, it was far from unusual.

Britain is not generally corrupt in the sense of cash-filled envelopes or offshore accounts. However, many committed public servants are hampered by militant mediocrity and poor process – 'muddling through', 'doing the bare minimum' and 'covering up' are part of the British corruption along with inflating budgets to flatter one's importance; stifling progress because 'no change' is easier; expensively obscuring a mistake rather than resolving it; overpaying salaries because of phoney private sector comparisons where rewards are linked to revenue generation which few officials do; exceptionally well-paid jobs awaiting decision makers after contract awards. No offshore accounts but there might as well be.

Licking our wounds, Nicholas invited me to join him sailing his boat in the archipelago south of Stockholm. It is magical in mid-summer, each island offering private haven for the short nights. Storms on the Baltic appear from nowhere and feet beneath the water's surface is a range of sharp topped mountains covered by the sea. I was lucky that Nicholas was in charge as we faced a ferocious storm on our final day's sailing.

When Maria and I were in London, we continued to take advantage of London's seemingly limitless menu of live performances of every sort. In 2008, we saw Michael Pennington playing Furtwängler in *Taking Sides*. When we were talking with Michael after the show, he asked about the young men sitting around us in the stalls. 'Were they American tourists from a Mid-West bible college?' He was delighted with the answer: they were young British soldiers identified as candidates to be plucked from the ranks and commissioned as officers, for which they were undergoing a cultural education. 'That's a great relief'. Michael explained that he'd been running a book in the wings during the performance and the Bible Belt option would have cost him dear.

Maria and I met Angela Hamlin one evening with Susan Horswood-Lee, whose email address identifies her as the Chelsea Doctor. Angela created Draycott Nursing, a domiciliary care agency without equal in London at the time.

Angela was frustrated in her attempts to establish a much-needed respite care location in central London. We knew a site owned by Luke and Brian Comer, unconventional and highly successful Irish developers of a host of exceptional properties. We met them in the context of the New Covent Garden redevelopment. We took Angela to see the site that night, our headlights illuminating the space. We imagined a mixed development: respite care beside luxury apartments for a community of older residents, with accommodation for nurses and carers. Using Angela's excellent existing numbers, we worked with the Comers to prove the expanded concept was viable. Meetings with the planners were OK, but there was resistance. There is now a wave of retirement villages, but our talks in 2008 drifted until, suddenly, the property market crumbled.

Timing is everything; a good idea at the wrong time is not a good idea.

WEATHERING THE STORM

2008 to 2012

On Friday 12th September 2008, Maria and I married at Hurlingham. It was a wonderful weekend with family and friends, excellent weather and beautiful music. Two hundred guests encompassing almost 30 nationalities meant we were busy. It was the happiest of days – the major milestone on an exceptionally special journey together. Maria's 85-year-old aunt, Dustrick, gave her away. The rooms were dressed in black and shocking pink; we had arias and a quartet during the afternoon, singing waiters during dinner and, with dancing late into the night, a DJ who managed much of Maria's colossal playlist.

Tony Hibbett, whom Maria had known for decades, tackled the first reading. We were not allowed anything religious, so I wrote a poem for Tony to read. It still feels relevant:

Will You Still Need Me? Will You Still Feed Me?

When the Beatles first asked the question,
They didn't expect love to last.
By the time that they got to sixty-four,
They assumed that all love would have passed.

For love was a simple equation,
In which one married one to make four.
If the sum of the ages makes more than a hundred,

They reckoned there must be a flaw.

But true love is no destination:
It's a journey that goes on and on.
So you catch the train when you get the chance,
And it carries you gently along.

If you catch the train in April,
Then your journey together drifts past.
But for those of us who embark in September,
The train rattles on very fast.

With our family and friends all together,
We sit back to savour the ride,
And the train whistles on through an Indian Summer,
The groom happy next to the bride.

During the reception Sophie's boyfriend, Drum, pulled me aside; he wished to marry Sophie. Charmingly old-fashioned, and I was thrilled. However, Maria sent out a search party as I had been missing for so long. I'd only met Drum once, briefly moving furniture. The conversation took time and would have been better enjoyed when we had no guests.

As 'newlyweds', we spent Saturday with the dozens of friends who had come from abroad. At the kind invitation of Lynda and Bill Luber, we were all entertained for brunch. In the evening, we took a large group to dinner and a musical in the West End. We returned, marching across St James's Square, arms linked with the three Bloch boys and singing inappropriately raucous songs that my very close friends from

Germany, Martin, Martina, and I had sung together in our early twenties.

On Sunday, my new bride and I flew to Soiana with Michael and Susan Moss for our honeymoon. Michael loves the morning news, especially the *Schadenfreude* of London traffic reports as he gazes at the rural tranquillity of deep Tuscany. That morning one item dominated – the collapse of Lehman Brothers.

The financial crash came close to ruining us. Client after client, most of which were financially sound, was pushed under or was subsumed into a pre-pack liquidation in which creditors lose almost everything. We had contracts generating monthly retainers from several client companies – that stopped almost overnight. Work we had done was due to be paid but invoices were not honoured as small companies failed; we had accumulated shares in client companies – these evaporated in restructurings or dwindled to pennies; we had invested savings in a portfolio of rental properties which no longer looked clever.

There were dark days, as grim as the aftermath of my first divorce, that left me once again with nothing material, except this time around, with Maria, I loved and finally felt loved, so anything was possible. It was a bit like Michael Finnegan in the nursery rhyme.

There was an old man named Michael Finnegan
He had whiskers on his chin-a-gen
Along came the wind and blew them in again
Poor, old Michael Finnegan, begin again.

At least we were alive and could have another go. I worked with Thierry Magon de la Villehuchet at CL. He was so urbane, charming and relaxed that it was hard to imagine he successfully ran the CL presence in New York's cut-throat financial market. He shifted comfortably between new world high finance, old-world aristocracy and the more mundane areas in which I worked with him. He retired from CL and founded Access, a grandees' fund manager; we lost touch. The business flourished and he restored the family fortune that had been lost over generations.

With a growing portfolio, he went into business with Bernard Madoff, operator of history's largest Ponzi scheme swindle. More than $50 billion vanished in Madoff's scam, including $1.4 billion belonging to Thierry and his clients. Thierry was wiped out; he had nothing left. He swallowed painkillers and slit his wrists; the first life lost to Madoff's crimes.

Thierry was the eighth person I have worked with who committed suicide because of the insupportable pressures of the business of money – eight financiers whose company I enjoyed, whose talent I admired and who have felt forced to end their own lives, not counting the far greater number whose early death was caused by the excesses of business stress, and often associated coping mechanisms of drink and drugs. It always helps to talk to somebody and in that too I have been lucky, with regular appointments in recent years.

Maria and I set about recreating our business. The post-crash world was difficult but there are always opportunities where there is hope. One lesson that I took a long time to learn was that a person who undervalues themself will always be busy but will never be rich. Luckily old clients reappeared, and new clients were introduced so we made progress.

Sophie and Drum's wedding was announced for early the next September. Maria and I were delighted and set about doing what we could. Soon there were pitfalls and obstacles; while our contribution was asked for and given, it seemed that our presence would be less welcome. Arrangements became transactional, an outcome I had sadly expected. Weeks before the wedding we were uninvited. It was hurtful but predictable having already been excluded from most of the milestones in the children's lives. When Sophie graduated, I bought a silver Fornasetti silk tie to wear at her wedding. It will never be worn.

From others, I learnt that Sophie and Drum were posted to Medicine Hat, a British Army base near Calgary; I introduced her to our Calgary cousins. The first response was a photograph of Tilly, shortly after she was born almost two years later. I was walking through Covent Garden when the photo of my first grandchild appeared.

After another gap, Sophie called, understandably distraught; pregnant with twins, one had been diagnosed *in utero* with hypoplastic left heart syndrome. The pain of losing a child is unimaginable. Sophie's courage was outstanding. We talked and talked. There are no answers to offer, only love.

Lyra and Bella were identical twins, born very prematurely on 17 August 2012. Lyra died ten days later. Drum wisely said, after the funeral, that being identical twins means 'we shall always know what Lyra would look like, but not who she would become'. I love Bella, as I love Tilly and their younger brother Wilf and would surely also have loved Lyra. Her name was inspired, I think, by Lyra Belacqua in Philip Pullman's *His Dark Materials.* I contemplated that Lyra is also the name of one of the oldest recognised constellations, visible only in late August.

In August Lyra glows in northern skies,
Outshining other stars of greater size.
A plucky little constellation, she,
Recorded by none less than Ptolemy.
Yet, just as August ends, her brightness fades,
Is lost from view out somewhere in the haze.
She has not gone – she's out there in the night,
Invisible, but always shining bright.

Drum read those words at the start of the funeral service. The poem sits on my desk with a photograph of Lyra and a picture of the stars. It must have been strange for two-year-old Tilly, running around after the burial, to meet her grandfather for the first time. It was wonderful yet strange for me, to start to know her; the wonder has grown with the years. Maria was not invited; it was some time before she met her step-grandchildren and lavished love on them as well.

I was 60. Maria arranged several wonderful dinners; on the day itself she invited the family that rescued me on my 12th birthday when I was left alone at school. Kiki, youngest of the four daughters, arrived with much conspiratorial shuffling. Later that evening, a chocolate cake was produced with a fire hazard of candles to extinguish. It was the same home-made recipe that I'd enjoyed in 1964. A fabulous evening. A ghost was laid to rest.

Our much-loved stepson, Sam, had ideas for a birthday mystery adventure. Perfectly planned, he got me to an airfield in Essex and revealed the surprise chance to drive a Ferrari, a Porsche and an Aston Martin at speed around a racetrack. It was a wonderful day out that I never would have thought of on my own. As I settled into the third car, the instructor commented that I was right at home in a DB9… I wish.

Keith Sykes invited me to the Guggenheim Dinner at Pembroke, my first such evening at a Cambridge college. To my right sat Dr Jean Ramjohn-Richards, First Lady of Trinidad and Tobago. We talked about republics, healthcare, grandchildren and dogs. She and I were soon in stitches as she described telling the Ministry of Works 'to replace the First Furniture because of the damage done by the First Dogs and to get it done before the next State Visit.' Her commitment and humour have touched very many lives. It was a long, happy night. Hungover at breakfast, I met Thierry Morel, curator of the spectacular Houghton Hall exhibition of many Hermitage treasures. He praised the merits of gentle lighting. Some months later, Thierry himself showed our group around.

THE GAMES OF THE XXX OLYMPIAD

2012

Originally, I did not want my hometown to suffer the chronic disruption that had so blighted Munich. On the day we won the bid, however, I yearned to be part of London 2012.

I enrolled as a Games Maker, initially auditioning as a dancer for the opening ceremony; I even had a call back a few days later. The mix of hopefuls (grooving to *Our House* by Madness) was fascinating. London would not be like the drilled automatons in Beijing's Bird's Nest Stadium, but clearly the standard was higher than I could achieve.

People came from all over the world to take part in the auditions. One man, a photographer, had arrived that morning; 'London's my home – it's where I was born, and I have to be a part of this.' He had lived in Toronto for 15 years but was determined not to be left out of something that so deeply affected his roots, even if he did have to pay all his own expenses and wouldn't get to keep rights to the photographs he took.

The Diamond Jubilee celebrations for Queen Elizabeth took place between the auditions and the Olympics. We went to as many events as we could, standing in indifferent weather in the Mall for the great open-air concert. We grabbed a great spot with Peter and Jane Jamieson and their twins, Poppy and Jamie, and waited. A German TV crew interviewed us at one stage, asking me why I was there… 'Because my wife told me we were invited' I said, and a short while later Martin and Martina in Hamburg phoned to say they knew where we were!

Back to the Olympics, I was offered a job as a driver. Enormous fun and quite a challenge – chauffeurs need to be assertive in traffic but calm in the car; intelligent enough to anticipate a passenger's needs and yet silent. As I say, quite a challenge! Another role, another uniform.

For more than an hour, I drove with an examiner between venues. There followed a 90-minute on-line theory test with game-style scenarios and tricky questions. Not having driven a manual car for 15 years, I was happy to have passed.

I learnt the routes by driving between the Olympic venues. At Eton Dorney Lake, an unaccredited photographer tried to bluff his way past the security detail, manned by soldiers from the Irish Guards. He spoke rapidly in French to a bewildered soldier until a fresh-faced young lieutenant stepped in to turn him away with immense courtesy and a flawless accent. 'Your officer speaks very good French,' I said to the soldier checking my credentials.

'Oh, 'im, Sir, 'e's from Luxemburg, Sir, 'e's got an excuse.' The young lieutenant was a member of Luxembourg's grand-ducal family, following a long tradition of service in that regiment.

Initially I was in a pool, available to chauffeur senior visitors – a B driver in a BMW series 5. A drivers, who drove identical vehicles, were individually allocated to celebrities, heads of state and top IOC officials. The third category, C drivers, drove series 3 BMWs and lined up in ranks to take groups of athletes between set points.

My greatest admiration was for one C driver, David

Watts. GB's fastest butterfly swimmer over 100 metres as an 18-year-old in 1964, he qualified for the Tokyo Olympics that year. However, the ASA budget apparently could fund travel for all the officials or all the swimmers, not both. He was not taken to Tokyo. Now aged 65, he decided, with great dignity and no rancour, that 2012 would be, in his own words, his 'final chance to be involved in an Olympics… albeit in a small, non-competitive way!' He was a delight.

My first dedicated passenger was Dr Alexey Pleskov, Chief Medical Officer for the Sochi 2014 Winter Olympics. He was in London with the Russian Federation team to observe the Games Maker programme, to understand the underlying culture and to experience the impact it would make. 'In Sochi we will have 50,000 volunteers. Is good to see programme at work in London.' I asked about the Russian tradition of voluntary work and Alexey said there was none, 'but no problem. 50,000 people will be sent letter saying, "you are volunteer".'

We went to many locations, including the shooting in Woolwich. 'No need to wait; I am supervising urine tests – sometimes human bladder refuses to stick strictly to timetable.'

For three days I ferried other medics, including Margo Mountjoy from Canada. There is a family of Olympic doctors who know each other from the Olympic, FIFA and other circuits. 'I'm not looking for pills and drugs, Julian; I'm looking for guys with hundreds of syringes and needles but only one hole in their arm or leg. They re-inject their own oxygenated blood but try to do it through the same hole every time to make us less suspicious.' Yuk!

In the ballroom of the Mayfair hotel where A and B drivers were based, the despatcher asked me to drive Count Jacques Rogge, Chairman of the International Olympic Committee, to Monument station so that he could be filmed on the tube between there and Tower Bridge, promoting the novel virtue of using public transport as an Olympic official. We drove in convoy, uniformed police and press photographers in a van at the rear, an unmarked BMW X5 vehicle in the middle with four armed, plain clothes policemen, each sporting a small enamel identification badge in his lapel. I drove the lead vehicle.

Lord Coe sent us on our way and as Jacques Rogge and his wife, Anne, climbed into the vehicle I said '*Bonjour, M le Président*.' A few moments later he changed from speaking indiscreetly in French to being similarly indiscreet in Flemish.

We hurtled through London, an armed, plain clothes policeman sitting beside me and urging that I drive through red traffic lights in Trafalgar Square at almost 40 mph. In my rear-view mirror I could see the word POLICE on the lowered sun visor of an otherwise unmarked car – I was chased through London at speed by armed officers.

It must be hard for sports functionaries to avoid feeling like royalty or minor gods (if they do indeed avoid it) when they inhabit a champagne bubble.

For more than three weeks, I was personal driver to Dame Kelly Holmes. 'Hi, I'm Kelly,' she said, 'Do you mind if I sit in front with you?' I called her Dame Kelly ('because you've earned it; a lot more than some I could mention') and when we met again in the following years, she gave me a big hug and whispered in my ear to insist, 'You're the only person to call me Dame Kelly, and I rather like it.'

When I first met Dame Kelly, I asked, 'How do you wish to be driven – fast, normal or slow?'

'Let's start fast and see how it goes,' so we drove everywhere as fast as the law and common sense allowed. Her timetable left little space for errors or delays, driving throughout London between the Games venues, sponsorship engagements and broadcasting studios. Mostly it was just the two of us; sometimes her devoted father and school friends joined us. Dame Kelly was tireless. Her palpable kindness and her selfless cheerleading (along with the presence of people like John Major, the Duchess of Cambridge and David Beckham) put medals on the table.

Dame Kelly is the same with everyone: charming, brave, cheeky and as pointedly purposeful as a pickaxe. The school friends in my car were the same ones who, as children, heard about her ambition to be an Army PE trainer and who, when she had just watched Seb Coe win, challenged her Olympic ambitions. 'But what about the army?' they asked; 'I can do both;' Double Gold, now a Colonel and with the comfort of those same childhood friends.

She was generous with photo opportunities at every security checkpoint, as the soldiers queued to have a cuddle on camera. 'That's enough, I think, chaps,' said one captain, as we returned to the Olympic Park.

'Perhaps just one more. Sergeant, here's my camera; do the honours, would you please.'

She is one of theirs; they love the fact that she never

forgets. In 2018 she was made an honorary Colonel with the approval of The Queen.

Volunteers collect pins; we exchanged them and stuck them on uniforms and hats. Dame Kelly was aiming for a BBC studio, with no time to spare as ever, when I noticed her Team GB lion was silver. 'You can't wear that, Dame Kelly. Wear mine, it looks gold,' and we swapped. Her warmth, drive and smile meant that I was rewarded more as a volunteer than most who were paid to work during the Olympics. And, when I dropped her and her luggage back home in Kent after the Games were over, the hug was Double Gold!

On the eve of Super Saturday, Number 10 asked me, via the despatchers, to drive Mo Farah from the Olympic Village to Downing Street on the day of the marathon. Mo was to address a conference on starvation in Africa. The PM's office wanted to harvest the political capital of association with a sporting legend combined with a Games Maker's uniform because, by then, GMs were publicly popular. I spent 18 hours practising the route to take account of all the obstacles that the marathon might cause; a dozen trips back and forth.

Mo is tiny and warm. He had a statesman-like presence, a sense of purpose and an unassuming awareness of his standing in the world; he was a giant at that moment, and he wanted to use that to do good. We met, were photographed, spoke for a few moments before I opened the door for him to board as planned… and then two policemen told me, without apparent reason or authority, 'Move aside, we're taking this one.' Mo was led to a marked police car where he was crammed uncomfortably in the back seat between grinning lads in uniform who appeared to be having more enjoyment from the arrangement than Mo was having. Mmm!

A shocker at the 2012 Olympics was G4S. The company's performance was abysmal, scandalous and, seemingly, reflective of a lazy, deceitful, venal corporate culture. G4S was contracted, for almost £300 million, to provide trained security personnel to mount the massive safekeeping process at Olympic sites in London and further afield. They failed.

I chatted to several G4S employees at security checkpoints. They described the perfunctory training as 'examiners give answers during tests and tell us to get one or two answers wrong, or they'll think it's a bit fishy'. Many employees claimed to be under 18 or paid less than the minimum wage. Almost all had issues with the supervisors and managers who showed little regard for proper security procedures. If even some reports were true, it was a scandal from which it appears that management walked away with more money than you'd find in a fleet of rusting G4S cash-in-transit vans.

It is bewildering that the regulatory layers are unable to pick up on failings that are so obvious on the ground. It happens with disturbing frequency, as the Covid, Windrush, infected blood, Grenfell and Post Office Inquiries show, caused perhaps by a merry-go-round of mutual supervision; remuneration committees whose independence is superficial; auditors who would rather tick Pandora's Box than open it; regulators who are 'not paid enough to care'; non-executives who turn up but do not switch on; or an inexperienced, over-promoted middle management cadre driven by resentment and entitlement rather than responsibility and purpose.

It is arrogant mediocrity, playing with other people's money. A tiny minority; of course, we are still a great country. But there are more than enough incompetents in public procurement and protected corporations to cause mayhem and injustice. There is no reason why the improper problems that ordinary people face daily cannot be managed with accountability.

Lutalo Muhammad was controversially picked to represent Team GB in Taekwondo. My fellow drivers watched the ferocious fighter, Muhammad, take the bronze medal. As the games wound down, I delivered a passenger to Paddington and saw a tall, slim, lonely 21-year-old going home with an impossibly big pile of kit emblazoned with the logo, Team GB. We chatted briefly and I shook his hand to congratulate him. My memory is of long delicate fingers, like those of a pianist, and an endearing, dignified shyness. I left and the world walked past him without a second look. How quickly the spotlight is extinguished.

SERVING THE SILVER AND THE GREY

2010 to 2018

Since we first met, fell in love and decided to grow old together, Maria and I have explored the enormous wants and needs of retired people and communities. The over-60s in the UK have traditionally been overlooked or sidelined, whereas in the USA, for example, they are mobilised by the giant AARP, and throughout much of the rest of the world they are valued and nurtured by younger generations.

The generalisation is borne out in many ways. For decades a single company, Saga, serviced the whole market with no significant competition. North America, Australia and New Zealand have retirement villages where more than five percent of the population lives independently; the equivalent in Britain houses less than half a percent of the British. Life expectancy in much of the country is for a further 25 to 30 active years on reaching retirement age. The over 70s occupy housing with 8 million spare rooms but are reluctant to move because of the fiscal friction as much as the fear of losing stuff when downsizing.

It is both an issue and an opportunity that the British have overlooked. We still see the over-60s as Darby and Joan with carpet slippers and Ovaltine; the reality is more likely to be Mick or Tina or Gilbert and George or any number of individuals and combinations with a long bucket list and the wherewithal to fulfil it.

We met several companies in financial services, publishing and advertising and drew up ideas for an approach and how we could deliver it. We experimented with creating websites that were easy and enjoyable to use; we explored advising companies on simplifying products and manuals for an older market; we looked at loyalty schemes and community structures. Years passed and suddenly we were given a practical challenge.

Shortly after the 2008 crash, Jayni Beecroft (a friend) asked for help with an idea that Hurlingham's committees and executive had dismissed. Anne French, a serene former model in her 80s, had suggested to Jayni that old films should be shown on wet winter afternoons, followed by tea. Such an innocuous idea had apparently led to raised voices and refusal.

I thought that the idea was not bold enough and, with Maria, wrote a two-page business plan, including proposals for talks, cabarets, book groups, lunches, visits to places of interest and outings to the theatre. Maria was full of superb ideas including the essential inclusion of transport for any outings. Two important thoughts completed the paper: (i) there would be no financial risk or extra work for Hurlingham and (ii) the concept delivered on unfulfilled promises made to members by the Club. We called the initiative Silver Screen as a nod to the original thought.

We were reluctantly given nine months to prove the idea's viability, and we underwrote the financial risk. Within two years, Silver Screen was the largest and most active social group within the club, with a full programme following the original two-page plan. We have hardly deviated from that plan in 15 years. Of course, it was a privileged community, but isolation is not cured by money alone. Our purpose is not the events, which are a vehicle, but the creation of a community within which every member can feel they belong if they wish.

We have hosted hundreds of events, with talks from public figures such as Quentin Letts and Jean Trumpington, as well as former ambassadors, authors, academics and prison governors. Our first lunch, addressed by Sir Terence Clark about the Arab Spring, caused a lively, well-informed debate about how Britain should respond to the situation in Syria – when I called for questions, five former British Ambassadors to Damascus stood to speak!

Terence was also one of our last authors to speak, several years later, when he talked about the Silk Road that linked trade between the East and the West over a thousand years ago. More than 300 attended the early evening talk, including dozens in their 20s and early 30s. Slightly surprised, I asked one younger member why; 'Well, Julian, it was really interesting but it's not what we were expecting. My generation knows of the Silk Road as the dark web, where money is laundered, and drugs and guns are traded.'

Lunches rapidly grew, with Roger Borges as head chef producing great meals every time. When Prue Leith spoke, Roger made two of her signature dishes for 300 and she called him onstage for a huge embrace of thanks. He still treasures the photograph of that kiss.

At an evening event we saw Claire Horton, then CEO of Battersea Dogs and Cats Home, trying to speak with a wriggling puppy in her arms. It was a 12-week-old Jack

Russell/Staffie cross who had been dumped two days after being born. He had big eyes, a crooked tail and irresistible charm, although few social graces. His name is Louis, and we adopted each other, joining our RSPCA 'rescue' terrier, Smudge. Smudge died some years ago; Louis is sitting by me, watching what I write. We've walked thousands of miles together to keep fit.

Our first out-of-town theatre adventure was to a matinée of *Singin' in the Rain* in Chichester. At 5.15 on the previous evening, the bus company called to cancel 'for technical reasons'! We made the trip in two leaky minibuses in appropriately driving rain and arrived late.

We did not lose sight of the original inspiration: films. *Carve her Name with Pride* is the 1958 story of Violette Szabo, played by Virginia McKenna. Virginia joined us to talk about the film over tea when we showed it. There were many personal links for me and for friends; for instance, our former house in Stockwell appears in the film's opening scenes. Of greater importance was Virginia's meeting with our friend Jacquie Isaac. Jacquie's father, 34-year-old Captain Desmond Hubble of the SOE, had been on a train to the death camps with Violette Szabo; he was tortured and shot a short while later at Buchenwald. Virginia, growing up as a child in South Africa, had met Jacquie's father while he was on leave from West Africa weeks before his final, fatal mission. History entered the room that day.

Through Silver Screen we met interesting, kind people by the score. Constance Halford Thompson, known to many as Spratt, was an artist with a delicious sense of humour and extraordinary resilience. Her eyesight failed while she was quite young and still exhibiting her compelling paintings and pastels of racing; when we met, she was in a wheelchair and effectively blind, magnetically engaging and without a speck of self-pity. She liked to sit in the theatre's front row 'so that I feel the warmth of the changing stage lights on my face'. She loved the company of young people. Her grandchildren all said of her, when I was preparing to speak at her funeral years later, that they could talk about anything and everything with her – 'Granny was unshockable; in fact, she was more likely to shock us than the other way around'.

On one occasion, I was wheeling Spratt around Kenwood House when one of our group pulled me aside and suggested I get somebody else to push. I invited them to walk with us for a while. We stopped by a painting by Reynolds or Gainsborough, a grand English family portrait with an imposing country house. 'Where are we now?' asked the invariably impatient Spratt and I gave the painting's title. 'Ah, there's a charming detail of a dog emerging from a bush on the right-hand side of the canvas' and she went on to give us a detailed explanation of the story and brushwork of a painting that she could not see and had not seen for more than thirty years.

Spratt listened to our newsletters using early text-to-voice software. It did not always work well. One morning she rang fretfully to ask, 'Why on earth are we going shopping in Majorca?'

Serendipity brought us an evening event, *Chopin in Majorca*. Rising pianist, Omri Epstein, was engaged to play the preludes that Chopin composed in 1838 in a monastery in Valldemossa. The recital was interspersed with letters and diary entries by Chopin and George Sand, read and expounded by Sir Humphrey Burton, Head of Music and Arts at the BBC. Hurlingham reluctantly allowed us performance space, but we were financially on the hook for the evening's costs. Omri required a concert grand piano that was beyond our means; the club only had an upright. An awkward moment until George Sand's 15-year-old son, Maurice, bailed us out. In 1839 he had drawn a sketch of his mother and Mallorquín villagers watching Chopin play on an upright piano. Omri was persuaded of the 'value of authenticity,' and our budget was rescued.

We began to build a collection of books written by members and invited the authors to address fellow members about their publication. One speaker, Arabella Dorman just back from painting soldiers in Iraq and Afghanistan, was asked if there is still a place for War Artists in an age of photography and video. She replied, 'a photo catches a single moment, a video can tell a story whereas a good painting can tell a story in a single image.'

The talks were popular; the first, *Social Kissing*, was a well-informed and humorous guide to manners around the globe. The author was retired entrepreneur Fred Marsh.

Fred arrived in Britain as a 14-year-old *Kindertransport* refugee called Otto Marx with a younger brother, no money and no English. After a year, he was apprenticed to a local bakery and began a career, becoming a successful business owner, that enabled him to race small aircraft and become vice chairman of the Royal Aero Club. He won the race on the sad day when Prince William of Gloucester died, and he changed the safety rules for air racing in such a way that the once-suspended Air Race continues as the Red Bull race around inflatable pylons.

I never spent a dull moment in Fred's company. His stories were hilarious; his delivery was wonderful. He was a happy step-grandfather, having eventually married the only person he ever loved (another utterly enchanting story). He gave me regular reports about one adventure. He contacted Buckingham Palace suggesting that Her Majesty might provide a cup for air racing, as her father and grandfather had done. After weeks of emails, Fred was eventually invited to the Palace to receive a fabulous Georgian cup, duly engraved and smartly boxed. His commentary about the misunderstandings was epic. Seeing the case, dumped casually in a corner of his trophy room, I asked what would happen next. 'I haven't a clue. I didn't expect them to give me anything.'

Silver Screen numbers grew for London outings. We were soon regularly 10 percent of an audience. Often the only restriction is the quality of available seats, resulting in three or four outings to the same show. Communicating with members of a certain age posed a challenge; fewer than one in five could, or wished to, use a computer. When the iPad was launched in 2010 everything changed.

That Christmas throughout the affluent world 'Granny got an iPad' but, sadly, no instructions on how to use it. Remember the saying 'in the land of the blind, the one-eyed man is king'. I learnt how to speak 'iPad' and how to teach 'iPad'. Different learning styles are defined as 'verbal, visual and kinesthetic' or 'read it, see it, do it'. I wanted to appeal to all three. Working through several nights, I was inspired by PADI's excellent diving manual to create a 100-page course offering descriptions, illustrations, diagrams and exercises, remembering the mantra I first heard from a Somali cabby, that 'a computer is a good servant but a bad master'.

I delivered dozens of iPad training sessions, starting with a simple 90 minutes entitled 'Getting it out of the box'. One member sat at the back of the room for the first talk and, more than an hour later, raised his hand. 'Julian, you haven't yet told us how to get it out of the box,' and in front of him lay his new iPad, still boxed in its original cellophane. Others found it easier; several hundred attended the courses. Only two percent of our mailing list now require printed newsletters; 80 percent of those online read every issue.

Liz Fraser demanded a printed copy. She had the capacity to retain close friendships over decades while being relentlessly infuriating; her funeral was packed with fellow actors and bridge players; everyone had stories of both sides of her character.

Liz was a very fine actor. She held a milestone birthday party for 20 friends surrounded by happy images from her career. Raising a glass someone said, 'The same as last year' and I instinctively murmured, 'Dinner for One' to the Queen Ratling, Audrey Maye, on my right. 'How on earth do you know about that?' she asked. *Dinner for One* is a short two-hander in English starring Freddie Frinton as the butler to Miss Sophie. I explained that I have German friends. The catchphrase 'The same procedure as every year, James,' is part of the German language.

Audrey said she played Miss Sophie on stage in *Dinner for One* with Frinton himself. Was that after the film was made? 'No, he offered me the film, but I was too young; I introduced him to my mother.' Audrey's late mother, May Warden, is watched by more than 50 million German speakers every New Year's Eve, including Martin and Martina in Hamburg.

We were in Paris with John and Mandy Peat on the day that HM The Queen became Britain's longest serving monarch. It was a day trip with, after lunch, a tour of the Ambassador's residence, Hôtel de Charost, led by Lady Ricketts. The house impresses, with a ballroom and throne ('retiring ambassadors may take it with them, but it wouldn't fit into our small house in Bromley'). We celebrated in the garden with a magnum of Pol Roger, Winston Churchill's choice.

I love the library given by Lady Diana Cooper (with Ministry of Works funding) to her husband, Duff Cooper, when he was ambassador in the late 1940s. Duff Cooper wrote several books including an immensely accessible biographical novel about the biblical King David. Papa worked alongside their son, John Julius Norwich, in Beirut. John Julius asked after Papa whenever we met; he was always a delight to see.

When I asked him to talk to our Silver Screeners, John Julius replied, 'Only if you guarantee more people than Artemis had at her talk'. One of his last talks before he died, it was delivered with all the boyish fun that made him so appealing. He opened with the words, 'Julian asked me to talk about my favourite subject, ME!'

Before lunch that day, I introduced John Julius to a friend and author, Alexandra Campbell, who was writing a biography about Earl Haig's wife. John Julius offered to introduce Alexandra to the librarian at Eton (where Duff Cooper's papers for his biography of Haig are kept). 'Thank you, I already know the librarian from when I was at Eton.'

'But you're a…' I had never seen John Julius lost for words.

Our near neighbour, Sir Eldryd Parry, gave a deeply personal talk about international aid. I lost him after lunch, moments before he was about to speak. He reappeared just in time, explaining that he recognised the geographical origin of the chef's name and had gone into the kitchens to thank him in Yoruba; their enthusiastic conversation had overrun, not least because the chef was surprised to hear a language he only ever uses when talking to his mother. Eldryd was rake thin and an inspiration, committing every drop of spare time or spare cash to improve training and the delivery of healthcare from Nigeria to Ethiopia. In 1976, he edited the first book of medicine for Africa, *Principles of Medicine in Africa*, which remains in print in its umpteenth edition although, since his death in 2022, without Eldryd's smiling wisdom and commitment at the editorial helm.

At this time, with Silver Screeners in mind, I wrote several articles. Gerald Wombwell, a fellow Hurlingham member, possessed the strongest laugh I have known. He was also sensitive and insightful. Gerald allowed me the privilege of reading 100 daily letters that his grandfather, Lt Col Gerald Madden of the Irish Guards, wrote to his wife from the Western Front. Written in pencil and scrutinised by military censors, the letters could be indiscreet (he consistently referred to future King Edward VIII as the 'Boy', using a respectful capital B), considerate and brave. His main thoughts were for the people who served him or were under his command, and to discourage his wife's extravagance at Harrods – monthly bills reached him in the trenches, to be paid between rounds of shell fire. Gerald's moving letters set the tone for our visit to the Somme in 2016.

That December we spent several days in the Venice studio of artist Ken Howard and his wife, Dora. We were, once more, with John and Mandy Peat (who won the stay in a raffle) and together discovered a different, winter Venice. When I gave Ken photographs of our stay, he thought they were watercolours, so diffused is the salt-bearing mist that keeps tourists away. We saw small ballet shoes hanging from the stone marking Diaghilev's grave on San Michele; then on to lunch at Locanda Cipriani on Torcello, sitting before a log fire in reception because the restaurant was shut. We watched *La Traviata* performed in the grand rooms of a tired yet elegant palazzo on the Grand Canal. Imagine Venice without the crowds or go in early December and experience it for yourself.

Movement is not a new concept in theatre; however, Toby Sedgwick raised it to a new level – he received the 2008 Olivier Award for Best Theatre Choreography because there is no award for Movement. He directed the puppet horses in *War Horse*, the people in *39 Steps* and in *Swallows and Amazons* and many phases of the Opening Ceremony for the 2012 Olympic Games. He is an actor and mime artist but above all a Director of Movement.

We invited him to speak. He was very good company at dinner beforehand – a small leather-bound book on the table, his speech neatly hand-written.

Then he stood to talk and almost froze. He stumbled over words until, as we held our breath, he walked across a stage with neither set nor props. 'I'm on a train in the Highlands…'; we didn't need telling; we knew the moment he started walking.

Toby spent months observing horses in the country; he took videos, sketches and notes and passes his knowledge onto team after team of puppeteers who bring horses to life. 'You must ensure that the audience invests their imagination,' was Toby's repeated mantra. Millions have invested their imagination at his bidding. It is possibly the greatest difference between a book, a play and a film. The same story can be told in all three ways (like *Rebecca* or *War Horse*) and yet with film the brain is generally relaxed and entertained; with the best books and plays, the mind is engaged, and the imagination invested. Uncle Ken's grandson, my cousin Corran Brownlee, is a storyboard artist for films. He expresses the idea thus: 'My aim is to not tell a story as much as stimulate one in the viewer's mind'.

In 2012 the *War Horse* puppet, Joey, appeared at the October Champion Stakes at Ascot. I watched him parading around the Grandstand Lawn, occasionally dropping his head to nibble softly at the manicured grass. A lady in a wheelchair, pushed by her husband, watched for a moment. I saw Joey swish his tail and shrug, cocking his head as she left. Neither she, nor her husband, noticed Joey following; with a shake of the head, Joey nudged the husband aside and nuzzled the lady's neck. For that precious moment, with the input of Toby's extraordinary alchemy, Joey was real, as were the smiles and tears of delight.

I met Kasper Holten while he was Director for Opera at Covent Garden. It was a small dinner at the Ivy Club, and one guest caused others to laugh when he asked, 'Why does it take so damned long for people to die in opera?' Kasper, usually eloquent, composed and urbane, sat sternly silent before giving a passionate answer, 'Have you ever sat and held the hand of somebody you love as they die. If so, you know that you experience every possible emotion, and it takes a heck of a long time.'

Meanwhile my corporate advisory work continued; business took me to Kyiv twice in 2014, just after Russia first invaded Luhansk and Donetsk and fraudulently seized Crimea. Kyiv was on alert, although nothing like February 2022. Ukraine is caught between the West and Russia; the language even differs at either end of the country. Kyiv had convoys of S-class Mercedes and Range Rovers ferrying oligarchs around a town where the average annual income for a highly qualified professional was about the same as a British graduate could expect in a month. Courteous students and young professionals solicited donations to fund paint to dress walls and street furniture in the national colours. The skyline was a billowing wave of blue and yellow flags. Fear, defiance and a very open trade in sex were the nation's response.

The city felt anxious but safe. We drove east for two hours to meet an entrepreneur and potential investor. Our route was deserted, apart from military vehicles rumbling in the same direction, and stretched between limitless birch-wood forests, hinting at the enormous size of the country. The road was straight but in poor condition; for an hour the outlook never changed. Conversation, when we arrived, was about the army, the opportunities of war and military contracts. Kyiv was home to a generation optimistically looking west; some hours to the east revealed an older generation, looking nostalgically eastward and mired in Soviet thinking.

Back in Kyiv, we met a Syrian businessman with interests in Ukraine, Saudi Arabia and Russia; two homes in Syria had been destroyed by the Russians. His Ukrainian wife, their adult children and family from Donetsk were staying with him in a Kyiv hotel, having fled Russian shelling. She joined us; as we chatted, she said, 'I can look my husband in the eye because, like him, I now know what it is like to have our family's home bombed by the Russians and to lose everything.'

At least in London the problems of ageing are not made worse by being bombed out of our homes.

ROOTS AND HOPE

2016

Bejay went into St Thomas' Hospital in late 2015, naming me as next of kin. We spoke late that evening, but the nurse asked me not to come in until the following day. The hospital called early next morning to say that he had died peacefully overnight. In his last few months, he had been in great pain, confined to a wheelchair. I called the boys and spoke to Bejay's other close friend (and at one stage fellow rough sleeper) Pluto. The Bereavement Team proposed a Hospital Funeral (the new expression for a pauper's grave) and suggested that the money I would have spent was better used for the boys.

I sorted his affairs and arranged his funeral, bringing the boys to London to identify anything they wanted me to take up to Norwich for them. Among his possessions were wrapped and labelled Christmas presents for the boys, for Maria and me and for Pluto. Beside the sofa on which he usually slept, was a book called *Pavement Poems*. It is a collection of verses by rough sleepers with a foreword by Glenda Jackson MP. The dedication, 'For those who live in doorways, but whose heads are full of dreams,' perfectly described my friend.

Bejay contributed three poems to this slim volume, and I wrote to Glenda Jackson about Bejay's death on the chance that they might have met. A week later I received a call from her in a few spare moments between performances as King Lear at the Old Vic. She asked about Bejay's life and talked of him with interest and warmth. He would have been so chuffed to know that she took time to remember him, having met him briefly 30 years before.

'Maybe', a poem by Bejay that appeared in the anthology, is regrettably as pertinent today as it was when he wrote it:

Maybe

By Bejay Wearn

Maybe I'm a tramp.
And maybe I'm not.
I don't turn with a key
Or fit into a slot.
I've nowhere to go,
But I'll get there tomorrow.
I don't live in a camp or
Suffer much sorrow.

The sky is my ceiling,
The stars are my light –
The things I've done wrong,
I thought they were right.
The sun casts a shadow,
The wind combs my hair,
Yet freedom's my banner
And no-one could care.

I don't live in a house,
But maybe I should.
If councils build enough
Then maybe I would…

St Thomas' introduced me to Greg at undertakers Albin's; he called me to discuss a 9.30 a.m. Hospital Funeral early in 2016. Greg always called Bejay 'Mr Wearn' and invited me to structure and conduct the service. I was early and unseen, well away from the crematorium, when the hearse arrived. Pallbearers stepped to each corner of the vehicle and bowed to the coffin. Bejay would have been proud. He loved to think of things 'bein' done proper-like.'

There were plenty of people to say goodbye, each with a story about my friend. There were service sheets with photos of Bejay; Greg played music by Santana; Emerson, Lake and Palmer; and, of course, Led Zeppelin's 'Stairway to Heaven' as the coffin disappeared. The service went without a hitch. Albeit trained as a priest, this is the only time I have officiated a funeral. Bejay himself introduced me to a poem that was read: 'The measure of a man' by Summer Sandercox:

Not 'how did he die?', but 'how did he live?'
Not 'what did he gain?', but 'what did he give?'
These are the units to measure the worth
Of a man as a man, regardless of birth.

Bejay was 63 when he died. I still miss him and think of him almost every day – how he valued his life and how he helped mine. Given the life dealt him, and how he lived it, 63 was a ripe old age. For more than 25 years he was another brother to me.

What of my own family? Papa came from Darvel in Ayrshire. He was educated at Loudoun Moor School, Darvel School and Kilmarnock Academy, where he said that he drove himself each day from the age of 14 – he never took a driving test (they were not mandatory until 1935 and by that time he was 17 and a veteran driver).

At 18, Papa came to London to read Law at King's College. He was very studious. He played the violin in an orchestra, played tennis at a high level and studied to be a certified accountant and a commercial lawyer. He was 22 when the war began, so all his plans changed. He was a very private man. I did not know that we had both gone to the same university college until he made a chance remark when I was in my 40s. We never played tennis together, nor did I know my uncles, aunts or cousins. He was the seventh of eight children.

More than 30 years before Papa, Cousin Alexander Fleming had attended the same three schools and left Scotland to work in London as a shipping clerk, starting his studies at St Mary's Hospital Medical School aged 22. It was at St Mary's that Fleming discovered penicillin, research for which he jointly received the Nobel Prize in Medicine, a knighthood and universal acclaim for discovering what *Time* magazine called, 'the most efficacious life-saving drug in the world'.

Emma grew up in the suburbs of Cardiff, moving to London before WWII. Her father, Wilfred, was English, her mother, Alice Marie, half French. Wilfred was a marine engineer who moved to north London in the 1920s when work dried up and worked for an electricity utility. Emma talked of being taught by a governess, but in fact she attended Haverstock School (a comprehensive whose distinguished alumni include David and Ed Miliband), studied acting and elocution, and worked in an estate agency. At the start of WWII, she joined the RAF press office of the War Department. Fusing my father's surname and her own, she adopted Sturdy-Morton as a stage name for a Pro-Am West End production the year before she married; she kept it and passed it to the next generation. She was the oldest of four children.

These two families are the source of my DNA, and I grew up as a stranger to them all. I was an adult with children of my own before I knew any of this. That may be why I feel that my roots grow in the soil of the countries where I have lived, in the shadows of the people I have met and in friendships that stick with me more than I deserve. Perhaps that is why I can be grateful for a childhood that gave me a love of travel and people, art and live performances, albeit with no sense of belonging. I spend no time on my own genealogy, and yet I know my friends' family stories so well.

Early in 2016, Maria and I decided to take a holiday in Beirut, travelling with our friend Marilyn Johnson, whose late husband, Ahmed, had sadly died before he could fulfil his promise to take her there. We took a large, serviced two-bedroom apartment in Verdun, with an infinity pool on the 23rd floor, overlooking both the sea and the mountains. We were a short walk from rue Hamra, where I spent some of my childhood. It was unrecognisable – a congregation point for Beirut's 300,000 Syrian refugees, many of them reduced to begging from each other. Beirut's magic began in the airport car park; the taxi we had booked failed to start and people appeared from all corners to push start it and smilingly wave us on our way.

On our first evening, we had dinner at Al-Mandaloun on the waterfront. Our taxi back demanded an absurd amount and was only discouraged by hotel security. The next morning, we took a taxi across town, and I gave Ali, the driver, $20 – more than twice what he asked. 'But sir, that is too much' – so I explained that it was also a payment for our next trip and asked him to collect us later that day. He returned and remained with us for our whole stay. $10 was a small gamble to confirm what I already believed – that Ali was reliable and honest.

At lunch in the Chouf Mountains, having walked among the Cedars of Lebanon and visited the President's Palace at Beiteddine, we heard schoolchildren dance in the next room: boys jousted with boys, girls stood to one side and swayed. I took photographs until beckoning hands took me onto the dance floor, onto the shoulders of the young and into their happy world, Christian and Muslim together before prejudice kicked in. Back at our table the children came, in small groups, to talk in English. One boy wore a Union Flag T-shirt and spoke, with an excellent accent, about London, the Royal Family and his ambition to do well so that he might visit. As we left, he held our hands and said, 'Thank you; I have always loved England, but you are the first English people I have met.' Tom Fletcher, our one-time ambassador in Beirut, talks about 'soft power'; this is how it works.

One Friday we travelled in a Nakhal tour coach with a dozen other 'tourists' from the Lebanese diaspora. We visited Anjar, an abandoned eighth-century city with a small, entirely Armenian population. Like so much else in this war-torn region, it is an unprotected UNESCO World Heritage Site. We then continued along the straight road through the Bekaa Valley towards Baalbek, the route once taken by Placido Domingo and Nina Simone, Lord of the Dance and the Ballet Rambert to reach the Festival. The Foreign Office advice regarding Baalbek was **DON'T GO THERE** in bright red letters, as if to ask, 'Have you completely lost your marbles?'

We passed the last army checkpoint into Hezbollah-controlled territory through a sea of flags on either side of the road. Inscribed with images of AK-47s and quotations from the Quran, there were yellow flags for Hezbollah (*The Army of God*), green for Amahl (*Hope*) and ominous black for Daesh or ISIS. From our high position, we could peer over the walls of the heavily guarded, luxurious villas of Hezbollah commanders. Terror greatly rewards some of its officers. Our Lebanese Armenian driver and our guide, a young archaeologist, decided to drive past the shrine of Sayyida Khawla, great granddaughter of the Prophet.

The building is as beautiful as any mosque in Iran, with gilded minarets and richly decorative blue tiling on the walls and towers. It is popular for Friday prayers with the elusive Shi'ite sheiks and mullahs that exercise oversight of Hezbollah's legions. We were stopped.

Several new SUVs blocked the road, fore and aft, and we were surrounded by a parade of high fashion and menace: young men in designer clothes, armed with much-used automatic weapons. Two armed men boarded our coach and, for 20 minutes, looked at each of the passengers, arguing with the guide that we should turn around. I looked down to avoid eye contact but could still see the guns, fingers on triggers, brushing against the passengers and inconsequentially saw that I wore two socks of different colours. Our guide argued that we were visitors and that this hostility was not the way of Islam; Arabic speaking fellow passengers told us that she debated with the gunmen that the Quran requires believers to treat visitors with respect and to welcome strangers. She was intense and brave; eventually they allowed us to pass.

Freed to drive through a cluster of Hezbollah fighters, we saw a bus full of children in school uniform happily arguing about football and homework; hatred does not start until they reach their early teens. We saw a painted statue of the Madonna and Child, the tidy vineyards on the surrounding hills and signs of the prosperity of terror. So much contradiction, living cheek by jowl; it perfectly encapsulates Lebanon. We visited the temples of Bacchus and Jupiter, two of the greatest remaining monuments of Roman times, one still intact after almost 2,000 years; they felt larger and more impressive than I remembered from childhood.

Returning, we stopped at the monastery in Zahlé where Ksara's cellars hold vast quantities of wine for export, made from grapes harvested in Hezbollah-controlled vineyards.

While Maria and Marilyn enjoyed the pool at the St George's or at our hotel, I explored with Ali, our loyal driver. At other times we explored together. It is a rich city with fabulous mosques, churches and Roman ruins, ultra-modern apartment blocks and blighted signs of endless civil wars such as Beit Beirut – a museum settled into the bullet-riddled ruins of an apartment building on the notorious Green Line. We went up to Shemlan, to the presidential palace at Beiteddine, to the grotto at Jeita and to Byblos. I spent hours in the Museum of Beirut with a rich collection of artefacts from the dawn of time, the Robert Mouawad private collection and the streets of Achrafieh.

When Ali and I were out together one afternoon, he asked if he might make a five-minute detour. Not a problem. When we set off again, he was very grateful; 'With all your work this week, Sir, I was just able to pay my daughter's tuition fees.'

Together we spent half a day in the newly refurbished Sursock Museum, which reopened in late 2015 after seven years of work. The harbour explosion of August 2020 destroyed much of the magic that we saw during our visit. Three years later, the Sursock Museum has been restored once more and is open again to the public at no cost, as it always has been. This is a perfect symbol of Lebanon. A gift from a Christian family to a diverse nation that has been destroyed by war and risen defiantly from the ashes several times in seven decades.

Almost the entire population of modern Beirut was born in the decades since I grew up there. Decades of war, wealth, tragedy and development have changed the city where I grew from infant to child. While my memories and love of Beirut shaped me, I realised that it had changed and so had I. At the airport, Marilyn and Maria sailed through departures. I was detained at passport control because of an illegible visa stamp and no evidence of my arrival. I was taken to a small, smoke-filled room where the only signs that I could understand said

'No Smoking!' For the next hour I was held in an intimidating space furnished with a metal desk and filing cabinet, a steel chair, a radiator and a fax machine, and populated with several heavily armed police and soldiers… all chain smoking. They did not speak to me but, while they tried to find evidence that I was not an illegal or a spy, they held the plane.

Later in the year, Maria and I took 34 Silver Screeners to the Western Front. We were led by the incomparable Andy Thompson, a former history teacher and headmaster turned tour leader. Based in a comfortable hotel on the edge of Lille, we visited the battlefields of Ypres and the Somme.

Preparing the itinerary, we realised that everyone had a family member in cemeteries near Lille. I do not know if any of my family fought in WWI, or if they lived or died. I was asked why I had never researched the topic to find out. Having grown up so detached from both families, I felt that conjuring up ancestors from the archives adds nothing to my story. I would rather get to know the living, as I gradually have done.

We selected six Hurlingham Heroes to celebrate, so that the group had a common purpose, and prepared a tour book with short histories of each, beginning with Francis Grenfell, the first gazetted VC of the war, a cousin of Joyce Grenfell and a man whose biography (combined with his identical twin Rivy) was written by their friend John Buchan.

In a week of moving moments, Andy brought the drama, fear, humour, bravery and determination to life with so many stories and so much knowledge. In Essex Farm

Cemetery, where John McCrae wrote 'In Flanders Fields' on witnessing the death of a childhood friend, Andy told us the story of the Canadian doctor. He then stood by the grave of Valentine Strudwick, possibly the youngest British soldier to die in battle. Andy spoke with passion about the 15-year-old's determination to serve, walking twice from mid-Surrey to the War Office to enlist while under-age; Andy's storytelling touched us. Six years later, we joined hundreds at Andy's memorial service near Dorking. He had evidently touched the lives of thousands. During that service, on a wall of Andy's local church, I read a plaque to Valentine Strudwick and heard his story again in my mind.

Each evening at eight, Ypres falls silent to mark the sacrifices of the 54,000 names of the missing dead listed on the Menin Gate. Local firemen play the Last Post, as they have done (almost without interruption) for more than a century. We heard film director Peter Jackson recite 'For the Fallen' and watched as wreaths were laid, including one from our group. A group of young British soldiers stood there, instantly recognisable in civvies. We spoke afterwards and they explained, 'We're in a training regiment, Sir. May I ask, Sir, what's the story behind the three in your party who placed a wreath?' I told them that all three had fathers who fought in the Battle of Ypres and survived. Given the carnage and the elapse of time the odds against such a group are stratospheric; there is a far greater chance of winning the top Lottery prize more than once. The young soldiers spontaneously stood to attention, and one spoke for them all, 'Sir, that's f***ing cool, sir.'

Our neighbours' building works got out of hand. The obnoxious young couple had introduced themselves with the words, 'We have great integrity.' That absurd claim should have been a warning. Their integrity did not extend to honouring their agreements or promises and the year was a nightmare. Our flat was extensively damaged (walls crumbled, floorboards broke, kitchen cabinets fell), and we largely funded the repairs ourselves. We had neither the time nor the emotional energy to go to court.

Our blind friend, Spratt, introduced us to Sue Dymoke, widow of the 34th Queen's Champion, a hereditary role with historic responsibilities, especially at the time of each coronation; the position has remained in one family since 1066. Before we met Sue, we had never heard of the post. Sue lent us a flat neighbouring Spratt and overlooking the Thames. The kindness of strangers is an unsinkable life raft.

The memorial service for my former father-in-law, Sir Timothy Bevan, took place at the Guards' Chapel; ex-wife Nicola asked us to attend because Sophie and Charlie would be there. I saw many of the people who had been my 'family' before the divorce and was happy to meet a small handful of them again. We had grown older in the intervening quarter century; some age better than others. I felt detached, yet I can survive even when several roots are cut. The Song of Solomon has a great line of hope, when quoted out of context – 'the day breaks, and the shadows flee away'.

CREATING A BUSINESS

2017 and onwards

We were invited to offer another club a service to match the breadth of Silver Screen; I concluded that it could be done commercially (i) with the blessing of Hurlingham – we created it for our fellow members there – and (ii) if we could invest in the systems and web presence needed to provide a first class, secure, and enjoyable experience. That sounds obvious, but we had built it as a very informal activity.

The Hurlingham CEO welcomed the idea, and it was endorsed by the Committee. We found enough capital in my pension pot and set out to create a business… in other words to do, for ourselves, what we had spent decades advising others to do: business plan, cash flow projections, marketing strategies, a working web presence, operating structures and the practicalities of fulfilment.

Sally Greengross regularly attended Silver Screen events, and we sought her guidance on what we had in mind. She talked about our plans frequently, at the start of the new venture and, subsequently, during Covid. Her time in the Lords was dedicated to issues of age from many angles, so her strong support from the outset was hugely encouraging.

Never underestimate luck. Samuel Goldwyn's line, 'the harder I work, the luckier I get', has its place but no hard work was involved when we met Nadia Xu through Penny Sloman… it was pure good fortune. Nadia created two websites, using the best options available, and wrote a perfect manual to enable me to run them. Without Nadia we would still be contemplating our navels.

While wondering about a name for the business, we led a group of 52 to Highgrove. The 'Thank you' letters were wonderful, and variations of one phrase appeared repeatedly – that people had felt enveloped in a bit of tender loving care. Bingo! A Bit of TLC Limited was born.

Company registration complete, we turned to our existing banks to open a business account. The lack of enthusiasm was extraordinary; the big banks didn't say 'no', they simply prevaricated and put obstacles in our way until, after several weeks, we turned to a Challenger bank. These are new banks that were set up in the aftermath of the 2008 crash, when hundreds of billions of pounds had been spent by government in life-support for those same major banks that had helped cause the crash. Our Challenger bank dealt swiftly and professionally with our request and within days we were underway.

Days later, after an event, Maria paid in our first TLC cheque. An exuberant member wrote the payee's name thus: 'A Wonderful Bit of Tender Loving Care, Thank you SOOOO much!'

The teller looked up, 'Awww! That's nice!' and processed the cheque.

It is strange, perhaps, to think of work as a privilege and pleasure yet that has been our experience of TLC, especially since we cut some ties and expanded our reach in 2021. It's hard work but above all immensely rewarding because of the people we have met, the shows and concerts we have seen, the events we have hosted, the individuals who have helped us, the lives we have touched and those that have touched us. I discovered as a student and have re-discovered in 'retirement' that London is the world's capital for live performances. I have also learnt that, for most, it is more enjoyable to attend in company than to be alone at events.

At its heart TLC is a community that, through enjoyment of events and live performances in company, enriches later life in London. It relies on the relentless use of technology (and the business disciplines about which I used to advise clients) to give us the freedom to host, spend time with individuals and 'do as we would be done by'. It results in a rich treasury of stories.

After watching David Haig's *Pressure* at Richmond Theatre, we were all aboard our coach, but Maria was missing. Suddenly she appeared at speed, chased by a suspiciously scruffy young man. David followed Maria onto the coach and answered members' questions for about 15 minutes. He is frequently incredibly generous with his time.

Reliable transport is a key ingredient of TLC, although Maria tells me it is a nightmare to organise in London. We have worked with two family-owned firms for more than a decade to ferry most of our members. With several pick-up points, we also use people carriers with drivers we know well and modern wheelchair-accessible taxis, which transform lives.

Business is all about the successful marriage of the big picture and the smallest details. In the late 1980s I met Sir Clive Sinclair, the ultimate big picture thinker, creator of affordable PCs, electric urban buggies, the folding A-Bike and the digital Black Watch. In each case he was pipped by a later, better product (Apple, Smart, Brompton or Swatch, for example). We talked about banks and why his business fortunes were so volatile, so beset by problems. 'Nobody ever asks about that,' he replied. 'It's partly the lack of funding and people to get the details right and partly because nobody ever tells me to stop when I wish they would.'

TESTING THE NHS IN LONDON

2017 and 2018

Three mini-strokes came in a cluster in 2014 and 2015. The first was so mild that I did nothing. The next two TIAs (Transient Ischemic Attacks or 'mini-strokes') were more robust. The worst registered well above 200 over 170 and severely affected my speech. Unaware of what was happening, I phoned the GP and spluttered incoherently, '*Bluh, bluh, bluh*'. The receptionist wisely replied that she couldn't understand a word, but it sounded as if I needed A&E.

Maria, equally wisely, assessed the situation – it was morning rush hour; an ambulance would take two hours to reach us; it would take more than an hour for her to drive me to the hospital; I'd do better on a bus. Three minutes later I boarded a 220 saying, '*Bluh, bluh, bluh*' again and the driver replied, 'You need A&E, mate. You're on the right bus.' I reported to reception 10 minutes after I had phoned the GP and was seen immediately. Ten minutes later I was in a hospital bed, wired up to every bit of kit they could find. I had no idea how serious the situation had become, but I knew that my afternoon meeting needed to be cancelled. A great pity as I was due to have coffee with Yotam Ottolenghi to discuss a possible project in Nine Elms… that meeting never happened.

For months as an outpatient, I received every imaginable test to discover why my blood pressure went through the roof, causing microscopic bleeds in the brain. Eventually, after two years, the Charing Cross stroke unit could still find no obvious cause. On an informed hunch, my wonderful NHS GP, Dr Alexandra Ryan, suggested that I see a cardiologist. Consultant Dr Ramzi Khamis picked up the file – how lucky was that? I believe that I am alive today because these two did not settle for '*enough*' but kept looking – thank you.

Meanwhile other issues popped up. At the end of a weekend in Madrid, I was paralysed with back pain and had to travel back in a wheelchair. We went from the airport straight to Harley Street, an MRI scan and more excruciating tests. Mr Dan Plev, a surgeon who does everything in his power to avoid back surgery, declared severe herniation of discs L4 and L5 as well as a compressed vertebra. It was a long and painful haul, frequently needing a walking stick, but I've avoided surgery so far and have only occasional relapses.

During one hospital stay for the back (rushed into Charing Cross by ambulance), the duty doctor spotted an irregularity on my chest. Numerous tests and scans left the medics convinced it might be cancer. Most men believe that we are immune from breast cancer; yet, while it is rare (fewer than 1% of cases), breast cancer can also be fatal for men. Still not believing the danger, I was sent to a breast cancer clinic for a biopsy. It was a wet morning, and I arrived wearing a raincoat and using a stick. As the only man in the room, I received hostile looks. Over the years, I have had many tests, treatments and interventions – the breast biopsy was in a league of its own for brutality.

A week later the consultant called me in to hear the results. I was calm as I waited, but when he announced it was 'Good news, it's not cancer,' I burst into tears, finally realising that there had been a realistic possibility that I might have harboured that fearsome terrorist of a disease.

The cardiology investigation (mostly at Hammersmith Hospital) continued for 18 months. Breathing tests, angiograms, electrocardiograms, echocardiograms, a transoesophageal echocardiogram and much else besides led doctors to conclude that my mitral valve was not functioning properly and that, without full open-heart surgery, I would soon die.

We were in the throes of launching A Bit of TLC Limited. I had difficulty breathing or walking any distance without a pause, stairs were a nightmare and yet I had work that I wanted to finish. So, it was irritating when, in February 2018, black spots scuttled endlessly across my right eye as I tried to finish the new website.

By the third morning I was fed up and called Specsavers for an eye test, which they did within two hours. An hour later I was in St George's Hospital having emergency laser surgery to prevent the retina from detaching completely (which would have meant blindness in that eye). The surgeon, a cheerful Liverpudlian with exceptional laser dexterity, kept me calmly chatting while delivering more than 200 zaps. 'Where did you learn to do this?' I asked conversationally to quell the fear.

'What? The zapping? I learnt that playing Space Invaders in the bar at Uni.' Strangely comforting.

Early in the year we had a surprise: an invitation to a Garden Party at Buckingham Palace in May. Breathless and leaning on a stick, I would not have missed it for the world, especially because of what it would have meant to Maria's mother, had she still been alive.

Maria's long-standing friend, Marilyn Johnson, was generous, courageous and strong. Shortly before her death, she joined us for dinner at Faheem and Shilpa's restaurant, Pure. She was in pain and smiling enigmatically as she so often did; she had not wanted to 'let us down'. She was a giant among casting directors, both for the stars and for the unknowns. She toured the country when casting a TV series about children with Down's syndrome. The convention at the time was to use makeup to make believe; Marilyn changed that and insisted on using actors who themselves live with Down's syndrome. She blasted open a door to a world of wonderful actors, gave opportunities for a generation of young talent (such as our friend Daniel Laurie) and helped to nudge attitudes in a better direction. When she died, weeks after that dinner at Pure, Marilyn dislodged President Trump from the leader board on Twitter. Hundreds of young and established actors posted their experience of the help she had given at the start of their careers. We had met many of them with her. Her voice lives on in my head with her numerous laconic comments: 'That's a first world problem, get over it,' 'So-and-so is just phoning in the performance,' and so much more.

We were introduced to our first TLC commercial partnership, with LifeCare Residences, by two friends who had recently moved to Battersea Place: Anne Hobson and the former mayor of Kensington and Chelsea, Christopher Buckmaster.

Battersea Place, overlooking the park, was London's first luxury retirement village; there are still fewer than 20. We signed our first contract as TLC during the summer and migrated the business, with its growing number of new members, across to the architecture of systems that Nadia had created. The programme was growing too, with 30 events between September and the year-end relying heavily on those new systems.

Our last personal outing, in the early autumn of 2018, was dinner with Martin and Martina Bloch to celebrate our 50 years of close friendship. We were joined by another doctor, Serban Stojakowits, marking 40 years of our joint friendship, and his wife Elvira. Out of my hearing Martin and Serban told Maria that, in their combined medical opinion, the situation was bad; so bad that, if there were no early date for surgery, they would send an ambulance from Augsburg and arrange for the operation to take place there.

It didn't reach that stage. The surgeon chosen by Dr Khamis, Mr Roberto Casula, is a world leader in minimally invasive open-heart surgery so I would not need to have my rib cage sawn open (a sternotomy) for the operation. Having got through the summer, struggling for breath as the heart faded and having to sit up to snatch sleep, I was given an early October date for surgery at Hammersmith Hospital. I would be in the same ward where, 30 years before, Emma had similar open-heart surgery for a congenital valve malformation.

We all die at some point. It is the only thing in life that is certain (as an acquaintance told me from his tax exile). I approached the possibility with a goal: to have a full diary and an empty in-tray. I learnt to live with the idea that I might die soon, by telling myself that fear of death is fear of life itself – you 'can't have one without the other'. I had at best a one in 12 chance of surviving the year if I didn't have surgery, so on this occasion I brushed aside the last minute, pre-op briefing in which my odds were set out as a one in 12 chance of not surviving the operation; statistically one person on that ward would not outlive the day, but I believed it would not be me.

The operation lasted for more than five hours, with my heart disconnected and cut open so that a valve could be repaired and partially replaced while I was kept alive by an external pump and a team of remarkable medics. There followed 48 hours in intensive care before I moved to a ward with three triple by-pass patients. We shared experiences (in Sri Lanka with one, Australia with another and Lebanon with the third – we'd both been detained in the same police facility!) so that we bonded as a team, supporting each other through the pains and doubts of the post-surgical roller-coaster. It might be more comfortable in a private room, but I was there to get better, not on holiday. A photo shows a motley, pyjamaed crew – it helped to share the early days of the journey.

I left the hospital in less than a week with a large parcel of medication and a thick pile of notes and instructions. One note said that I had Grade 3 Intubation so I asked if I could have a certificate, as I had for Grade 5 Music Theory and Grade 3 Piano, to put on the loo wall. Apparently, it doesn't work like that with Intubation – Grade 3 means that it was almost impossible to insert a breathing tube because my tongue got in the way… little surprise, really, as it is my most exercised muscle.

Like Jerome K Jerome, writing as himself in *Three Men in a Boat*, 'the only malady I could conclude I had not got was housemaid's knee'. By the end of 2018, the 70th anniversary of the NHS, I'd been in more departments than most people see in a lifetime. Almost all the superb medical and ancillary staff have a real vocation, and it shows even when dealing with the Worried Well. There are also, however, many jobsworths who undermine the pursuit of excellence by their colleagues. I fervently hope that the NHS survives but that grows more unlikely while it is exposed to polarising politics, short term gimmicks and a revolving door of mediocre managers undermining brilliant practitioners. Please will a handful of leading politicians have the courage to work across the House to get it right.

During the summer, a TLC member mentioned that the Parliament Choir was due to perform Mozart's Requiem with the Bundestag Chor in Westminster Hall on 31 October to mark the 100th anniversary of the end of WWI; would we like some tickets? We always like to add value – the best seats in the house, a discount, a reception before the event, that sort of thing. Walking slowly with the dogs one morning, I saw Norman Fowler and asked if he could introduce me to somebody at the Palace of Westminster who might help. 'As Lord Speaker, I have an anteroom you're welcome to use, if that helps.' I must have sounded ungrateful when I replied that we had 80 tickets. 'That's lucky; the River Room only takes 80 people.' I was still in recovery when the concert took place in the presence of German and British leaders. I was disappointed not to have been there, not least so that I could have thanked Norman in person on the day for his characteristic kindness.

BACK IN THE SADDLE

2019

It was many weeks before I was allowed out. Maria managed a well-curated diary of visitors and otherwise I divided my time between sleeping, reading and trying to keep the business up to date. Somehow, I sent out 10 emailed TLC newsletters between the operation and the summer, suggesting that Maria was working incredibly hard, and I had time on my hands. We already had dozens of events lined up for 2019, including a three-day trip to Yorkshire and an outing to West Horsley Place to see Grange Park Opera's new home as a group.

We had a flurry of Silver Screen events. Most featured Vincent di Maio, the club's head barman and beating pulse. He approached Jeffrey Archer before one lunch, placed a glass beside him and poured, with the words, 'Your usual, my Lord.' Archer asked how Vincent knew and was told, 'It is what I used to serve you regularly 20 years ago'. They reminisced. Vincent had already met Charles Moore, talking about Margaret Thatcher, whom Vincent looked after at the club in her later years. At another talk by Charles Moore, Vincent joined us for lunch and was rightly applauded by Charles in his opening remarks.

Richard Harries, formerly Bishop of Oxford and one of Radio 4's best known voices as a regular on *Thought for the Day*, is a prolific author and keen on theatre. He wrote a play for which we organised a rehearsed reading with a first-class Pro-Am cast. The transition from page to the spoken word is magical and the audience was delighted. It would be good to see this intriguing and well-written play performed on stage.

Chef Roger Borges delivered consistently fabulous meals for these lunches. While discussing a menu, I mentioned a four course 'picnic' for 40 at Grange Park Opera in June: roast beef or poached salmon as the main course. Roger asked when we would cook it. Unasked, he appeared that evening with a vast roll of knives and his usual energy.

It is several years since that evening, and we have cooked dozens of kilos of fillet of beef as we were taught: succulent, rare, flavoursome every time and not less than two hours in the oven. That was the best cooking course I could have wished for, in great company. I missed Roger when he felt forced to move after some very poor management decisions.

We began to travel again, for short stays with life-long friends in France, Italy, Germany and Spain, where we spent an idyllic first week of 2020 with Peter and Jane Jamieson.

Weeks spent in hospital had given me plenty of thinking time. I jotted down an idea for an event or even a TV show and Sue Lawley kindly agreed to discuss it. One morning I went to her house, near where I had lived when at university, and went through my idea for *In Case of Fire*. In brief, what single inanimate object would you rescue from a burning house and why? Sue's input was wise and encouraging; the idea remains a work in progress.

WHAT'S A PANDEMIC?

2020

In early March, it was unclear to most in Britain whether Covid was a real threat. Robin in Italy (where the pandemic first reached Europe) told me of the problems facing hospitals there – his son, Alberto, was a doctor on the front line in a major hospital in Bologna. Robin himself was very aware of the situation in hospitals in Rome. His advice to isolate was clear. On the other hand, the British government had not decided and most of our members wanted to see what they had paid to see; we obliged.

On Saturday 14 March, we took 20 members to see the Pimlico Opera production of *Hairspray* performed by professionals and prisoners at HMP Bronzefield. By Monday evening, the theatres had decided to shut. We had two major tasks: what to do for our members during what soon became known as Lockdown and what options we had (and could offer) for the 2,500 tickets we had already purchased for our members.

I was engaged to advise a small recycling company at the time, so it was the tail end of 'business as usual', although I was wary after my last meeting with them in St James's. I stood on the platform at Green Park and watched hundreds, many in masks, shoving their way onto a tube train. The driver had a foot on the platform and was shaking his head. 'Have you got room for one passenger up front, please?' was meant to be a joke, before I left the station. 'Where to, mate?' came the reply and moments later I was in the driver's compartment, being told not to touch anything.

It was fascinating. Tube lines have sharp corners, changes in elevation, speed limit signs and, appearing briefly on the right, the defunct Down Street station. I've been up front in Concorde at Mach 2, on a TGV at full speed and on a Cathay Pacific flight into Hong Kong's Kai Tak ('*Heart Attack*') airport. Green Park to Earl's Court was as exciting and more frightening – the terror of watching passengers crowd towards the platform edge as the train approaches – will this one jump? Will that one slip into our path? My driver (I'd better not name him – it was illegal for me to be there) was a keen Arsenal supporter and a teacher who could earn so much more driving a train than teaching. As he missed the classroom, he volunteered to coach youngsters at weekends. Apparently, there can be dozens of candidates for each trainee tube driver's job, but less than one candidate for each teaching vacancy in his subject. My driver's priorities for his family were well thought through but, as a society faced with those statistics, where are our priorities?

Maria had already thought about TLC members; we emailed a 'watch this space' about theatre tickets and offered vulnerable members help with shopping and prescriptions. We organised deliveries of a short list of essentials on Tuesday and Thursday. Immediately, we had 25 addresses to supply; it was neither sustainable nor scalable. Our kitchen couldn't cope with sorting and packing; my head couldn't handle the invoicing.

I met the local Waitrose manager at 6.30 one morning. He was sympathetic to our proposal of pre-ordering for distribution but, after consulting HQ, replied that collectively supermarkets would stick to till limits and early morning shopping for the elderly.

Chris and Judy's son introduced us to the chairman's office at Sainsbury's. Baroness Greengross had a top-level conversation with them and Nicholas Saphir spoke with his very senior connections in DEFRA; all were led to believe that the companies and the Ministry were in favour of ideas like ours (about order consolidation for groups of older people). One DEFRA official described shops as 'a petri dish for the virus'. In the end, however, it was the same answer: there would be no ministerial intervention, and no supermarket was motivated to resolve somebody else's problems.

After a week of chaos at home, I sat down to analyse our situation as best I could.

Firstly, there was no shortage of any produce or product; it was just in the wrong size or the wrong place. Simplistically for example, suddenly a whole nation went to the loo at home instead of at the office or factory; commercial loo rolls don't fit domestic holders. Less popcorn and fewer energy drinks will be consumed if cinemas and gyms are shut.

Secondly, supermarket distribution algorithms use historic patterns to determine how much to load onto a delivery lorry for any store on any given day. Initially the stores near the workplace received 'normal' deliveries, even after people stopped going to work. Whereas there was no increase in deliveries to residential areas. Changing an algorithm takes time or informed early intervention! Executives do not like overriding computers. Beware AI.

Thirdly, of course, restaurants, clubs and cafés were shut and food destined for public consumption was stranded in the wholesale markets. I knew from NCG that up to a third of all food consumed in the southeast is usually eaten outside the home.

Next, the supermarkets together had far fewer than one million delivery slots available each week (compared with four million now and multiple food delivery services). I ran numbers and concluded that an improbable number of vans and trained staff would be needed immediately to fill the gap.

Finally, there was no shortage of volunteers. People wanted something to do – the NHS sought 250,000 volunteers and received 750,000 applications.

I worked out what we needed to do at about the same time as the announcement of Lockdown on Thursday 26 March. At 3 a.m. that Friday morning, I had a conversation with Jason Tanner, owner of Britain's largest independent fresh produce wholesaler at the time with annual sales of £100 million. By 3.15 a.m., we had the foundations of our plan in place.

I dipped into our pension pot once more to fund the venture, and again Nadia was brilliant. She had moved to Seattle to take a master's degree in computer science, in particular the sort of work that brings the benefits of the internet to older people who otherwise struggle to get online. I sent sketches of what I had in mind; we phoned regularly and overnight she sent back an initial explanation of the IT suppliers we required and the budget. At 2 or 3 each morning she would insist that I get some sleep, promising more for me to go through first thing. I skipped a lot of sleep whereas

Nadia always did exactly as she promised.

On Friday and Saturday, Maria and I phoned around to find the right suppliers. We already had fruit, veg and dairy. We added Marrfish (the top trawler-owning wholesaler), The Bread Factory (sister company and supplier to Gail's) and Springvale (a general supplier to small shops). We had our own account with Ashby's, a meat and poultry supplier to the City's clubs and directors' dining rooms. I worked on the web content, images and descriptions for everything we were to sell (350 lines of produce when we were at full tilt), researched and wrote up our legal obligations and restrictions, created contracts and order sheets for each wholesaler, agreed prices and payment arrangements, sought and bought packaging, opened a bank account, commissioned a logo for TLC during COVID and wrote to possible users.

Hurlingham was persuaded to let us work from the Club while it was shut, on one condition – given our contract, we should 'not make a profit'. The thought had never occurred to us. We contacted TLC members to invite children and grandchildren as volunteers, eventually amassing a fabulous corps of 150. The number included 12 Club employees on furlough; we had worked closely with Birsen, Marli, Jason, Martin, Ringo and all of them in the past.

I created a functional database and wrote a manual for the volunteers and a contract for each to sign. Maria allocated tasks and managed the team day to day, calling in enough to meet all our selection, packing and delivery requirements and doing one of the very many things she does so well – managing and motivating people.

With an operating space, we designed the produce-flow to be efficient and respect Covid restrictions; work-stations well apart, air flow ensured, and signage throughout our Packing Shed encouraging best practice. Walk-in fridges needed to be prepared and split between different produce types. We ordered gallons of hand sanitiser and thousands of latex gloves – I am proud that not one of 150 volunteers contracted Covid in four months of operations (including Maria, who shopped at local supermarkets daily for items that were cheaper there than through a wholesaler!).

The daily (sometimes twice daily) visits by Maria to a supermarket were time-consuming and undoubtedly a risk. Not least because she relied on finding a friendly cashier to avoid the computer restrictions on the number of items being bought. However, four weeks after we started, a letter arrived from the office of the Sainsbury's chairman, requesting that the local store should provide whatever we needed, overriding limits, and opening a dedicated till for Maria. I think the manager stood to attention when he read the letter; he complied.

Everything was in place by Tuesday evening. By Wednesday morning, Nadia had created a Beta version of the website that was tested by two dozen of our members, with valuable feedback. By Thursday afternoon, we were drafting emails to go to TLC and Hurlingham members and to promote our temporary trading name, TLC during COVID, on the wonderful social network of Radio HP (a website and nothing to do with radio at all). We launched the site on Friday and took orders over the weekend for our first deliveries on Monday.

TLC DURING COVID

2020

After a reasonable night's sleep (the first in nine days), I drove 300 yards to Hurlingham's main gate by 7 a.m. on Monday morning. Security was unlocking the chains as I turned the corner. The first deliveries were about to arrive and Birsen, the head banqueting porter with whom we had worked so well for several years, was already in place as a volunteer to help us set up. I put together a small office to keep on top of the paperwork and then the first Premier lorry arrived.

They unloaded 400 flat pack delivery boxes and dozens of containers of fresh produce. Strawberries that smelled of… strawberries. Each leek weighed a kilo and was the size of a bulbous Victorian dining table leg. There were 25 kilo bags of spuds, and everything was on a massive scale. We were the lucky recipients of ingredients that were destined for dishes in Michelin starred restaurants. We had already received almost all that we'd ordered, and it was going smoothly until the driver started to use a small forklift to move a pallet from deep within the lorry.

'What's that for?'

'It's fer the eggs, mate.'

'But we've only ordered 13 boxes of eggs; that's 78 eggs.'

'Nah, Mate; there's 180 eggs in a box; that's 2,340 eggs and that's why I need this to shift the bloomin' pallet.'

Divided by a common language, I kept one box and returned the rest.

Each day brought challenges, surprises and fun, although few days brought much sleep. We added new suppliers, introducing people to Jenkyn Place (a fabulous award-winning producer of wines competing sip-for-sip with the best champagne), the Abbeville Supper Club, Nutbourne Heritage tomatoes and the joys of smoked German ham with white asparagus and new potatoes.

Volunteers arrived singly and in families. We could not have started without Chrissie, Ella and Harry Horowitz (and numerous friends of Ella); Ella was in her first year studying Nutrition at university. She designed the content for boxes that were distributed *gratis*, so that families could eat well, cultural needs were respected, and Ella added treats to 'put a pep in their step'. We could not have functioned without three Bircher sisters and their children; we could honestly boast that 'all our Muesli is packed by real Birchers,' direct descendants of the creator of that breakfast cereal.

Mati Glassborow identified serious hardship cases that were off-the-radar for conventional help; in all we had more than 100 families in need. Mati delivered a first unsolicited box of produce to an 80-year-old living half a mile from our base. Gary occupied half a garage which served as his workshop (to make and repair furniture) and living quarters. Apparently he liked to cook, so Ella ensured that the first box, with a week's supply of fresh produce, included fresh chicken fillets and a tin of sweetcorn. It was placed outside the door as requested by a hesitant voice from within.

When Mati returned, she and Maria discussed whether he might have a tin opener, and one was supplied with the second delivery. This time the door was opened, and Gary said how much he'd enjoyed cooking the chicken with sweetcorn. Then he spotted the utensil on top of the box. 'Is that a tin opener? I've never had a tin opener.' Then how had he opened the sweetcorn? 'With a 'ammer and chisel, like I usually do.' Gary slept on a mat on the floor and cooked on a single electric ring. By the end of lockdown, he had a bed and linen, a small cooker and his first fridge.

Volunteers brought their own vehicles for deliveries. We had the largest Mercedes people carrier and the smallest Smart car. One mother and daughter used Daddy's Car for a delivery to the White City housing estate; the Porsche Panamera looked incongruous but apparently attracted an admiring crowd at its destination. Then there was Milo, who passed his driving test a week before lockdown and had been given a second-hand run-around, his pride and joy. He was an insatiable delivery driver ('I can manage a few more boxes, please'), covering dozens of miles each day, but in mid-July I saw his car had been in a crash and asked how; 'When lockdown lifted, nobody told me there'd be other blooming idiots on the roads' – he'd never encountered traffic.

A London Air Ambulance helicopter landed periodically on open land next to the Packing Shed. With two flight crew and two doctors, their visits could be long or short, always waiting for a call. We fed them while they waited and provided fresh food to deliver to a fire station, where they also landed occasionally; apparently it made a pleasant change from a diet of pickled onions provided by a local shop. The Air Ambulance deals with horrendous car crashes in normal times. During lockdown most of their calls were for domestic violence cases – to the team's visible distress, they did not always arrive in time.

Labelling was a challenge. We learnt about 14 categories of allergens as well as other regulations. Wonderfully patient Mary Badenoch produced more than 1,000 ready-meals for delivery, and the volunteer chefs at Hurlingham produced thousands of meals using ingredients in the stores that might otherwise go to waste. We distributed industrial quantities of ready meals to nursing and care homes in the borough and to Royal Trinity Hospice across the river.

For four days each week we called our working area the Packing Shed. However, just before midday each Friday, several A-level students arrived, released from the last of the week's on-line schooling. They were enthusiastic and delighted to be in mixed company after a week locked up at home. The Packing Shed morphed into Hormone House as we tried to maintain the two-metre rule.

Throughout the week, one of us hand-delivered a hot meal to Spratt at lunchtime but on Fridays the refrain was 'please may I take lunch to the blind lady?' and typically four or more of Britain's brightest youth managed the task. Concerned about their welfare, or nervous about the answer they might give, I asked why. 'Because she is genuinely interested in what we are doing and where we hope to go in life. She remembers what we've said, and nothing ever shocks her when we answer.'

Several of the Friday team went on to university together or have kept in touch and developed lasting friendships. Many continue to volunteer (we are asked for references from time to time) and a few used the experience as part of their Duke of Edinburgh challenges, when more conventional tasks were not available. Maria and I loved working with all of them; we learnt so much from a generation that sees the world in a differently valid way and has so much to offer.

Through four months of Lockdown, we sent out weekly newssheets and monthly newsletters. Clara Strunck wrote the weeklies, bringing the disciplines of a successful young journalist. I wrote the newsletters, beefed up with occasional guest articles from generous contributors, including Prue Leith and Quentin Letts. Our publications bore a strapline, 'We sell great food to those who want it so that we can give to those that need it'.

In early July, Mati took her final delivery to a single mother with several children. The mother had been thrilled to be able to provide good home-cooked meals and had been grateful for every delivery. What threw Mati, on that last day, was the appearance of one of the children who emerged from behind his mother with hand-drawn cards from each of the family and the heart-melting words, 'Thank you for making my mum very happy'.

While it is possible to mobilise kindness in those that have it, one cannot delegate kindness to be performed by those that have none. We had the privilege of working with 150 kind people. We have a long way to go before we live in a just society. In the box-ticking world where we try to delegate kindness, often those that need help do not get it and those that get help do not need it. I think kindness is underrated, undervalued. The Dalai Lama wrote, in an article published in 1990, 'Kindness is my true religion.'

An Australian friend, Rod Whyte, led me to Adam Lindsay Gordon's poetry. Dead at 36 in 1870, Gordon is the only Australian commemorated in Poets' Corner, Westminster Abbey. His bust has the rugged features of a drover. Towards the end of his short life he wrote, in 'Ye Wearie Wayfarer':

Life is mostly froth and bubble.
Two things stand like stone:
Kindness in another's trouble,
Courage in your own.

Perhaps the most frequently read verses in the Bible are from 1 Corinthians chapter 13: the bit about faith, hope and charity, or love as it is often translated. The Greek word in the verse is αγάπη, one of several Greek words that we translate as 'love'. A fuller translation is 'selfless or universal love'. Possibly the best translation would be 'kindness'. In my mind, verse 13 reads, 'And now these three remain: faith, hope and kindness. But the greatest of these is kindness.'

Harry joined his sister, Ella, and mother whenever schoolwork permitted, to keep me alert. He mastered the statistics, with a natural grasp of numbers, logging the tens of tonnes we delivered, the households we served and encapsulating our stats in a poem:

TLC during COVID Food Facts

by Harry Horowitz

The apple juice weighed as much as an adult panda.
The asparagus weighed as much as half a pig.
The avocados weighed twice as much as an octopus.
Total bananas weighed as much as 30 bowling balls.
The carrots weighed 20,000 times as much as a human eye.
The eggs could have made more than 1,000 omelettes.
The lemons could have made more than 200 lemon meringue pies.
The tomatoes of all types were equivalent to a million raindrops.
The milk could have filled 12 baths.
The oranges would have squeezed into 84 litres of orange juice.
The various apples weighed as much as 500 human hearts.
The raspberries weighed as much as 7,000 golf balls.
All the different potatoes weighed as much as 15 million rice grains.
The sausages stretched to five lengths of an Olympic-sized swimming pool.
The strawberries weighed as much as 40,000 sheets of paper.

With hindsight we could have done more. We talked with community groups, in and around London, but were in too steep a learning curve to be able to pursue other areas.

The experience ended on a sour note that caused us to terminate our contract with Hurlingham, offering to deliver projects in the pipeline but nothing further. An isolated misunderstanding is fine; decent people can settle a dispute politely. This was worse than that, with repeated instances of a lack of good faith and rudeness. We gave notice.

The year's challenges (both negative and positive) continued. Regulations kept changing but, in essence, the Two Metre and Plenty of Fresh Air rules remained in force.

Tom Littler, then Artistic Director of the Jermyn Street Theatre, called our friend Martin Bishop about putting on a new play at Hurlingham. Actor Charles Ward wrote *Renaissance* about a week in 1502 in which Cesare Borgia, Niccolò Machiavelli and Leonardo da Vinci were housed under the same roof… fact! The trap was baited with a strong cast led by Haydn Gwynne and James Corrigan.

With Martin, we persuaded Hurlingham to allow eight performances in the Club's grounds, with 100 seats two metres apart for each show. The play went ahead in late September 2020, in the wake of Hurricane Sally, which led many to ask, 'What is Plan B if the weather turns bad?' Our answer? 'There's a free poncho with each ticket', and the actors put a single prop on stage… a mop. The setting was a sunken garden, probably designed by Gertrude Jekyll in the 1910s. It was beautiful, especially with light lifting through the trees at night. The play was engaging; 666 tickets were sold. *Renaissance* was a courageous and enjoyable success. My enduring memory, striking the set after the last performance, was of Haydn up a wobbly ladder dismantling lights with a huge smile and the words 'I haven't had to do this since I was at school.' She is much missed.

We had two more productions before the year end. First, the exceptionally talented and warmly human Janie Dee asked if she could put on a performed reading of *Lettice and Lovage* with friends including Rupert and Emma Vansittart. It was great fun, even with social distancing in the audience, and raised thousands for Hurlingham's new foundation. Our experience during Covid enabled us to provide the committee with a template for the foundation's creation, unlocking years of stalemate over how the club might pursue a charitable purpose without using members' subscriptions. This event provided some of the foundation's first funding, in time for Christmas.

Secondly, Fiona Hamilton asked if we could host a Christmas concert for some of her Opera Prelude singers – talented young professionals at the start of their careers who had been without the vital oxygen of an audience response for months. Applause is an energy source that fuels performance. As usual, Maria chose a programme with great appeal and the singers added two of the Scottish Songs of Beethoven: 'Come fill, fill my good fellow' and 'Music, love and wine'. If you don't know them, they are worth looking up. The evening was less fun for the young mezzo-soprano, who soldiered on without missing a beat of an exquisitely well-sung *Voi, che sapete* while competing with a fire alarm in a different key.

Building on these remarkably rewarding experiences, Martin Bishop, Maria and I had an idea.

CREATING A FESTIVAL

2021

With a blank sheet of paper and facing a post-Covid world, the three of us thought of creating, curating and hosting a new festival of the performing arts with 30 performances in five venues over five days… all to be created, curated and carried out in less than a year.

All we needed for the festival to be a success was to persuade Hurlingham to provide the space, notwithstanding our disagreements, to map out a balanced programme with something for all ages, to identify and invite the best artists we could imagine, to engage professionals and volunteers to deliver the events, to factor in some participation for the local community, to connect with a charity as beneficiary and to arrange the finances so that the Club might profit but would not be at risk. Of course, we would do all this for no personal gain, while getting A Bit of TLC back up and running and continuing to advise clients. Diary management is not my forte.

The journey was a rollercoaster ride; the festival itself was an extraordinary joy.

Maria and I had a clear idea (usually, but not always, the same idea!) of what we wanted to achieve and a very good understanding of what the target audiences might appreciate. Martin had his own ideas from a different, and therefore very valuable, perspective.

Martin had run a large business, but his heart had been in singing and acting for a long time. He is blessed with a rare voice (I could happily listen to him reading the *Yellow Pages*). When he retired, he went to drama school and now he is an actor with a long string of credits on stage, screen and TV (such as *The Crown* and *Ted Lasso*). He was also a past chairman of Hurlingham.

While Martin, Maria and I were chasing our individual responsibilities, we agreed that the venture needed a chairman – somebody away from the coal face who could provide insight, perspective and endorsement for an ambitious project that would inevitably trigger doubters. One Covid volunteer driver happened to be between senior positions. Chantal Rickards had returned in late 2019 from being a very successful CEO of BAFTA in Los Angeles with a bulging CV as an executive producer of well-known TV programmes. Her experience, diligence and kindness brought much more to the table than we had realised we would need.

When mapping out a project, I have been taught a simple approach; fortunately, Martin's views were similar. There are two initial questions: 'to what problem is this a solution?', and 'what would you do if it were your own money?' Both questions were easily answered.

The three of us worked in harmony so that the Hurlingham Club Arts Festival (HCAF) was rapidly planned, with objectives, benefits, budgets, explanations, spreadsheets, timings, diagrams, and an indicative line-up of performers. Everything was ready in October for our first and worst hurdle – committees. 'A committee is a group of people who keep minutes and waste hours.' Approval arrived in late February for an event at the end of August!

HCAF was billed as a 'family friendly, country house arts and music festival in the heart of London'. It fulfilled that billing in its first happy year with something for everybody.

The last bits of the scene-setting were a printed programme and dressed interiors and gardens. We created the programme with the publisher of official programmes for the Jubilee and the Coronation. We created the outline for a logo, a rainbow of nine Matisse-style figures (the Greek muses?), that appeared everywhere. We dressed the spaces. The grounds were richly populated with floodlit sculptures, and the main hall was festooned with multi-coloured fabric banners to display the sponsors' logos and improve the acoustics of the barrel-vaulted glass ceiling.

A 1 o'clock on Tuesday, 31 August, the first of 600 people started bagging seats for the opening event. On stage, in front of a nine-foot concert grand piano, Kadiatu Kanneh-Mason talked easily with John Suchet about *House of Music: Raising the Kanneh-Masons*, her book about her life and her incredible family of seven exceptionally talented musicians.

By picking up a phone, Maria arranged for all seven children to support her with a concert. She also organised a Kanneh-Mason Green Room (with their favourite biscuits!) and a Rolls-Royce to bring Kadi and her husband Stuart, with Aminata and Mariatu, from their London hotel. The older children were to make their own way from various parts of London. We forgot about social media! The two youngsters instantly contacted their siblings and when the car arrived four leapt in with their instruments, telling their parents, 'Follow us in a taxi'. I was there to greet them as the young musicians tumbled out of the vast Cullinan, a London cab wheezing in minutes behind to deposit two serene parents.

Their concert was magical. They played solo and in twos, threes and fours as well as all together. When not performing, they sat on two rows of chairs in the wings with Isata in the second row. I watched as she placed an encouraging hand on each sibling's shoulder before they took to the stage and a congratulatory pat on their return. When we watch Isata perform now, she attacks the keyboard at lightning speed and has quietly championed the work of women (such as Clara Schumann) and black musicians (such as Samuel Coleridge-Taylor) by making us fall in love with their music. However, for me, all that talent is enhanced by the memory of her gentle kindness.

It was the last time (to date) that all seven siblings performed together in public in the UK. Kadi signed hundreds of books and, at a table next to her, Braimah, Sheku, Konya, Jeneba, Aminata and Mariatu added their names to each book (Isata had left to play in a Prom). It was magical – and when later I gave each a programme and volunteer T-shirt, the grittily determined Mariatu repeated her familiar war cry that one day she will be 'a better cello player than Sheku!' When I last spoke to Sheku and Braimah both reported that, while Mariatu is catching up, Sheku is still ahead.

The backbone of the festival was theatre and opera, cabaret and music.

Diva Opera performed *Carmen* and *Don Giovanni* superbly in the theatre; and we hosted Tom Littler's 1920s production of *She Stoops to Conquer* in the Gertrude Jekyll-designed sunken garden, a perfect period setting for the piece.

In the nightclub atmosphere of Palmer's, a room we dressed in black with small red table lamps and large neon signage, Kit & McConnel entertained (in place of our fabulously talented friend Janie Dee), Alistair McGowan performed his *Piano Show* and Gyles Brandreth gave a preview of his autobiography, *Odd Boy Out*; hundreds of copies were sold and signed although it was still officially a fortnight before the publication date. As I was on stage introducing Gyles, I heard Jeffrey Archer engage him in reminiscences of Jeffrey teaching Gyles athletics at school. That held us up for more than a moment.

That evening, my son Charlie attended as a volunteer. I was delighted that he accepted the invitation. After the show finished, we talked for hours but with so much more to say. Rebuilding bridges is a slow, hard process that does not happen in a single evening – it can take years and a willingness to see things from another perspective. Most disagreements stand a better chance of resolution when the two sides find the areas and goals on which they agree and then build on those.

I had long wanted to see the Ward Thomas twins live. I once interviewed their father, Anthony. He tried to row across the Atlantic and, when he needed help, the nearest person was apparently on the International Space Station and not on Earth. The twins sing an unusually attractive mixture of Nashville and Hampshire with success and respect on both sides of the pond. They generously allowed Katya Janoff (one of our aspiring singers) to be their warm-up act with great help from their road manager, Bryony October.

We had recitals by students at the Yehudi Menuhin School, thanks to Geoffrey Richards, a long-standing governor of the school and trustee. Kingsley Lin and his sister Laura played a charming programme closing with Bela Bartok's *Romanian Folk Dances* played on the Rosa Levinsky (or Cumming) Violin. This ornate instrument escaped in 1918 from St Petersburg, where it was used to teach the Tsar's children; it later survived Kristallnacht and WWII in camps including Auschwitz and Belsen. The instrument has its own biography (*The Fiddle* by Natalie Cumming) and can rightly be described as awesome.

Our other YMS students were Coco Tomita and her younger sister Yume. Coco had just won the strings section of BBC Young Musician with an outstanding performance including Jenö Hubay's *Carmen Fantaisie Brillante*, that she played for us. To my surprise, when I asked, she had never seen the opera. We arranged for the family to watch Diva Opera's production that evening but first Coco, Yume and their parents watched *Carmen* in rehearsal, and the *Carmen* cast listened to Coco playing the formidable *Fantaisie*. There were several emotional moments that day.

Charlie Grave, the sponsorship whizz guiding us, delivered great partners in a tremendous vote of confidence. Sponsorship partnerships are an invaluable set of transactions. In return for funds, they require a privileged package for their own patrons and a powerful presence. Our role was to meet the sponsors' demands without diluting the character of the festival. It can be a challenge. Charlie found five ideal partners including Rolls-Royce.

Delphine Gray-Fisk, one of Britain's first female commercial airline pilots, arrived for one opera in a two tonne 1934 yellow Rolls-Royce Phantom, which she parked alongside two modern RR models and a four-foot tall 1930s sculpture of the Spirit of Ecstasy. The most photographed moment of the week, it was a devil to park on grass without power steering.

Thursday was exceptionally warm; people ate and drank under the trees and stars until midnight, imitating the South of France. My highlight that day came just after lunch. Our vision was that one in 12 HCAF tickets would be available to the community, especially for disadvantaged youngsters with no chance to see live shows.

That afternoon several local kids came to watch and listen to SK Shlomo, the beatbox wizard. I found a group, aged 12 to 14, waiting quietly as directed in a corridor and, after a bit of banter, led them to the courtyard where three mighty RR Cullinans were parked. As we gingerly approached, the Rolls-Royce drivers opened the doors and invited the young to sit inside. It was a moment of awe for all of them, looking up at the star-cloth ceilings and feeling the soft leather of each car's seats, being shown how to use the ultra-sophisticated sound system and move the seat positions; for once they were in complete control, smiling in happy disbelief – 'This is the best day of my whole life… ever,' said one as we walked back in to hear SK Shlomo. Hats off to those drivers.

We ended the week with a wrap-up party to thank the performers, the sponsors, the charity Acting for Others, the volunteers and those who had made HCAF successful, including my son Charlie and his partner, Lula, who came back up to town to take part. The night began with some home team performances: artists Katya Janoff and Louise Welby, and Martin performed.

Then Clive Rowe arrived, hot from *The Prince of Egypt* in the West End with his black tie undone and hanging round his neck. 'Maria darling, I need prosecco please' were his opening words. Pedro the barman poured a glass, and Maria handed it to a shocked Clive. 'Not a glass, darling… I need a bottle!' He'd had the journey from hell to reach us.

Maria had arranged that Clive would sing 'Great Balls of Fire', a second song and then finish with his Olivier Award-winning performance of 'Sit Down You're Rocking the Boat'. 'But darling, I can't do that without my backing singers,' he'd said on the phone, but he trusted Maria when she said it would all work on the night. And it did. Diva Opera's cast for their fabulous performance of *Carmen* that evening were persuaded to provide the backing, and it was roof-raisingly sensational. The opera singers, most holding the sheet music, loved every minute (including the encore) and their voices were the perfect foil for Clive.

We were thrilled to have achieved what we set out to deliver. It had been ambitious so we followed David Lloyd George's dictum: 'Don't be afraid to take a big step if one is indicated; you can't cross a chasm in two small jumps'. With our focus on quality, we achieved diversity and satisfied every appetite, delivering a programme encompassing most tastes 'from woke to bloke' and excelling in the middle ground. We'd had a ball.

Remarkably HCAF made the club a decent profit in year one. We identified lessons, passed on a comprehensive report with a handbook, and left strong foundations. We intended to play no further part in year two. I believe management and marketing are the most important contributors to any success in business. It is not enough to know financial reporting standards, for example, without understanding their purpose. A modest idea can flourish with good management; a good idea (as HCAF was) can fail when handed over to an inadequate team and lose, as the second year of the festival lost, tens of thousands of pounds. QED.

The remains of the year were busy. I received an email in error commissioning another Julian to write programme notes for an Opera Gala at the Cadogan Hall. When I pointed out the mistake I was asked to submit my own notes, which were duly used in the programme. Such fun to research, write and see in print. We organised 27 TLC outings before Christmas, with numbers nudging closer to pre-pandemic levels; members overcame fear to return to the theatre.

I repeatedly see reasons not to prejudge; seldom more starkly than when a couple returned with us to the Cadogan Hall, their first cautious post-Covid foray. He was bent double, and she moved slowly behind, adjusting his slipping face mask. She had been the first female Judge at the International Court of Justice and its president. He had won a Silver Medal in the 4 x 440 yds relay in the 1950 Empire Games and was

5th in the 1952 Olympics before I was born. They are both giants.

We received an offer on our flat that eventually ended in a sale.

In November, two official letters arrived together, one addressed to each of us. 'If we were to offer you an honour, would you accept? You may not mention this to anyone, or we may decide not to make the offer. Anyway, you won't know which way we've decided until midnight on 31 December, when the list is published.' I paraphrase.

The letters were much more generous and courteous. Having read and re-read them, our first question, 'What is a British Empire Medal?', was quickly answered online. Our second thought, 'Why us?', remains much harder to grasp. The official explanation was, 'for services to the community in the London Borough of Hammersmith and Fulham during Covid-19'. It was very emotional to receive an accolade from strangers: happy, odd and emotional. On top of that, I was not allowed to talk about it, which is difficult for me!

AN UNEXPECTED HONOUR

2022

We were on the phone to Martin and Martina just before midnight on New Year's Eve. An advantage of having such close friends on the other side of the time zone is that they could report from 2022 while we were still in the last throes of 2021. While we chatted, Maria scrolled through the *Official Gazette* online and found our names at the end of the New Year's Honours list. It was real! We were taken aback by the number of letters and emails we received. Pippa and Dickie Dutton delivered the first letter before 7 a.m., in the rain. The phone rang and emails pinged for days.

Having sold our flat, we prepared to move; we decided not to buy our next flat until the cash was in the bank. The first stage was a rental overlooking Putney Bridge and the Thames, one floor above the Dymokes and a dash downstairs to Spratt's. We knew the owners; it was an excellent arrangement for us all. We took it unfurnished and moved most of our possessions into the small space, knowing we might be there for a year. However, rather than knock holes in the walls for paintings, we moved them and some decorative objects into a locked garage. The flat was a happy place.

By contrast, the wider world was in turmoil. Russian troops amassed on the north and east borders of Ukraine in vast numbers. Apart from the UK, Canada, Denmark and the Baltic states, the EU and wider west were caught napping… or perhaps chose to look away. It seemed inevitable that Putin wished to complete the land grab that he began in 2014, threatening everywhere as a distraction from his desire to create a land bridge between Russia and Crimea. The February invasion was no surprise. Interest rates rose as did inflation. We were lucky to have completed our sale.

Louis played a large part in the next stage. Few London blocks of flats accept pets. Maria identified one and we made an offer on one flat, then another, being outbid in each case. By then we knew what to do. We saw another flat, offered and were accepted on the same day. It overlooks the Thames and Barnes Wetlands to the West and, across the Victorian and Edwardian rooftops of London, to the Shard and City skyscrapers in the East.

I created drawings for cupboards, bathrooms and kitchen, floorplans, removing a wall, wiring plans and every imaginable permutation of the space available to take everything we owned, without swamping the flat. We gave Sophie and Charlie furniture and several paintings that we liked but could not accommodate and brought Tomasz and Wojciech in to turn our ideas into reality. Together with these two brothers, Maria has transformed 15 properties over 17 years, with my input when they were our properties.

Spratt died. She was the last woman living to have been awarded the Burma Star in her own right, as a member of the Women's Auxiliary Service (Burma), the WAS(B)s. So often we attend funerals and memorials with only a handful of people present. That was never going to happen with Spratt, who connected with a third and fourth generation to the day she died, happy to have run her full course on her own terms, yearning to be reunited with her late husband and son. She had been a wonderful friend, and her memorial was a chance to hear and pass on more stories about 'the blind lady' who so enchanted teenagers at lunchtime on Fridays during lockdown.

In April, we went to the Tower of London to receive our medals from the Lord Lieutenant, Sir Ken Olisa. We took two grandchildren, Tilly and Bella. Two friends kindly came unannounced to support us – Mike Dudgeon and Sandy Cahill were London Deputy Lieutenants with easy access to medal presentations. It was a very chilly day and a fascinating and uplifting experience.

The 65 recipients included a cross-section of Britain's exceptionally diverse population: Jews, Christians, Muslims, Hindus, Sikhs and those of other faiths or none. We shared the day with people who had been born in Britain, continental Europe, Africa and Asia. The ages ranged from an extraordinary teenager to Holocaust survivors.

Each presentation lasts for two minutes. A 60-second citation is read, photos are taken, and the next name is called. This was not the Britain of newspaper headlines, but the inspiring stalwarts of communities, beacons of tolerance, commitment and hope. Long before our names were called, we looked at each other and whispered, 'Should we stay?' We felt like imposters. We then heard the words, 'Maria and Julian Sturdy-Morton, BEM, are an exceptional couple...' and stood without hearing another word. We still don't know what else was said; GDPR demands that citations are destroyed.

The grandchildren behaved impeccably. A few photos (including one with a Beefeater at the Tower) and we began a short walk to lunch. 'We're taking a cab!' said Maria. Even the cab driver thought us daft; the walk takes three minutes and the drive 10 to 15.

When we were seated, I clicked. 'May we have the heat on full blast please'. A chance to thaw.

In a private room in the quirky Georgian house of the City University Club, Roger Borges and Marli Neves, two of our closest working companions for years, had organised a fabulous meal for the four of us and Sophie. Roger prepared a delicious run of surprises for the adults and spag bol and fish and chips for Tilly and Bella.

We received an invitation to a Garden Party at Buckingham Palace at the end of May. At the last minute we were able to invite a substitute guest, Ella Horowitz, who had been so important for everything we did during Covid. Her parents were abroad when she messaged, 'May I please use your card to buy a hat'. They thought she planned to elope.

The crowd is shaped by gentlemen-at-arms to resemble the banks of a meandering river, with the Royals weaving comfortably along the stream. We watched as the Duchess of Cambridge enchanted two young guests before Prince William came back to fetch her. A young Ukrainian refugee stood immediately in front of us; Prince William came over to talk with her. He listened intently, gently urging her to speak freely. Eventually he took both her hands in his, saying 'I hope you know that here you are surrounded by friends'. For all its ambiguities, our royal tradition has the potential for such comforting and lasting reassurance.

David Hearn, a retired captain of industry, phoned to say he'd miss an event because he'd bought an ambulance and would be driving it to Ukraine. He travelled in convoy ('We're not sure if any of the ambulances will break down so we're sticking together'). After handing over the ambulances in Lviv, they went to a show, which began with a reminder to turn all mobile phones on: 'on' not 'off'. In a modern war, air raid warnings arrive by phone.

David had a simple reason for giving an ambulance. He says that life has three phases: 'you learn, you earn, and you return' and, he said, he is now in the 'return' phase.

We went to a dinner at which Bill Browder, author of *Red Notice*, talked about his shocking experiences at the hands of Putin's agents. Bill slips into an evening unannounced and evaporates before the last course; that is how he survives. At the end of the evening Marina Litvinenko, who lost her husband to similar agents, talked briefly. Her final, memorable words were 'be happy, and please remember that all most people want is to be happy themselves.'

2022 was a Royal Year, starting for us with an investiture at the Tower and a Garden Party at Buckingham Palace. Sophie's husband, Drum, was then Major of the Parade at Trooping the Colour for an unusual second year in succession; in 2021 he undertook the role on foot in the presence of HM The Queen at Windsor Castle, and in 2022 he was mounted for the traditional ceremony on Horse Guards Parade, the last of Her Majesty's reign. After the Colonel's Parade, we all gathered for lunch: three sets of grandparents, Sophie, Drum and the grandchildren. It was a very happy day; the first and only time we were all together.

We found a perfect spot to watch the parade on Jubilee weekend as history joyously edged past. The most moving moment was a lady of the Windrush generation, festooned in Union Flags holding a framed portrait of The Queen up to the screen as she briefly appeared on the balcony, calling, 'Mamma, Mamma Queen, we love you Mamma.'

I was in St James's Piccadilly, at a service commemorating the tercentenary of Grinling Gibbons' death, when the rector, Lucy Winkett, announced, 'I have just been informed of the death of Her Majesty The Queen.' Muffled sobs punctured the silence as civilians and soldiers in the congregation dabbed at their eyes; many had served her in a personal capacity. Flowers carpeted Regent's Park and crowds came up to London to pay their respects there if they could not file past the coffin. Can one love a stranger? For the tens of millions who mourned her, the answer is surely 'yes'. The Queen's Funeral was an exceptional public display of widespread and private grief.

In July we were asked, 'What would you do if you were a charity?' We were not but eventually outlined what we might do and thought no more about it. Until, that is, a significant sum appeared in our bank account. We set out to register a charity by setting out our aims in writing, inviting trustees to join us and creating the necessary paperwork for the Charity Commission process.

Towards the year end, I reached 'three score years and ten'... According to Psalm 90, verse 10, I am now officially 'out of warranty'. To celebrate, Maria and I took Sophie, Drum, Tilly, Bella and Wilf out for an exotic lunch. Not yet teenagers, all three children have a taste for sushi and sashimi!

We gutted, reconfigured and recreated our new flat. Following the advice of the Turin fashion manufacturer, we aimed to mix some expensive features with inexpensive essentials, which meant B&Q kitchen units with beautiful granite worksurfaces. One weekend, Maria and I each ordered an additional item. On the following, busy Saturday morning, I went to B&Q to collect. There was no issue with the first item (for which I had presented my driving licence) but the second was in Maria's name and they refused to hand it over without additional ID... With a long queue building behind me, and not wanting to spend hours returning, I said, 'Maria's the name I use at weekends.' GDPR didn't stand a chance against identity politics. I was given the parcel with a smile.

FACING MORE OF THE UNEXPECTED

2023

Having spent months wrestling with paperwork without blowing donations on lawyers, we filed an application with the Charity Commission. It is a complicated process with the great advantage that, by doing it ourselves, we tested every assumption and ambition.

On 5 March, I walked Louis just before midnight as usual and returned to make tea before bed. We were in our pyjamas when the smoke alarm began to scream for no apparent reason. Moments later I saw smoke seeping under a cupboard door. 999 on the landline did not work – the phone was dead. 999 on my mobile connected immediately, and I peeped inside the cupboard to see the fuse box ablaze. I tried to smother the flames with coats, and we got out fast waking the neighbours as we went. We were moments from being burnt alive, and yet I feel strangely detached from the drama and horror.

Minutes after we left, the cupboard burst into a fireball with temperatures estimated at 300°C, hot enough to crack the concrete ceiling and blast the study window frame out of the wall and onto the lawn two floors below. Flames leapt up 20 feet from the gaping hole.

Four minutes after starting that call, the first fire engine arrived. Appliances appeared from Fulham, Chelsea, Hammersmith and Wandsworth, and 25 firemen quickly and calmly got on with their work. Although our rented flat was 'completely destroyed' in the words of the LFB report, they successfully stopped it from spreading to any other property.

Having faced financial wipe-out before, the fire felt strangely less dreadful than growing up, my first divorce, redundancy or the 2008 crash. We were both alive, as was Louis. We had the pyjamas and jumpers in which we stood, our keys and our mobile phones and not one other item of the day-to-day stuff on which we rely to run our lives; we had lost virtually all our paperwork, computers, photograph albums, clothes, kitchen equipment, furniture and many books and mementoes. But in a way, that's beside the point… we still had our lives. Unlike previous crises, the fire had only taken things, and it was not personal.

Our local pub (I'd love to name it, but best not) had a lock-in that night and they were happy to provide tea for the firemen and something stronger for the evacuated residents. It is hard to be 'collateral damage' in a fire; we feel great sympathy for those neighbours. One mentioned our BEMs to Steve, head of Fulham Blue Watch. He asked me to describe where the medals were kept. As I stood by the smouldering door, his team found them, boxes destroyed but medals intact. Steve invested us for a second time. Sadly, the adjacent Premier Inn turned us away when asked by the Fire Brigade: 'No dogs allowed'. The pub was breaking the law while the hotel was 'within its rights'. I know which was the kinder; as for the other, we were too tired to care.

In the small hours, reeking of smoke and having seen the embers and ashes of almost all our possessions, I lay awake on a mattress in a vacant storeroom and wrote some words to help find a reason to get up in the morning.

After the fire

The smoke has gone and only dust remains,
With ashes and the fingerprints of flames,
Accumulated proof of past obsessions...
A man is not defined by such possessions,
But by kindnesses received and those bestowed,
By every footstep taken on his road,
By memories he stores of love and sorrow.
What he was worth, he still is worth tomorrow.

There are many variations of the mantra, 'It's not what you have that matters, it is what you do.' Early the next morning, the firemen returned to check again that there were no hot spots – I donned protective clothes and went inside for a few minutes to see the extent of the devastation and then be given the LFB report and number. Having scarcely slept, and still in my pyjamas and jumper (with a borrowed pair of jeans) I arrived at the Army & Navy Club in St James's to host a talk at 11 that morning. People can be very polite – nobody mentioned that I smelled like a bonfire and was in breach of the club's dress code. Having just been shown the blackened and ravaged cinders of our lives by the fire brigade, my task was to introduce a talk about the elegant interiors of Robert Adam.

With our landlord's welcome help, we moved into a short-term rental that would accept our dog, Louis. Then we received emails from our two earliest partners, Battersea Place and Riverstone Living, each offering accommodation in their respective retirement villages. Had we not been committed we would happily have stayed in either. We were astonished by the generosity and kindness of friends, strangers and colleagues. Anthony Sharp appeared with a toolbox and the words, 'You're going to need this'. Every tool we could possibly need is there. We share an absurd sense of humour that has kept us close for decades, but when it comes to matters practical, Anthony does not mess about. Maria and I also dashed into a discount shop for emergency clothing.

It was days before I remembered the long conversation with Sue Lawley about *In Case of Fire.* I still like it as a vehicle for getting to know more about people, but it is of limited practical use… When I ran from the flames, I never once thought of what I had decided to rescue. As the 19th century Field Marshal Moltke is so often quoted as saying, 'No plan survives the first contact with the enemy.'

We experienced so much kindness.

Our experience caught many friends off-balance. Several called the Fire Brigade for a check, replaced smoke alarms and sought advice. Others talked of their own experiences with fire and of family members who had died in their sleep in very similar circumstances to our own. Katie Coventry, a more recent friend, had lunch with somebody we had never met, Charlotte MacClure, whose husband Charles had died in 2021. Over lunch, Katie talked about the fire; that afternoon, Charlotte left a large case of clothes for me to wear. Charles had been a very snappy dresser and from the first week I was dressed in Savile Row and TK Maxx!

At the end of that first week after the fire, I received an email invitation with the hallmarks of a scam. It included the words, 'recipient only with no plus one'. Before discarding it, I called Maria; she also had one. Then I called the Cabinet Office in case the email really was about the Coronation. Confirmed... we had both been invited. We were happily bewildered. To give that context, 2,200 people attended, including '16 monarchs, 70 heads of state, and 10 prime ministers.' Even with all the Royals, world figures, guests from almost 200 countries and celebrities, there were fewer than 100 couples in the Abbey. We were among the very few attending with partners... cue tears of delight.

The fire occupied almost every waking hour: there were forms to fill in, reports to write, people to notify (DVLA, Companies House, insurers, pension providers, utilities), things to replace, computers and files to rebuild, the new flat to complete, the move (which now only required a minivan) and all our existing obligations to fulfil. There was no time to manage the trauma of escaping death by moments or the excitement of our surreal invitations.

We were caught on the hop when, late on the Thursday before Good Friday, Maria received a call from DCMS, the government department tasked with organising BEM attendance at the Abbey. Would we be available to be interviewed by the BBC for Breakfast TV on Easter Saturday? The caller let slip, in outlining arrangements, that she had been calling people all day, but most did not answer or had already left for the country or abroad. We might have been in the fourth wave of invitations; it was still exciting.

By the time the make-up was on, and microphones attached, Maria had established that she'd been Sales and Marketing Director of a company where the cameraman had worked. At our age, it's more important to have the cameraman onside than the interviewer. The interview lasted an hour, followed by a tour of the newsroom. The 45 second recording went out at 7 on Saturday morning.

Our first text message that morning was from Charlotte: 'Just wondering if you need Charles' morning coat etc?' At that point we still had not met. Calls and emails arrived for days, from several countries. Our builders, in Poland for Easter (trying to get away from us!), reported seeing us on Polish news headlines. Martin and Martina rang to say that his whole family was 'so proud', whereas he thought Emma would simply have asked, 'Why them? Why not me?' What had been a private surprise for us was apparently also a source of delight for friends.

The week that followed was cluttered with calls from television stations at home and abroad, requesting interviews on camera closer to the day. Without much thought, pre-occupied with the move, we agreed to talk closer to the event and then got on with life.

In April, a month after the fire, we moved into our new home. I'm used to new beginnings; with all the support we received, this was a good restart.

'Where's the kettle/corkscrew/coat/passports?' Months after the fire there were things that we'd forgotten to replace. There were also that things that were irreplaceable – certificates, files, treasured books, favourite outfits, cufflinks, past projects and photographs. All my silk ties (mostly Hermès from when I was in the City) had been irreparably damaged, so we rescued snippets of silk that Caroline Hamilton kindly turned into patchwork cushions. We painstakingly assembled lists: 'what we need', 'what we'd like' and 'what we miss or don't miss'. We mapped out furniture, clothes, utensils and electronics needed to keep going.

Strangely, photographs were the least difficult problem. In 2012, I gave Maria an album of photographs from the previous year. I uploaded them to a website, and they were printed as an album/coffee table book. It was a hit, so I made albums of our major trips and of Maria's childhood and before. A shoe box of photos from since before the war required scanning, cleaning, enhancing and identifying. It took time. I created albums of occasions, holidays and memories; images of our families and our history together were caught in 40 albums, all destroyed by flames; gulp. One call and each album was diligently reconstructed and reprinted by the marvellous Harvey at PhotoBox, which had originally printed them.

Of course, there were irritations – predictably BT got everything wrong. After 45 years with BT, a switch was quickly achieved. The new provider sent engineer Amadeusz, who asked if he could discuss the wiring with our electrician, Lukasz. I connected them and, although they are both Polish, they talked in English. Why? These were not the jobs they did in Poland, 'so we don't know the words in Polish'.

CORONATION RAIN

2023

Our invitations arrived: stiff boards, 9" by 10" and exquisitely decorated with heraldic significance and humour. They are intended for framing and were accompanied by sheets of guidance notes (nothing about loos!) and a mundane invitation slip for use on the day.

By mid-April, appearance requests resulted in arrangements with one Italian, one Spanish and two French TV channels as well as the BBC (on Coronation Day). The Spanish conversation came out as a very full article, heavily illustrated with photographs of our endeavours. One French camera-journalist followed us everywhere he was allowed on the Friday and Saturday, which was surreal.

Following our Easter Saturday BBC interview, the fire and our burnt-out wardrobes were public knowledge; not surprisingly, one sentence was repeated in every broadcast… *'j'ai rien a porter', 'non ho niente da mettere', 'no tengo nada que ponerme'* or simply, I've got nothing to wear. We talked about the late Queen, the King, his exceptional environmental and youth employment work over five decades and the great honour of our invitation, reflecting the volunteering of 150. Editors left it all on the cutting room floor and focussed on clothes!

My wonderful NHS GP gave sensible advice, adjusting my medication so that I wouldn't search for a loo every two minutes (she even asked the Abbey where I could find one). Thank you again.

We stayed at the Army and Navy Club overnight, so that we could stroll across St James's Park at dawn on the day. Mistake: that route was closed. Following a former Chief of the General Staff, we took the tube. Being filmed throughout, we walked to Piccadilly Circus, 'took a carriage' to North Lambeth station, walked in the damp past St Thomas' Hospital and Lambeth Palace and crossed Lambeth Bridge with the composer Roxanna Panufnik, hearing about the King's keen interest in her music for the service. We took photos and spoke with Nick Cave (to the joy of the Weinstocks in Sydney). We were in the Abbey by 7.45 am. It was buzzing and most unallocated seats were taken.

An elegant young lady, dressed in blue wearing a large Royal Ascot hat, floated in and out, periodically whispering into her wrist and looking unlike any security bouncer I have ever seen. Some people caught up with old friends or turned to neighbours and made new friends, others searched for a seat with a view, past Gentlemen-at-Arms, Yeomen, Archers and others in glorious historic uniforms, each carrying out duties that had not been called for in 70 years. Potentially chaotic, it was reassuringly calm.

We chatted to those around us: a distinguished scientist with the Order of Merit, the dignified Māori Kīngi Tūheitia VII and his wife next to us, an ebullient Melanesian Bishop, a Solomon Islands security team, and grittily determined Molly Fenton, founder of the Love Your Period Campaign, who was there with her delightful mother. Six feet away was a TV cameraman, past whom streamed, one way, the celebrities, peers and cabinet ministers who were not in the procession, and the other way, the dignitaries and guests needing the loo in the cloister.

Shortly before 9 a.m., we settled quietly for the day's first music from the English Baroque Soloists and Monteverdi Choir: a concert of Bach, Bruckner, Byrd, Elgar, Handel, Holst, Parry, Purcell, Richard Strauss, Vaughan Williams and pieces composed at the King's request for the Coronation. We heard three concerts back-to-back (before, during and after the religious and constitutional ritual). There was familiar music, new music, uplifting, joyous and martial music and…

…then there was Iain Farrington's infectiously exuberant new composition, *Voices of the World*, played as though the Abbey's 7,000 pipe organ were a Mighty Wurlitzer, rising from the priceless Cosmati Pavement before the High Altar. Ceremonial plumes and great hats bobbed with the beat and our neighbouring TV cameraman almost danced, while the organist celebrated musical energetic rhythms from throughout the Commonwealth.

We grew up with rerun highlights of the first televised Coronation. Crackly renditions of Parry's 'I Was Glad', with the shout of '*Vivat! Vivat Regina!*', and *Zadok the Priest* are part of our history. Hearing them blasted with such passion, in the room, caused goosebumps. It took a moment to adjust to the changed lyrics and melody at the heart of the Parry.

We watched proceedings on large screens subtly hanging throughout the Abbey, moved by the disrobing of the King before he was anointed, as though vulnerably surrendering himself to the office of service he is about to take on.

The moment the pageantry concluded, King Charles processed smiling gently out of the Abbey, preceded by the extraordinary Penny Mordaunt still holding that sword!

We have been asked how many bowed or curtsied as the newly crowned King and Queen walked past. Most did not, although that meant no disrespect. It was the most diverse Coronation in our history, including a huge number from other countries and other traditions who express their respect in different ways. There were also hundreds in the congregation who, like us, could never have dreamt of being in such a situation or needing to learn it's arcane etiquette. Finally, the event cleverly merged a sense of colossal historic and spiritual significance with a celebration of all that is good about our diversity and those who serve it. Many were caught in the awe of the moment.

We remained in the Abbey for an hour after the King's departure. Music continued and the atmosphere went up a notch as people chatted or lobbied – Rishi Sunak was still there when we left. I spotted an old friend, Tim Duke, now Clarenceux King of Arms, but lost him in the crowd by the west door where, under a transparent awning against the rain, Chief Constable Lucy d'Orsi was smilingly taking selfies for her social media presence. I went back inside and bumped into Gyles Brandreth, already wearing make-up for broadcasting; I walked him briskly to be introduced to the head of British Transport Police. The photo she took with Gyles starred on her account and caught the day's happy mood.

I had no time, in the moments it took to guide Gyles across to meet Lucy, to congratulate him on how effective advertising can be. In his after-dinner show, Gyles brags about being the daytime television voice-over advertising luxury incontinence pants – I suspect most people in the Abbey had them on that day… we certainly wore them!

We emerged into rain to find cheerful, soaked young Scouts and Guides handing out ponchos.

Our French tele-journalist was waiting, following us to a café to warm up and wrap up his day's transmission, which provided a third of a one-hour programme that weekend. The coffee shop was almost empty apart from two others from the service – another BEM and an enigmatic lady in a pale grey coat. The cameraman asked her about her day, and she was polite and precise, softly giving her name. Dame Anne Rafferty, PC, was one of those who had signed the Proclamation of Accession.

The BBC checked we were on our way to Green Park. Wrapped in transparent ponchos against the pouring rain, Maria's hat in a bin liner, we pushed through crowds and were repeatedly instructed by policemen to go a long way round that would add more than an hour to our walk and cause us to miss the BBC broadcast. Luckily, there was at least one police or Army officer at each point who intervened. Common sense prevailed; we arrived in time.

We stood on a platform, Buckingham Palace as the backdrop, waiting to be interviewed by Katty Kay and Christian Fraser. Occasionally a small group hollered, 'Not My King!' – their sound swiftly overwhelmed by crowds singing 'God Save the King'.

We were made to feel comfortable. The interview lasted six minutes, which could feel like a lifetime. Christian

Fraser asked if, besides the King, there was 'anyone famous that you saw?' Maria replied that we were 'in the cheap seats opposite Ant and Dec', leading Christian to ask if they had bowed when the King went past. 'We didn't see them bow, but they're quite short!' Maria was outstanding throughout. It was fun.

It was an extraordinary day; a day when I should have felt most like a fish out of water, yet an occasion when we were both made to feel part of the magic.

A few weeks later, at Gifford's Circus, we met Declan Donnelly (as in Ant and Dec), and I told him the story with an apology. He replied with a smile, 'As it happens, we did bow, and that makes us even shorter!'

Gradually we got back on track. Again, we spent time with friends in France, Germany, Italy and Spain. We went to Scotland, both to build bonds with family and for business; we still have clients to nurture. Maria helped to organise the Brain Tumour Research Campaign Dog Show, attracting thousands to Parson's Green on a brilliant late September afternoon; it had been an exercise in crisis management. The first BTRC Dog Show, in 2022, was almost cancelled because of the Queen's death but instead served as a dignified, joyful celebration of her love of dogs and charity. The second, in 2023, was postponed because temperatures rose to the high 30s.

Blue Watch, from LFB Fulham, brought their fire engine to the Dog Show on its new date and let children clamber over it. The team leader, Steve, had been in charge on the night of our fire; it was, he said, the worst they attended all year. We chatted about his London childhood, his son's army career, his work. I mentioned the BBC documentary, *The Night Notre-Dame Burned*. Steve's Blue Watch had been in Paris for a cultural stag weekend; 'We're too old for all the drinking and stuff.' They saw the smoke rising above the city and moved towards it. We were interrupted by cries of '*Shout! Shout!*' and he was gone, blue lights working in earnest. Steve told me, when we met by chance some weeks later, that the documentary is now used for training at the station.

Anthony Sharp was to fly to Tel Aviv on 7 October. He administers an exceptional charity that funds small businesses in Israel, irrespective of race or religion. After a successful career in the arid zones of accountancy and compliance, Anthony's DNA activated the kindness that I have known in him for decades. Hester Grant's *The Good Sharps* describes how 18th century members of his family combined innate decency, courage and fun to do lasting good, triggering Abolition and launching a precursor of the RNLI. My friend upholds that tradition and recently, as executor of his late brother's estate, funded and movingly launched a new Shannon Class lifeboat in Hartlepool that bears the name of his brother, John Sharp, which was also the name of the forebear who commissioned the first recorded lifeboat.

In a Sainsbury's car park, a lady stopped loading her car and approached Maria and me. 'I know who you are,' she began smiling, then momentary hesitation. 'You're Thingummy and Whatsit'; she paused, turned and walked away. Fame at last?!

LATERPRENEURS

2024 and beyond

Old age is easier to face with someone to talk to, something in the diary, a sense of humour and a responsibility. It is the advice we offer others and, rarest of things, advice we try to heed ourselves.

We enjoy being *laterpreneurs*, part of the statistic of working retirees who have created businesses. Our work serves hundreds of kindred spirits in later life as well as most of the new wave of London's upmarket retirement villages and care homes, providing more than two internal or external events each week, procuring thousands of tickets and seeding innumerable memories. I loved hearing Maria interview the BBC's arch interviewer, Mishal Husain; going around Westminster Abbey on a private tour with choristers one evening; or sitting next to Dame Norma Major at dinner just before Christmas; listening to Quentin Letts interviewing Jeremy Hunt with probing questions and rich humour; taking our eighth group to see Nicholas Hytner's production of *Guys and Dolls* (we took 500 members in all and I never once tired of the show); sitting in the intimacy of the Jermyn Street Theatre or the Orange Tree Theatre to watch world class theatre within touching distance; hearing some of the greatest musicians play; and meeting many of the performers. All these memories and more are seeded by what we do. I can confidently echo Alexei Navalny's words: 'I know one thing for sure: that I'm among the happiest 1% of people on the planet – those who absolutely love their work.'

London is the only city in the world where we could do what we do.

Our world is returning to a new normal despite the apocalyptic wave of wars, Covid, starvation and global warming trending towards destruction. One member asked to see *Hello, Dolly!* and was reassured that she already had tickets. 'I don't remember doing that. When did I pay?' It had been pre-Covid, 235 weeks before we finally saw the show. Online systems have allowed our business to grow despite the double hit of a pandemic and a fire that destroyed all paperwork.

Listening to Beethoven's Fifth Symphony in the Festival Hall, I sat next to a dear Austrian friend in her 90s and she sat by a Ukrainian refugee, a working mother of three girls whose husband is on the front line. Dorry and Natalya chatted; both have experienced Russians invading their country. Dorry remembered creeping into the attic with her father to listen illegally to news from London… it began with da-da-da-dum; dot-dot-dot-dash; Churchill's V for Victory. For Natalya, the concert 'opens my eyes and my soul to British culture' and was 'a time for myself and my feelings'. Special.

We spent an evening with Johnson Beharry, VC, an embodiment of redemption. We talked about his brief, highly lucrative life as a drug dealer and gang leader when he first reached London from Grenada. A conversation with his adored grandmother shamed him into turning his life around… She was struggling to pay for food, and he knew she would rather starve than accept dirty money. He is one of only three men living in the UK with a VC, and one of only seven living VCs in the world. Many charities give young people opportunities once they have turned the corner. Johnson's charity, JBVC Foundation, is a catalyst for the harder challenge of triggering a Damascene conversion, like his own, among committed members of today's increasingly violent gangs. He is a celebration of re-purposing a once flawed life. He is also great company.

In 2022, two generous families had put a significant sum into our account to create a charity. After substantially more than a year of filing applications, I more recently received the registration number, 1205113, for the charity that we created to fund transport, care and access to live performing arts for disadvantaged young people with physical (deaf, blind or wheelchair bound) or neurological difficulties. There is work to do, and enjoyment, challenges to overcome and possibly successes, sadness to face and joy. As ever, we shall work with professionals and volunteers, hoping to harness and catalyse kindness; if we can positively touch one life we shall have scored a goal. That is the hope of 'Christmas yet to come'.

Sadly, confirmation of TLC Live Events' registration as a charity arrived on the weekend that a trustee died. Anthony Holden, writer and critic, cruelly confined to a wheelchair by a stroke, did not live to see our work begin. He was an inspiration; his emotion at a concert at Cadogan Hall, after five years deprived of live performances, motivated us.

Perhaps, half a century after answering a wobbly calling, I now have my parish. Perhaps this is what it is all about – the transformation of hope into reality, fulfilling a purpose and being fulfilled.

In late 2023, I received a call from Robert Verdier, a former CL colleague now living in Tokyo. In 1993, Robert was new to the UK and had asked me how the British celebrate Christmas. I wrote a four-page manual detailing every tradition, hour by hour, with instructions for how to celebrate, when to attend church and adding menus and recipes for all the seasonal excesses. It was, he said, a manual that his Franco-Japanese family had followed to the letter for 30 years, and that his three children now follow in Tokyo with their own children. He had called, he said, because there were absolutely no Brussels sprouts available in Tokyo that year and what should he use as a substitute?

He then asked if I could introduce an English public school that might wish to set up in Japan with backing from investors he knew. No experience need go to waste; that is the huge advantage of an eclectic life like mine, coupled with a lively imagination. Remembering my missed months at Salem and Kurt Hahn's values, that in some ways resemble the Samurai code or Bushido, I instead approached a Scottish school, Gordonstoun, and set negotiations in train, including a memorable evening in Elgin when the distinguished Japanese contingent obliged us all to engage in wanton karaoke. Within six months the first stages of a contract had been signed.

In August 2025, the project was agreed with Osaka Christian College and announced. Thanks largely to my erstwhile colleague Robert and the highly professional team at Gordonstoun, a new Gordonstoun School will open in Wakayama Prefecture, Japan, in September 2027.

Late in 2024, after I finished writing this book, I was diagnosed with prostate cancer. So many friends have faced cancer with incredible courage and strength: Diana, Hugh, Jenny, Jon, Lynn, Marilyn, Martina, Rita, Suellen, Vivien and so many more… It can be a relentless, sapping battle that is not easily won and is sadly often lost; cancer took the lives of half of the friends named in this sentence. My own situation is nothing like as challenging.

My NHS GP again acted with exceptional speed, and an early diagnosis means I was treated with radiotherapy at the Royal Marsden during the opening weeks of 2025. My consultant's first words after a biopsy were, 'Very many years from now you will die with cancer, but not from cancer.' Most men of a certain age die with prostate cancer but (if caught early) very, very few die of it. My good fortune is that this is cancer with a very small 'c'; something to fight, nothing to fear.

Cancer is the terrorist of illnesses, an enemy sleeper that follows no logic and obeys no rules of war. My life-long friend, Martin Bloch, was President of the Association of German Urologists almost 20 years ago. He told me to follow the protocol, reminding me that he himself was responsible for its introduction in Germany. His friendship and guidance are comforting for Maria and me; after all, even 'cancer with a very small c' does not just attack the body, the mind and the emotions… It thinks nothing of causing collateral damage to everyone you love as well.

I cannot imagine that a finer facility exists than the Royal Marsden. Care is calmly delivered; however, the most valuable quality is the kindness with which the vocation of care is fulfilled. Is that kindness the difference between *curing* and *healing*? That, with the wonderful encounters with other patients in the period each day while the body is prepared for radiation, provides the best foundation for effective therapy. Even so, as treatment progressed, I felt hollowed out by tiredness. Thoughts floated aimlessly like plastic bags caught on a gust of breeze, never in one place for long enough to form into action. And yet I am truly lucky.

In 2024 Cousin Joe died, after defiantly mocking fate during years of suffering from the hateful motor neurone disease. I had enjoyed time spent with him, radiating his jocular defiance of both convention and the rotten death he bravely faced 'with Darvel humour'. His death means that, for the first time in 350 years, there is no directly related Morton living in Darvel. 100 family, friends and colleagues attended Joe's humanist funeral celebrating an unconventional life of implacable commitment to people, always loving on his own terms. Joe would have believed in Hal David's lyrics for Burt Bacharach's finest song, *Alfie*, including the lines 'I know there's something much more / Something even non-believers can believe in / And I believe in love...'

AND THEN?

Most people suffer bumps and bruises; compared to the world's real misery, I have a privileged life, made immeasurably better by sharing the last 25 years and more with Maria. Facing death from cancer aged 47, American IT and VR professor Randy Pausch said, 'We cannot change the cards we're dealt, just how we play the hand.' Towards the end of my game, I feel I have been dealt a good hand.

Three decades ago, a friend sent me the words of Charles E. Raven, a distinguished 20th century theologian, who wrote elegantly that, 'Most people have, at some time or other, to stand alone and to suffer, and their final shape is determined by their response to their probation; they emerge either the slaves of their circumstance or, in some sense, the captains of their souls.'

Rabbi Hillel, a Jewish scholar at the time of Christ, wrote, 'If I am not for me, who will be for me? Yet, if I am only for me, then what am I?' It makes me ask:

Did we do enough?

People die; that's what we do –
All of us… them, me and you –
Yet when we die, was life enough?
I don't mean all the 'stuff',
The bits and bobs
Collected on the way,
Exams and jobs

And things that we display.
But did we use our breaks?
Do what it takes
To make a difference
To some other person's day?

There is still much to do. Milan Kundera wrote, in his 1984 novel *The Unbearable Lightness of Being:* 'What can life be worth if the first rehearsal for life is life itself?' It is a thought that has been with me since I first read it, and it is widely and repeatedly recycled. For all the self-examination and study, I am no nearer to knowing if there is a next life, another chance; however, by virtue of age and questionable health, I'm closer to finding the answer.

Perhaps the best category for me is one I heard recently: I am a 'God-fearing agnostic'. I suppose this is a modern equivalent of Pascale's Wager, whereby if I live life as though there is a God and yet there is none then I have lost nothing, whereas if I live life as though there is no God and yet there is one, then I have lost everything for infinity.

A believer in the idea of a god but not in religion, Voltaire was urged by a priest at the end to renounce Satan and allegedly replied, 'This is no time to make new enemies.' It is a time to hope.

On paper I am Julian Sturdy-Morton, BEM, BD, AKC, ACIB: the post-nominals define me as a former ordinand, a banker and a frequent volunteer and in recent years I have been a *laterpreneur.* Most of my hopes have been fulfilled. Above all, for this past third of my life, I am where I belong, with Maria, loving and feeling loved, happy in who

I am and what I do, which I might describe as being pastor to a parish of later life. My life has turned out all right in the end. I am not rich but live with the richness of a diverse family of friends, proudly watching a new generation carrying my blood.

Everybody wants to belong; it is one of the most natural of human needs.

ACKNOWLEDGEMENTS

In one sense, this book encompasses my acknowledgement of the gratitude that I owe to those who have helped and shaped me through their kindness or their example. There are, however, several people who have been instrumental in helping me to turn my story into this publishable work, and I take great pleasure in recording my thanks here:

Rosemary Sandberg, one of the finest literary agents of her generation, for encouraging me to write this book almost ten years ago and for her gentle guidance. It is a great sadness that she is not alive to see the result of her encouragement in print…

Jane Fior, an experienced senior editor for reading an early collection of my short stories and anecdotes, and for pointing me in the direction of writing a full-blown autobiography.

Anne Abel-Smith for helping me to navigate the world of publishing and for her enthusiasm and encouragement once I had a manuscript to offer to publishers.

Sonia Ingram, who has listened over the years as I ironed out some of the chunkier challenges in my narrative; it is always important to have somebody to talk to.

Jan Gayner and Alexandra Campbell for reading the manuscript in its earlier (probably rather indigestible) form.

Ella Horowitz and Lottie Fauvelais for their support and interest and for reading this manuscript just before it went to the printer.

Harry Horowitz, for his encouragement and for allowing me to use his wonderfully imaginative verse about our pandemic efforts.

Cate Myddleton-Evans, my editor, for the generosity of her questions and suggestions and for painstakingly polishing the final version to the point where I (and she) can feel proud of the end product.

Todd Swift, my publisher, for believing in the manuscript that I submitted, long before we even had a title for the book or were ready for take-off.

And above all I wish to record once more, my infinite gratitude to Maria for everything at every step along the way. As we said as children, 'by hook or by crook, they're the last words in my book.'